Honolulu, Waikiki & Oahu

Here's what the critics say about Frommer's:

"Amazingly easy to use. Very portable, very complete."
—Booklist

♦

"The only mainstream guide to list specific prices. The Walter Cronkite of guidebooks—with all that implies."
—Travel & Leisure

♦

"Complete, concise, and filled with useful information."
—New York Daily News

♦

"Hotel information is close to encyclopedic."
—Des Moines Sunday Register

Other Great Guides for Your Trip:

Frommer's Hawaii

Frommer's Hawaii from $70 a Day

Frommer's Maui

Frommer's Portable Maui

Frommer's Portable The Big Island of Hawaii

Frommer's®

6th Edition

Honolulu, Waikiki & Oahu

by Jeanette Foster & Jocelyn Fujii

MACMILLAN • USA

ABOUT THE AUTHORS

A resident of the Big Island, **Jeanette Foster** has skied the slopes of Mauna Kea—during a Fourth of July ski meet, no less—and scuba dived with manta rays off the Kona Coast. A prolific writer widely published in travel, sports, and adventure magazines, she also co-authored *Frommer's Hawaii from $70 a Day* with Jocelyn Fujii.

Kauai-born **Jocelyn Fujii,** a resident of Honolulu, is one of Hawaii's leading journalists. She has authored *Under the Hula Moon: Living in Hawaii* and *The Best of Hawaii,* as well as articles for the *New York Times, National Geographic Traveler, Condé Nast Traveler, Travel Holiday,* and other national and international publications. She is a contributing editor to *Spirit of Aloha,* the in-flight magazine of Aloha Airlines.

MACMILLAN TRAVEL

Macmillan General Reference USA, Inc.
1633 Broadway
New York, NY 100019

Find us online at **www.frommers.com**

ISBN 0-02-862985-X
ISSN 1064-1238

Editor: Kathy Iwasaki
Production Editor: Carol Sheehan
Photo Editor: Richard Fox
Design by Michele Laseau
Staff Cartographers: John Decamillis, Roberta Stockwell
Page Creation by Dave Faust, Sean Monkhouse, Carl Pierce, and Linda Quigley
Front cover photo: Waikiki Beach at dusk
Back cover photo: Surfing at Pipeline, North Shore

SPECIAL SALES

Bulk purchases (10+ copies) of Frommer's and selected Macmillan travel guides are available to corporations, organizations, mail-order catalogs, institutions, and charities at special discounts and can be customized to suit individual needs. For more information, write to: Special Sales, Macmillan General Reference, 1633 Broadway, New York, NY 100019.

Manufactured in the United States of America

5   4   3   2   1

Contents

v

List of Maps

An Invitation to the Reader

In researching this book, we discovered many wonderful places—hotels, restaurants, shops, and more. We're sure you'll find others. Please tell us about them, so we can share the information with your fellow travelers in upcoming editions. If you were disappointed with a recommendation, we'd love to know that, too. Please write to:

Frommer's Honolulu, Waikiki & Oahu, 6th Edition
IDG Travel
1633 Broadway
New York, NY 10019

An Additional Note

Please be advised that travel information is subject to change at any time—and this is especially true of prices. We therefore suggest that you write or call ahead for confirmation when making your travel plans. The authors, editors, and publisher cannot be held responsible for the experiences of readers while traveling. Your safety is important to us, however, so we encourage you to stay alert and be aware of your surroundings. Keep a close eye on cameras, purses, and wallets, all favorite targets of thieves and pickpockets.

What the Symbols Mean

✪ Frommer's Favorites

Our favorite places and experiences—outstanding for quality, value, or both.

The following abbreviations are used for credit cards:

AE	American Express	ER	enRoute
CB	Carte Blanche	JCB	Japan Credit Bank
DC	Diners Club	MC	MasterCard
DISC	Discover	V	Visa
EC	Eurocard		

Find Frommer's Online

Arthur Frommer's Budget Travel Online (**www.frommers.com**) offers more than 6,000 pages of up-to-the-minute travel information—including the latest bargains and candid, personal articles updated daily by Arthur Frommer himself. No other Web site offers such comprehensive and timely coverage of the world of travel.

The Hawaiian Islands

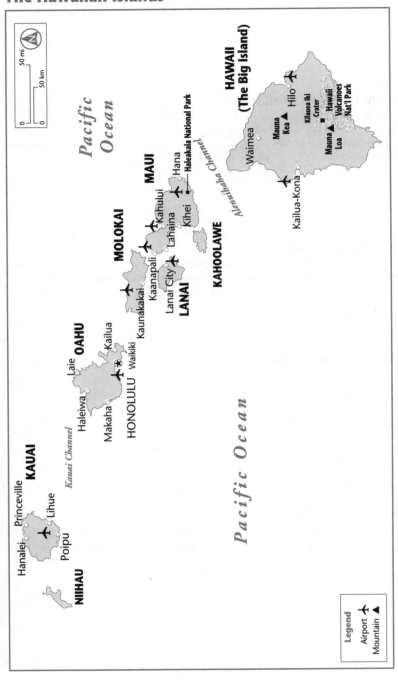

The Best of Oahu

by Jeanette Foster and Jocelyn Fujii

The island of Oahu, located literally in the middle of the most remote chain of islands on the planet, doesn't just offer a respite from work or a travel adventure, but also a sojourn into a dreamlike paradise. Imagine yourself hovering weightless over a rainbowed sea of tropical fish, sitting in a kayak watching the brilliant colors of dawn etch themselves across the sky, sipping a mai tai while you take in sweeping views of the south shore and the Waianae Mountains, battling a magnificent game fish on a high-tech sportfishing boat, or listening to melodic voices chant the stories of a proud people and a proud culture that was overthrown little more than a century ago.

Everyone ventures to Oahu seeking a different experience. Some talk about wanting to witness the "real" Hawaii, some are looking for heart-pounding adventure, some yearn for the relaxing and healing powers of the islands, and others are drawn by Hawaii's aloha spirit, where kindness and friendliness prevail.

This book is designed to help you have the vacation of your dreams. For those too excited to page through from beginning to end, this chapter highlights what we think are the very best of what Honolulu and Oahu have to offer.

1 The Best Beaches

To anyone unlucky enough to be landlocked, a beach is just a beach. But to Oahu residents, there are beaches of all sizes, shapes, and colors, each one offering something different. Here's a list of our favorite ones.

- **Lanikai Beach:** Hidden, off the beaten tourist path, this beach on the windward side has a mile of powder-soft sand that's safe for swimming and—with the prevailing trade winds—excellent for sailing and windsurfing. It's the perfect isolated spot for a morning of swimming and relaxation. Sun-worshipers should arrive in the morning, as the Koolaus' shadow blocks the sun's rays in the afternoon. See chapter 7.
- **Kailua Beach:** Imagine a 30-acre public park with a broad, grassy area with picnic tables, a public boat ramp, rest rooms, a pavilion, a volleyball court, and food stands. Add a wide, sandy beach, great for diving, swimming, sailing, snorkeling, and board and windsurfing, and you've just described Kailua Beach. On weekends, local families consider it *the* place to go. Great on weekdays, when you practically have the entire place to yourself. See chapter 7.

- **Kahana Bay Beach Park:** If you didn't know you were in Hawaii, you would swear this beach was in Tahiti or Bora Bora. Picture salt-and-pepper sand, a crescent-shaped beach protected by ironwoods and *kamani* trees, and as a backdrop, a lush junglelike valley disturbed only by jagged cliffs. Kahana offers great swimming (even safe for children), good fishing, and perfect conditions for kayaking. Combine that with picnic areas, camping, and hiking trails, and you have one of the most attractive beaches on the island. See chapter 7.

- **Malaekahana Beach:** If you would like to venture back to the Hawaii before jet planes brought millions of people to Oahu, back to the days when there were few footprints on the sand, then go north to the romantic wooded beach park at Malaekahana. This is a place to sit in quiet solitude or to beachcomb along the shore. Good swimming most of the time, good snorkeling when it is calm, but no lifeguard here. Surprisingly, very few visitors come to Malaekahana Beach, one of the best on Oahu—it's a true find. See chapter 7.

- **Waimea Bay:** Here is one of Oahu's most dramatic beaches. During much of the winter—October to April—huge waves come pounding in, creating strong rip currents. Even expert surfers think twice when confronted with 30-foot waves that crash on the shore with the force of a runaway locomotive. It's hard to believe that during the summer this same bay is glassy and calm—a great place for swimming, snorkeling, and diving. Oh, and by the way, despite what the Beach Boys croon in their hit song "Surfin USA" (Why-a-*mee*-ah), the name of this famous surfing beach is pronounced Why-*may*-ah. See chapter 7.

- **Pokai Bay:** If your dream is of a powdered-sugar sand beach, a place you can swim, snorkel, and probably be the only one on the beach (on weekdays), try this off-the-beaten-path shoreline. Surrounded by a reef, the waters inside are calm enough for children and offer excellent snorkeling. Come with the aloha spirit and a respect for local customs—the local residents here don't see too many visitors. See chapter 7.

- **Sunset Beach:** Surfers around the world know this famous site for the spectacular winter surf—the waves can be huge, thundering peaks reaching up to 15 to 20 feet. During the winter surf season, the best activity here is watching the professional surfers attack the giant waves. In the summer months, Sunset lies down and becomes a safe swimming beach. Great place to people-watch year-round, everything from wanna-be *Baywatch* babes to King Kong surfers. See chapter 7.

2 The Best Oahu Experiences

To have the absolute best experiences on Oahu, be prepared for a different culture, language, cuisine, and way of doing things. Slow yourself down—you're now on an island that operates on its own schedule. To really experience the islands, we recommend the following:

- **Get Out on the Water:** View the islands the way Mother Nature does—from the sea. There are many different boats to choose from, ranging from tiny kayaks to 100-foot sightseeing vessels. Even state-of-the-art boats guaranteed to prevent seasickness are available. You'll take home memories of an emerald island rising out of the cobalt sea with white wispy clouds set against an azure sky or the Waikiki shoreline colored by the setting sun. See chapter 7.

- **Plunge Under the Water:** Don mask, fins, and snorkel and dive into the magical world beneath the surface, where clouds of colorful tropical fish flutter by, craggy old turtles lumber along, and tiny marine creatures hover over exotic corals. Can't swim? No excuse—take one of the many submarines or semi-submersibles, but don't miss this opportunity. If you come to Hawaii and don't see the underwater world, you're missing half of what makes up this paradise. See chapter 7.

- **Meet Local Folks:** If you go to Hawaii and see only people like the ones back home, you might as well stay home. Extend yourself, leave the resorts and tourist quarters, go out and learn about Hawaii and its people. Just smile and say "howzit?" which means "how is it?" "It's good," is the usual response—and you'll usually make a new friend. Hawaii is remarkably cosmopolitan; every ethnic group in the world seems to be here. It's delightful to discover the varieties of food, culture, language, and customs. The best place to start is Oahu's Polynesian Cultural Center. See chapter 8.

- **Drive to the North Shore:** Just an hour's drive from Honolulu, the North Shore is another world: a pastoral, rural setting with magnificent beaches and a slower way of life. During the winter months, stop and watch the professionals surf the monster waves. See chapter 8.

- **Watch the Hula Being Performed:** This is Hawaii, so you have to experience the hula. There's no excuse—many performances are free. For just about as long as we can remember, the Eastman Kodak Company has been hosting the **Kodak Hula Show** at Kapiolani Park. The show is really more '50s nostalgia than ancient culture, but it's a good bit of fun any way you slice it. Some 1,500 people flock to the shows at 10am every Tuesday, Wednesday, and Thursday; they last until 11:15am. See chapter 8.

- **Experience a Turning Point in America's History—the Bombing of Pearl Harbor:** The United States could no longer turn its back on World War II after December 7, 1941, the day that Japanese warplanes bombed Pearl Harbor. Standing on the deck of the USS *Arizona* Memorial, which straddles the eternal tomb for the 1,177 sailors and Marines trapped below deck when the battleship sank in 9 minutes, is a moving experience you'll never forget. Admission is free. See chapter 8.

3 The Best of Natural Oahu

This is Oahu as it was created by Mother Nature: the remains of once-steaming volcanoes, thundering waterfalls, the dazzling array of tropical flora in full bloom, and the wonderous pockets of beauty that continue to amaze us all.

- **Volcanoes:** Oahu was born of volcanic eruptions, so don't miss the opportunity to see the remains of a volcano up-close-and-personal. You can actually walk into the crater of Diamond Head. See chapter 7.

- **Marine Life Conservation Areas:** Oahu's underwater parks have a unique marine environment protected by state law. Submerged in a Neptunian underworld, these parks possess a sensual serenity unmatched in life above the waves. There are three underwater parks along Oahu's shorelines: Waikiki, Hanauma Bay, and Pupukea. See "Beaches" in chapter 7.

- **Gardens:** Flowers are what Hawaii is about and there is no shortage of gardens on Oahu. Foster Garden is a 14-acre, leafy botanical oasis amid the high-rises of downtown Honolulu, showcasing 24 native Hawaiian trees and the last stand of several rare trees, including an East African species whose white flowers bloom only at night. See chapter 8.

- **Natural Wonders:** Forget Old Faithful; the Halona Blowhole on the southeast side of Oahu features a geyser shooting into the air through a vent in the lava cliffs. See chapter 8. Other not-to-be-missed phenomena are the waterfalls that seem to flow uphill along the Nuuanu Pali highway. Gale-force winds sometimes howl through the mountain pass at this 1,186-foot-high perch guarded by 3,000-foot peaks; the result is waterfalls that are blown back up the mountain. See chapter 8.

4 The Best Snorkeling & Diving Sites

A different Hawaii greets anyone with a face mask, snorkel, and fins. Under the sea, you'll find schools of brilliant tropical fish, lumbering green sea turtles, quick-moving game fish, slack-jawed moray eels, and prehistoric-looking coral. It's a kaleidoscope of color and wonder.

- **Hanauma Bay:** It can get very crowded, but for clear, warm, calm waters, an abundance of fish that are so friendly they'll swim right up to your face mask, a beautiful setting, and easy access, there's no place like Hanauma Bay. Just wade in waist deep and look down to see more than 50 species of reef and inshore fish common to Hawaiian waters. Snorkelers hug the safe, shallow inner bay—it's really like swimming in an outdoor aquarium. Serious, experienced divers shoot "the slot," a passage through the reef, to gain access to Witch's Brew, a turbulent cove, and other outer reef experiences. See chapter 7.
- **Wreck of the *Mahi:*** Oahu is a wonderful place to scuba dive, especially for those interested in wreck diving. One of the more famous wrecks in Hawaii is the *Mahi,* a 185-foot former minesweeper, which is easily accessible just south of Waianae. Abundant marine life makes it a great place to shoot photos—schools of lemon butterfly fish and *taa'pe* are so comfortable with divers and photographers that they practically pose. Eagle rays, green sea turtles, manta rays, and white-tipped sharks occasionally cruise by, and eels peer from the wreck. See chapter 7.
- **Kahuna Canyon:** For non-wreck diving, one of the best dive spots in the summer is Kahuna Canyon. In Hawaiian, *kahuna* translates as priest, wise man, or sorcerer. This massive amphitheater near Mokuleia is a perfect example of something a sorcerer might conjure up: Walls rising from the ocean floor create the illusion of an underwater Grand Canyon. Inside the amphitheater, crab, octopi, slipper, and spiny lobsters abound (be aware that taking them in the summer is illegal), and giant trevally, parrot fish, and unicorn tangs congregate. Outside the amphitheater, you're likely to see the occasional shark in the distance. See chapter 7.
- **Shark's Cove:** The braver snorkelers might want to head to Shark's Cove, on the North Shore just off Kamehameha Highway, between Haleiwa and Pupukea. Sounds risky, we know, but we've never seen or heard of any sharks in this cove, and in summer this big, lava-edged pool is one of Oahu's best snorkel spots. Waves splash over the natural lava grotto and cascade like waterfalls into the pool full of tropical fish. There are deep-sea caves to explore to the right of the cove. See chapter 7.
- **Kapiolani Park Beach:** In the center of this beach park, a section known as Queen's Beach or Queen's Surf Beach, between the Natatorium and the Waikiki Aquarium, is great for snorkeling. We prefer the reef in front of the Aquarium because it has easy access to the sandy shoreline and the waters are usually calm. It has the added advantage of being right next door to the Aquarium in case you see any flora or fauna you would like more information about. See "Walking Tour: Kapiolani Park" in chapter 8.

5 The Best Golf Courses

Oahu is golf country, with 5 municipal, 9 military, and 20 private courses to choose from. The courses range from 9-hole municipals, perfect for beginners, to championship courses that stump even the pros. Below is a range of selections; one will be just right for your game.

- **Ko Olina Golf Club** (☎ 808/676-5300): Here's a course that's not only in a beautiful setting, but is also downright challenging. In fact, *Golf Digest* named this 6,867-yard, par-72 course one of "America's Top 75 Resort Courses" when it opened in 1992. The rolling fairways and elevated tees and a few too many water features (always where you don't want them) will definitely improve your game or humble your attitude. See chapter 7.

- **Hilton Turtle Bay Resort** (☎ 808/293-8574): Of the two courses to choose from here, we recommend the 18-hole **Links at Kuilima,** designed by Arnold Palmer and Ed Seay; *Golf Digest* rated it the fourth best new resort course in 1994. Palmer and Seay never meant for golfers to get off too easy—this is a challenging course. The front nine holes, with rolling terrain, only a few trees, and lots of wind, play like a course on the British Isles. The back nine holes have narrower, tree-lined fairways and water. In addition to ocean views, the course circles Punahoolapa Marsh, a protected wetland for endangered Hawaiian waterfowl. See chapter 7.

- **Sheraton Makaha Golf Club** (☎ 800/757-8060 or 808/695-9544): The readers of a local city magazine recently named this challenging course "The Best Golf Course on Oahu," and the readers of *Golfweek* rated it one of Hawaii's top 10. Away from the crowds of Honolulu and about an hour's drive, this William Bell–designed course is in Makaha Valley on the leeward side of the island. Incredibly beautiful, sheer, 1,500-foot volcanic walls tower over the course, and swaying palm trees and neon-bright bougainvillea surround it; an occasional peacock even struts across the fairways. "I was distracted by the beauty" is a great excuse for your score at the end of the day. See chapter 7.

- **Olomana Golf Links** (☎ 808/259-7926): This is a gorgeous course located in Waimanalo, on the other side of the island from Waikiki. The low-handicap golfer may not find this course difficult, but the striking views of the craggy Koolau mountain ridges are worth the greens fees alone. The par-72, 6,326-yard course is popular with local residents and visitors. The course starts off a bit hilly on the front nine, but flattens out by the back nine. The back nine have their own special surprises, including tricky water hazards. See chapter 7.

6 The Best Walks

The weather on Oahu is usually sunny, with trade winds providing cooling breezes—perfect conditions for a walk. Below are some of our favorites, from city strolls to trails through rainforests.

- **Diamond Head Crater:** Most everyone can make this easy walk to the summit of Hawaii's most famous landmark. Kids love the top of the 760-foot volcanic cone, where they have 360-degree views of Oahu up the leeward coast from Waikiki. The 1.4-mile round-trip takes about an hour. See chapter 7.

- **Makiki–Manoa Cliff Trails:** Just a 15-minute drive from downtown Honolulu, you'll find a walk through a rain forest and along a ridgetop with nonstop views. This somewhat strenuous loop trail is one you'll never forget, but it's more than 6 miles long, gains 1,260 feet in elevation, and takes about 3 hours to finish. The trail is part of the labyrinth of trails in this area. The views of the city and the shoreline are spectacular. See chapter 7.

- **Manoa Falls Trail:** This easy .8-mile (one-way) hike is terrific for families; it takes less than an hour to reach idyllic Manoa Falls. The often-muddy trail follows Waihi Stream and meanders through the forest reserve past guava and mountain apple trees and wild ginger. The forest is moist and humid and inhabited by nothing more dangerous than giant bloodthirsty mosquitoes, so bring repellent. See chapter 7.

- **Chinatown:** Honolulu's Chinatown appeals to the senses: The pungent aroma of Vietnamese *pho* mingles with the ever-present sweet scent of burning incense; a jumble of streets come alive every day with busy residents and meandering visitors; vendors and shoppers speak noisily in the open market; retired men talk story over games of mah-jongg; and the constant buzz of traffic all contribute to the cacophony of sounds. No trip to Honolulu is complete without a visit to this exotic, historic district. See chapter 8.

7 The Best Views

Oahu has many extraordinary lookouts. How can you have a bad view in paradise? Here are just a few of our favorites.

- **Puu Ualakaa State Park:** Watching the sun set into the Pacific from a 1,048-foot hill named after a sweet potato is actually much more romantic that it sounds. Puu Ualakaa State Park translates into "rolling sweet potato hill," which was how the early Hawaiians harvested the crop. Don't miss the sweeping panoramic views, which extend from Diamond Head across Waikiki and downtown Honolulu, over the airport and Pearl City, all the way to the Waianae range. Great photo opportunities during the day, romantic sunset views in the evening, and starry skies at night. See chapter 8.

- **Nuuanu Pali Lookout:** Oahu's best-looking side, the windward coast, can be seen in its full natural glory from the Nuuanu Pali Lookout, a gusty perch set amid jagged cliffs that pierce the puffy white clouds that go racing by. A thousand sheer feet below, the island is a carpet of green that runs to an azure Pacific dotted by tiny offshore islets. You'll feel like you're standing on the edge of the world. See chapter 8.

- **Diamond Head Crater:** The view from atop this world-famous 720-foot-tall sleeping volcano is not to be missed. The 360-degree view from the top is worth the 560-foot hike. You can see all the way from Koko Crater to Barbers Point and the Waianae mountains. See chapter 8.

- **Lanikai Beach:** This is one of the best places on Oahu to greet the sunrise. Watch the sky slowly move from pitch black to wisps of gray to burnt orange as the sun begins to rise over the two tiny offshore islands of Mokulua. This is a five-senses experience: birds singing the sun up; a gentle breeze on your face; the taste of salt in the air; the smell of the ocean, the sand, and the fragrant flowers near by; and the kaleidoscope of colors as another day dawns. See chapter 8.

- **Puu O Mahuka Heiau:** Once the largest sacrificial temple on Oahu, today Puu O Mahuka Heiau is a state historic site. Located on a 300-foot bluff, the Heiau encompasses some 5 acres. People still come here to pray—you may see offerings such as ti leaves, flowers, and fruit left at the Heiau. Don't disturb the offerings or walk on the stones (it's very disrespectful). The view from this bluff is awe-inspiring, from Waimea Bay all the way to Kaena Point. See chapter 8.

8 The Best Adventures for Thrill-Seekers

- **Soar in Silence in a Glider:** Imagine soaring through silence on gossamerlike wings, with a panoramic view of Oahu. A ride on a glider is an unforgettable experience. Glider rides are available at Dillingham Air Field, in Mokuleia, on Oahu's North Shore. The glider is towed behind a plane; at the right altitude, the tow is dropped, and you (and the glider pilot) are left to soar in the thermals. See chapter 7.

- **Surf Waikiki in a Hawaiian Outrigger Canoe:** It's summertime and there's a South Pacific swell rolling into Waikiki from Tahiti; here's your chance to try surfing—in a Hawaiian outrigger canoe. Numerous beach concessions on Waikiki Beach offer the chance to paddle an outrigger canoe and surf back into Waikiki. Not only do you get a great view of Waikiki Beach from offshore, but also the thrill of actually catching a wave and gliding back into shore. See chapter 7.

- **Float on the Thermals on a Tandem Hang Glider:** See things from a bird's-eye view (literally) as you and an instructor float high above Oahu on a tandem hang glider. See chapter 7.

- **Leap into the Ocean:** Even though all the signs say DANGEROUS, STAY OFF THE ROCKS, a favorite pastime on Oahu is climbing the stone precipice next to Waimea Bay and leaping into the ocean. This is for experienced swimmers and is a summer-only experience, as the thundering winter waves drive everyone from the sea, except the professional surfers and the very, very stupid. See chapter 7.

- **Venture into the Neptunian Underworld:** It's Hawaii—you have to see what it's like under the waves. Try scuba diving; you can enjoy a "scuba experience" with absolutely no previous diving experience. Here's your opportunity to glide weightlessly through the ocean while you admire the multicolored marine creatures. See chapter 7.

9 The Best Places to Discover the Real Oahu

Oahu isn't just any other beach destination. It has a wonderfully rich, ancient history and culture, and people who are worth getting to know. If you want to meet the "local" folks who live on Oahu, check out the following:

- **Watch the Ancient Hawaiian Sport of Canoe Paddling:** From February to September, on weekday evenings and weekend days, hundreds of canoe paddlers gather at Ala Wai Canal and practice the Hawaiian sport of canoe paddling. Find a comfortable spot at Ala Wai Park, next to the canal, and watch this ancient sport come to life. See chapter 7.

- **Attend a Hawaiian-Language Church Service: Kawaiahao Church** (☎ 808/522-1333) is the Westminster Abbey of Hawaii; the vestibule is lined with portraits of the Hawaiian monarchy, many of whom were coronated in this very building. The coral church is a perfect setting to experience an all-Hawaiian service, held every Sunday at 10:30am, complete with Hawaiian song. Admission is free; let your conscience be your guide as to a donation. See chapter 8.

- **Buy a Lei from Vendors in Chinatown:** There's a host of cultural sights and experiences to be had in Honolulu's Chinatown. Wander through this several-square-block area with its jumble of exotic shops offering herbs, Chinese groceries, and acupuncture services. Before you leave, be sure to check out the lei sellers on Maunakea Street (near North Hotel Street), where Hawaii's finest leis go for as little as $2.50. See chapter 8.

- **Observe the Fish Auction:** There is nothing else quite like the Honolulu Fish Auction at the United Fishing Agency, 117 Ahui St. (below John Dominis Restaurant), Honolulu, HI 96814 (☎ **808/536-2148**). The fishermen bring their fresh catch in at 5:30am (sharp), Monday to Saturday, and the small group of buyers wanders from big fat tunas to weird-looking hapupu, bidding on the price of each fish. Don't be surprised if you don't recognize much of the language the bidders are using; it is an internal dialect developed over decades, which only the buyers and the auctioneer understand. The auction lasts until all the fish are sold. It is well worth getting up early to enjoy this unique cultural experience.
- **Get a Bargain at the Aloha Flea Meet:** For 50¢ admission, it's an all-day show at the Aloha Stadium parking lot, where more than 1,000 vendors are selling everything from junk to jewels. Go early for the best deals. Open Wednesday, Saturday, and Sunday from 6am to 3pm. See chapter 9.

10 The Best Luxury Hotels & Resorts

No Hawaiian king or queen ever had it this good. Great luxury resort hotels stand like temples of hedonism on the waterfront. Here are our favorites:

- **Halekulani** (☎ **808/923-2311**): For the ultimate in a "heavenly" Hawaii vacation, this is the place. In fact, Halekulani translates into "House Befitting Heaven," an apt description. When money is no object, Oahu's only five-diamond resort is the place to stay. This luxury 456-room resort is spread over 5 acres of Waikiki beachfront property. The atmosphere of elegance envelops you as soon as you step into the lobby. Even if you don't stay here, drop by at sunset to sip on a mai tai and listen to Sonny Kamehele sing Hawaiian songs as a graceful hula dancer sways to the music. See chapter 5.
- **Kahala Mandarin Oriental Hawaii** (☎ **800/367-2525** or 808/739-8888): Formerly the Kahala Hilton, this luxury property reopened in March 1996, after $75 million in renovations. Since 1964, when Conrad Hilton first opened the hotel as a place for rest and relaxation, far from the crowds of Waikiki, the Kahala has always been rated as one of Hawaii's premier hotels. A venerable who's who of celebrities have stayed at the hotel, including every president since Richard Nixon, a host of rock stars from the Rolling Stones to the Beach Boys, and a range of actors from John Wayne to Bette Midler. The Mandarin has retained the traditional feeling of an earlier time in Hawaii, which defined the Kahala for a generation, and has combined it with exotic Asian touches, creating a resort hotel for the 21st century, but with the grace and elegance of a softer, gentler time in the islands. See chapter 5.
- **Royal Hawaiian** (☎ **800/325-3535** or 808/923-7311): Hidden in the jungle of concrete buildings that make up Waikiki is an oasis of verdant gardens and a shockingly pink building. The Royal Hawaiian Hotel, affectionately called the "pink palace," is known around the world as a symbol of luxury. Since the first day it opened in 1927, the Royal has been the place to stay for celebrities, including Clark Gable, Shirley Temple, President Franklin Roosevelt, the Beatles, Kevin Costner, and others. The location is one of the best spots on Waikiki Beach. See chapter 5.
- **Sheraton Moana Surfrider Hotel** (☎ **800/325-3535** or 808/922-3111): Step back in time to old Hawaii at the Sheraton Moana Surfrider Hotel. Built in 1901, this was Waikiki's first hotel. Those days of yesteryear live on today at this grand hotel. Entry is through the original colonial porte-cochère, past the highly polished wooden front porch, with white wooden rocking chairs, and into the

perfectly restored lobby with its detailed millwork and intricate plaster detailing on the ceiling. Time seems to slow down here, tropical flowers arranged in huge sprays are everywhere, and people in the lobby all seem to be smiling. At check-in guests are greeted with a lei and a glass of fruit juice. This is a hotel not only with class, but with historic charm. See chapter 5.

- **Hilton Hawaiian Village** (☎ **800/HILTONS** or 808/949-4321): This is Waikiki's biggest resort—so big it even has its own post office. Some 2,545 rooms, spread over 20 acres with tropical gardens, thundering waterfalls, exotic wildlife, award-winning restaurants, nightly entertainment, 100 different shops, children's programs, fabulous ocean activities, a secluded lagoon, three swimming pools, Hawaiian cultural activities, two mini-golf courses, and Waikiki Beach. This place is so big and so complete, you could spend your entire vacation here and never leave the property. See chapter 5.

- **Ihilani Resort & Spa** (☎ **800/626-4446** or 808/679-0070): Located in the quiet of Oahu's west coast, some 17 miles and 25 minutes west of Honolulu International Airport—and worlds away from the tourist scene of Waikiki—the Ihilani (which means "heavenly splendor") is the first hotel in the 640-acre Ko Olina Resort and features a luxury spa and fitness center and championship tennis and golf. It's hard to get a bad room here; some 85% of the guest rooms have lagoon or ocean views. The luxuriously appointed rooms are larger than most (680 square feet), with huge lanais complete with comfortable cushioned teak furniture. Luxurious marble bathrooms have deep soaking tubs and separate glass-enclosed showers. Who misses Waikiki with luxury like this? See chapter 5.

11 The Best Moderately Priced Hotels & Resorts

It is possible to stay in paradise without having to take out a second mortgage. You can choose from an elegant boutique hotel in Waikiki, a historic bed-and-breakfast in Manoa, or a tropical accommodation reminiscent of the Hawaii of yesteryear, all at affordable prices.

- **The Royal Garden at Waikiki** (☎ **800/367-5666** or 808/943-0202): Deals, deals, deals—that's what you'll find at this elegant boutique hotel, tucked away on a quiet, tree-lined side street in Waikiki. There's a deal for everyone: room/car packages start at $135 (that's a $130 standard room, plus a car for only $5 extra); a family plan, which gives you a second room at 50% off the rack rate; and the Young-at-Heart Package, which allows seniors to book rooms starting at $91 (they also get a 10% discount at Royal Garden restaurants). See chapter 5.

- **New Otani Kaimana Beach Hotel** (☎ **800/35-OTANI** or 808/923-1555): This is one of Waikiki's best-kept secrets: a boutique hotel just outside Waikiki nestled right on the beach at the foot of Diamond Head. The airy lobby opens to the open-air Hau Tree Lanai restaurant, under the same tree that sheltered Robert Louis Stevenson a century ago. Double rooms in this quiet section of Waikiki start at $115. Since the hotel overlooks Kapiolani Park, guests have easy access to such activities as golf, tennis, kite flying, jogging, and bicycling. See chapter 5.

- **Hawaiiana Hotel** (☎ **800/535-0085** or 808/923-3811): The lush tropical flowers and carved tiki at the entrance on tiny Beach Walk set the tone for this intimate low-rise hotel. The hotel's slogan says it all: "The spirit of old Hawaii." From the moment you arrive, you'll experience the aloha spirit here: At check-in, guests are given a pineapple; every morning, complimentary Kona coffee and tropical juice are served poolside; at check-out, flower leis are presented to the women as a fragrant reminder of their vacation at the Hawaiiana. The concrete hollow-tile rooms, which start at $85 double, feature a kitchenette and a view of the gardens and swimming pool. See chapter 5.

• **Outrigger Prince Kuhio** (☎ **800/OUTRIGGER** or 808/922-0811): The Prince Kuhio is one of the best hotels in the Outrigger chain, which is famous for comfortable accommodations at reasonable prices. Up the escalator to the second-floor lobby, the marble floors, chandelier, handwoven rugs, and artful decor offer a hint of your accommodations. Completely renovated in 1997, the 37-story Prince Kuhio is located just blocks from Waikiki Beach, the Honolulu Zoo, and the heart of Waikiki shopping. A room for two starts at $150. See chapter 5.

• **Manoa Valley Inn** (☎ **800/535-0085** or 808/947-6019): It's completely off the tourist trail and far from the beach, but that doesn't stop travelers from heading to this historic 1915 Carpenter Gothic home on a quiet residential street near the University of Hawaii. This eight-room Manoa landmark—it's on the National Register of Historic Places—offers a glimpse into the lifestyles of the rich and famous in early Honolulu. Each room has its own unique decor and has been named for a prominent figure in Hawaii's history: The John Guild suite, for instance, has a turn-of-the-century parlor with antiques and old-fashioned rose wallpaper; the adjoining bedroom has a king-size koa bed, and the bath features an old-style tub as well as a separate modern shower. As the sun sets, complimentary wine and cheese are served on the quiet veranda. Rates are $99 to $120 double with shared bath; $140 to $190 double with private bath. See chapter 5.

12 The Best Places to Stay Beyond Waikiki

Waikiki is the draw, but other parts of Oahu are worth equal consideration. There are adorable B&Bs on the North Shore, practical two-bedroom apartments in Honolulu, a studio with a swimming pool overlooking Pearl Harbor, and a luxury resort on the north end of the island.

• **Santa's by the Sea** (☎ **800/262-9912** or 808/885-4550): This certainly must be where Santa Claus comes to vacation, and for good reason—$110 for two for this apartment right on the ocean on the North Shore. The location, price, and style make this place a must-stay if you plan to spend time on the North Shore. Santa's is not located on just any beach, but the famous Banzai Pipeline. You can go from your bed to the sand in less than 30 seconds to watch the sun rise over the Pacific. See chapter 5.

• **Rainbow Inn** (☎ **808/488-7525**): This private tropical garden studio, downstairs from the home of retired military officer Gene Smith and his wife Betty, has panoramic views of Pearl Harbor, the entire south coast of Oahu, and the Waianae and Koolau mountains. A large deck and full-size pool are just outside the apartment's door. Located close to Pearl Ridge Shopping Center, Rainbow Inn is freeway-close to all of Oahu's attractions, yet far enough away to provide you with lots of peace and quiet. At $65 a night, this is one of Oahu's best bed-and-breakfast deals. See chapter 5.

• **Lanikai Bed & Breakfast:** (☎ **800/258-7895** or 808/261-1059): This old-time bed-and-breakfast, a *kamaaina* (native-born) home that reflects the Hawaii of yesteryear, is now into its second generation. The recently renovated 1,000-square-foot upstairs apartment is decorated in an old Hawaii bungalow style and rents for $90 for two. Or you can follow the ginger- and ti-lined path to a 540-square-foot honeymooner's delight, at $80 for two. Access to picture-perfect white-sand Lanikai Beach is right across the street, bus routes are close by, and a 2½-mile biking/walking loop is immediately accessible. See chapter 5.

- **Hilton Turtle Bay Resort** (☎ **800/HILTONS** or 808/293-8811): An hour's drive from Waikiki and eons away is this luxurious oceanfront resort out in the country. Sitting on 808 acres, this is a resort filled with activities: 27 holes of golf, 10 tennis courts, and 5 miles of shoreline with secluded white-sand coves. Choose from the spacious guest rooms, suites, or oceanside cabanas—all have oceanfront views starting at $165 for two. See chapter 5.

13 The Best Culinary Experiences

Great news on Oahu's dining front: George Mavrothalassitis has moved back from Maui and opened his own Chef Mavro Restaurant, sending atwitter his throngs of worshipful foodies. A few long blocks away, Sushi Sasabune is redefining sushi from its nondescript Pawaa location, spurning all that is not authentic, Japanese, top-drawer, and fresh. (No mayo or California rolls there.) Sasabune and Chef Mavro are only two of Honolulu's stellar newcomers. Around them, Oahu's dining scene continues to fall into the general categories of Waikiki restaurants, chef-owned glamour restaurants, neighborhood eateries, fast-food joints, and ethnic restaurants. One of Honolulu's greatest assets is the range of restaurants in all of these categories. Watch for Kelvin Ro's (of the erstwhile Kahala Moon Café) soon-to-open new restaurant, where the legendary old Willows used to be. Meanwhile, here's a sampling of Oahu's finest.

- **Akasaka** (1646B Kona St.; ☎ 808/942-4466): The spicy tuna hand roll, hamachi sushi, clam miso soup, and sizzling tofu and scallops are among life's greatest pleasures. The tiny sushi bar is hidden among the shadowy nightclubs of Kona Street—off the beaten track, yet always jumping with regulars. See chapter 6.
- **Alan Wong's Restaurant** (1857 S. King St., 3rd Floor; ☎ 808/949-2526): Master strokes at this shrine of Hawaii Regional Cuisine: crisp ahi lumpia; warm California roll made with salmon roe, wasabi, and Kona lobster instead of rice; and fresh "day boat" scallops in season. The menu changes daily, but the flavors never lose their sizzle. See chapter 6.
- **Chef Mavro Restaurant** (1969 S. King St.; ☎ 808/944-4714): This is the perfect balance of soigné and sumptuous without being intimidating: elegant fare (Mediterranean/French with Hawaii regional elements), a cordial ambience, with food-and-wine pairings and three prix-fixe menus. A great concept, executed in the Mavrothalassitis way: brilliant and approachable. See chapter 6.
- **Hawaii Seafood Paradise** (1830 Ala Moana Blvd.; ☎ 808/946-4514): Nine kinds of roast duck, including a peerless Peking, are reason enough to go there. But the sizzling platters, seafood fried rice, spicy prawn soup, and kung pao scallops take Cantonese/Szechuan to new heights. A few Thai dishes spice up the menu. See chapter 6.
- **Jimbo's Restaurant** (1936 S. King St.; ☎ 808/947-2211): Life's simple pleasures: homemade broth, homemade noodles, light-as-air tempura, nabeyaki of the gods. All in a cozy room accented with bamboo, calligraphy, and folk art. See chapter 6.
- **Hoku's** (5000 Kahala Ave.; ☎ 808/739-8777): Bamboo floors, a soothing ambience, tandoor oven, and a menu that combines European finesse with island ingredients make Hoku's a Honolulu treasure. Cross-cultural dishes (Szechuan

wok-cooked prawns, peppered ahi steak, steamed whole fresh fish, baked Caesar salad) are creative, appealing, and stunningly executed. See chapter 6.

- **Olive Tree Cafe** (4614 Kilauea Ave.; ☎ **808/737-0303**): Bravo to this sensational cafe of big flavors, fresh ingredients, and unbelievably affordable prices. A tiny cafe with a sprinkling of tables outdoors, Olive Tree is the peerless purveyor of Honolulu's best fresh fish souvlakis, spanakopita, tabouleh, and hummus. Daily specials include lamb shank in herbs, lemon chicken, and other tender mercies. BYOB. See chapter 6.

- **Roy's Restaurant** (6600 Kalanianaole Hwy.; ☎ **808/396-7697**): The pioneer of Hawaii regional cuisine still reigns at his busy, noisy flagship Hawaii Kai dining room with the trademark open kitchen. Roy's deft way with local ingredients, ethnic preparations, and fresh fish make his menu, which changes daily, a novel experience every time. See chapter 6.

- **Sushi Sasabune** (1419 S. King St.; ☎ **808/947-3800**): "Trust me" sushi means eat what the chef serves you, and it will be fresh, shipped in that day. (If you want to order à la carte, you can, but sit at a table.) From the first bite of bluefin tuna in ponzu to the Nova Scotia salmon and delicately translucent king clam, Sasabune serves sushi nonpareil, thrilling in its freshness and integrity—and the warm rice is the clincher. See chapter 6.

14 The Best of Oahu for Kids

Oahu isn't for adults only—there are plenty of activities to keep the keikis (kids) as well as the kids-at-heart busy.

- **Swim at Waikiki Beach:** Waikiki Beach offers a lot more than just swimming for the kids; they can boogie board, learn to surf, take a ride on an outrigger canoe or sailing catamaran, snorkel, or build sand castles. See chapter 7.

- **Snorkel at Hanauma Bay:** Kids will be enthralled at the underwater world they can see in this marine park teeming with tropical fish. The shallow waters near the beach are perfect for neophyte snorkelers. The long (2,000 ft.) beach has plenty of room for kids to take off and run. Get there early; it can get crowded. See chapter 7.

- **Explore the Depths in a Submarine Dive:** Better than a movie, more exciting than a video game, both the *Atlantis* and *Voyager* submarines journey down to 100 feet below the waves and explore the Neptunian world of tropical reef fish, turtles, huge manta rays, and even an occasional shark or two. See chapter 7.

- **Explore the Bishop Museum:** There are some 1,180,000 Polynesian artifacts, 13,500,000 different insect specimens, 6,000,000 marine and land shells, 490,000 plant specimens, 130,000 fish specimens, and 85,000 birds and mammals all in the Bishop Museum. Kids can explore interactive exhibits, see a 50-foot sperm whale skeleton, and check out a Hawaiian grass hut. There's something for everyone here. See chapter 8.

- **Walking Through a Submarine:** The USS *Bowfin* Submarine Museum Park offers kids an interactive museum and a real submarine that served in some of the fiercest naval battles in World War II. Kids can explore the interior of the tightly packed submarine that housed some 90 to 100 men, and see the stacked bunks where the men slept, the radar and electronics in the command center, and where the torpedoes were stored and launched. See chapter 8.

- **Dream at the Hawaii Maritime Center:** Kids will love the Kalakaua Boathouse, the two-story museum of the Maritime Center with exhibits that include the development of surfing, the art of tattooing, and artifacts from the whaling industry. Next door is the fully rigged, four-masted *Falls of Clyde*. Built in 1878, it served as a cargo-and-passenger liner and a sailing tanker before being declared a National Historic Landmark. If it's not out sailing, moored next to the *Falls* is the *Hokule'a*, the re-creation of a traditional double-hulled sailing canoe, which in 1976 made the 6,000-mile round-trip voyage to Tahiti, following only ancient navigational techniques—the stars, the wind, and the sea. See chapter 8.

- **Watch the Fish and Sharks at the Waikiki Aquarium:** Much more than just a big fish tank, the Waikiki Aquarium will astound and, at the same time, educate your youngsters. They can probably sit for hours staring at the sharks, turtles, eels, rays, and fish swimming in the main tank. For a few laughs, wander out to the monk seal area and watch the antics of these endangered seagoing clowns. See chapter 8.

- **See Sea Creatures at Sea Life Park:** Kids will love this 62-acre ocean theme park that features orca whales, dolphins, seals, and penguins going through their hoops to the delight of kids of all ages. There's a Hawaiian reef tank full of native tropical fish, a "touch" pool where you can grab a real sea cucumber (commonly found in tide pools), and a bird sanctuary where you can see birds such as the red-footed booby and the Frigate bird that are usually seen overhead. The chief curiosity, though, is the world's only "wolphin"—a cross between a false killer whale and an Atlantic bottle-nosed dolphin. See chapter 8.

15 The Best Shopping

Products of Hawaii now merit their own festivals and trade shows throughout the year. "Made in Hawaii" is a label to be touted as aloha shirts, textiles, craft items, fine arts, and food products burgeon throughout the Islands. This has immeasurably enhanced the world of shopping. In this land of the alluring outdoors, few people like to admit that shopping is a major activity—or, some would say, distraction. The proliferation of top-notch made-in-Hawaii products, the vitality of the local crafts scene, and the search for mementos of the islands lend a new respectability to shopping here.

- **Academy Shop** (900 S. Beretania St., Honolulu Academy of Arts; ☎ **808/ 523-8703**): What's here: ethnic and contemporary gift items representing the art and craft traditions of the world, from books and jewelry to basketry, beadwork, ikats, saris, ethnic fabrics, and fiber vessels and accessories. What you'll want: everything. See chapter 9.

- **Alii Antiques of Kailua II** (9-A Maluniu Ave., Kailua; ☎ **808/261-1705**): Abandon all restraint, particularly if you have a weakness for vintage Hawaiiana— koa lamps and rattan furniture from the '30s and '40s, hula nodders, rare 1940s koa tables, and a breathtaking array of vintage etched-glass vases and trays are some of the items in this unforgettable shop. See chapter 9.

- **Avanti Fashion** (2229 Kuhio Ave., ☎ **808/924-1688;** 2270 Kalakaua Ave., Waikiki Shopping Plaza, ☎ 808/922-2828): In authentic prints from the 1930s and 1940s reproduced on silk, Avanti aloha shirts and sportswear elevate tropical garb from high kitsch to high chic. Casual, comfortable, easy care, and light as a cloud, the silks look vintage but cost a fraction of collectibles prices. The nostalgic treasures are available in retail stores statewide, but the best selection is at the retail stores in Waikiki. See chapter 9.

- **Bibelot** (1130 Koko Head Ave.; ☎ **808/738-0368**): Bibelot is the perfect local gallery: tiny, tasteful, and luminous with fine works of glass, paintings, ceramics, jewelry, textiles, and other objects of beauty. Kudos to Paul Sakai and Tom

Tierney for giving Island artists this new and refreshing venue. More than 30 artists, some of them the finest in the Islands (Doug Britt, Margaret Ezekiel, Charles Higa, Kenny Kicklighter) make their works available here. Fantastic gifts to go. See chapter 9.

- **Contemporary Museum Gift Shop** (2411 Makiki Heights Rd., Contemporary Museum; ☎ **808/523-3447**): It gets our vote as the most beautiful setting for a gift shop, and its contents are a bonus: extraordinary art-related books, avant-garde jewelry, cards and stationery, home accessories, and gift items made by artists from Hawaii and across the country. Only the best here. See chapter 9.

- **Four Calling Birds** (619 Kapahulu Ave., upstairs; ☎ **808/735-6133**): From designer birdhouses to lamps, retro-aloha welcome mats, mochi demonstrations, and objects that are collectible, antique, or recycled, this unique atelier is a treasure trove of finds. Mailboxes, utensils, leather coats, jewelry, beads, purses, greeting cards—they're all wonderful, made or collected by local artists. Open only 2 days a week, so call ahead. See chapter 9.

- **Island Provision Co. at Vagabond House** (1200 Ala Moana Center, Ward Centre; ☎ **808/593-0288**): Gracious island living is translated here into home accessories, one-of-a-kind island crafts, fine porcelain and pottery, children's books, luxury soaps, hand-screened table linens, china, furniture, and designer toys and teapots. A browser's (and shopper's!) paradise. See chapter 9.

- **Native Books & Beautiful Things** (Ward Warehouse, 1050 Ala Moana Blvd., ☎ **808/596-8885;** 222 Merchant St., Downtown, ☎ 808/599-5511; Bishop Museum, 1525 Bernice St., ☎ 808/847-8288): Hawaii is the content and the context in this shop of books, crafts, and gift items made by island artists and crafters. Musical instruments, calabashes, jewelry, leis, books, fabrics, clothing, home accessories, jams and jellies—they're all high quality and made in Hawaii—a celebration of Hawaiiana. See chapter 9.

- **Strawberry Connection of Hawaii** (1931 Kahai St., Kalihi; ☎ **808/842-0278**): This is paradise for foodies, chefs, aspiring chefs, and those on the hunt for the best in Hawaii food products. This warehouse in industrial Honolulu rewards your search with thousands of the best gifts to go, from tropical fruit vinegars and preserves to gourmet honeys, chocolates, and made-in-Hawaii sauces and marinades. A new tea salon, Way of Tea, and a top-notch gourmet deli with avant-garde warehouse seating are wonderful, down to the last grain of Petrossian. See chapter 9.

16   The Best Spots for Sunset Cocktails

Need we say more?

- **Sunset Lanai** (2863 Kalakaua Ave., New Otani Kaimana Beach Hotel; ☎ **808/923-1555**): The hau tree shaded Robert Louis Stevenson as he wrote poems to Princess Kaiulani. Today it frames the ocean view from the Sunset Lanai, next to the Hau Tree Lanai restaurant. Sunset Lanai is the favorite watering hole of Diamond Head–area beachgoers who love Sans Souci Beach, the ocean view, the mai tais and sashimi platters, and the live music during weekend sunset hours. See chapter 5.

- **Jameson's by the Sea** (62–540 Kamehameha Hi., Haleiwa; ☎ **808/637-6272**): The mai tais here are dubbed the best in surf city, and the view, although not perfect, isn't hurting either. Across the street from the harbor, this open-air roadside oasis is a happy stop for North Shore wave watchers and sunset-savvy sightseers. See chapter 6.

- **House Without a Key** (2199 Kalia Rd., Halekulani; ☎ **808/923-2311**): Oahu's quintessential sunset oasis claims several unbeatable elements: It's outdoors on the ocean, with a view of Diamond Head, and it offers great hula and steel guitar music—and one of the best mai tais on the island. You know it's special when even jaded Honoluluans declare it their favorite spot for send-offs, reunions, and an everyday gorgeous sunset. See chapter 10.
- **Mai Tai Bar** (2259 Kalakaua Ave., Royal Hawaiian Hotel; ☎ **808/923-7311**): This bar without walls is perched a few feet from the sand, with sweeping views of the South Shore and the Waianae Mountains. Surfers and paddlers ride the waves while the light turns golden and Diamond Head acquires a halo. This is one of the most pleasing views of Waikiki Beach; sip a mighty mai tai while Carmen and Keith Haugen serenade you. See chapter 10.
- **Duke's Canoe Club** (2335 Kalakaua Ave., Outrigger Waikiki Hotel; ☎ **808/ 923-0711**): It's crowded at sunset, but who can resist Moe Keale or Brother Noland's music in this upbeat atmosphere a few feet from the sands of Waikiki? Come in from the beach or from the street—it's always a party at Duke's. Entertainment here is tops, and it reaches a crescendo at sunset. See chapter 10.

2 Planning a Trip to Oahu

by Jeanette Foster

Oahu has so many places to explore, things to do, sights to see—planning your trip can be bewildering with so much vying for your attention. Where to start? That's where we come in. In the pages that follow, we've compiled everything you need to know to plan your ideal trip to Hawaii: airlines, seasons, a calendar of events, and much more (even how to get married in the islands). We'll show you how to do it without going broke: You'll find lots of great money-saving tips and insider advice on how to get the most out of your vacation time and money.

Remember, the planning process can be part of the excitement of your trip. So in addition to reading this guide, we suggest you spend some time on the Internet looking at sites (we've included Web site addresses throughout this book) or calling and writing for brochures. We fully believe that searching for the best bargains and planning your dream vacation to Hawaii should be half the fun.

1 Visitor Information & Money

SOURCES OF INFORMATION

For information about traveling in Hawaii, contact the **Hawaii Visitors and Convention Bureau (HVCB),** Suite 801, Waikiki Business Plaza, 2270 Kalakaua Ave., Honolulu, HI 96815 (☎ **800/ GO-HAWAII** or 808/923-1811; www.gohawaii.com). Among other things, the bureau publishes the helpful *Accommodations and Car Rental Guide* and supplies free brochures, maps, and the *Islands of Aloha* magazine, the official HVCB magazine.

The HVCB also has a U.S. mainland office at 180 Montgomery St., Suite 2360, San Francisco CA 94104 (☎ **800/353-5846**). All other HVCB offices on the mainland have been closed because of budget constraints.

If you want information about working and living in Hawaii, contact **The Chamber of Commerce of Hawaii,** 1132 Bishop St., Suite 200, Honolulu, HI 96815 (☎ **808/545-4300**).

You can also surf the Web for information on Hawaii:

- Hawaii Visitors & Convention Bureau: www.gohawaii.com
- Hawaii State Vacation Planner: www.hshawaii.com
- Planet Hawaii: www.planet-hawaii.com/travel
- Oahu Visitors Bureau: www.visit-oahu.com
- State of Hawaii: www.hawaii.gov

- City and County of Honolulu: www.co.honolulu.hi.us
- Hawaii Yellow Pages: www.surfhi.com
- Weather information: http://lumahai.soest.hawaii.edu/index.html or www.weather.com/weather/us/states/Hawaii.html or www.cnn.com/WEATHER/cities/us.hawaii.html

MONEY
ATMs

Hawaii pioneered the use of automatic teller machines (ATMs) nearly two decades ago, and now they're everywhere on Oahu. You'll find them at most banks, in supermarkets, at Long's Drug stores, at Honolulu International Airport, and in some resorts and shopping centers, like Ala Moana Center and Aloha Tower Market Place. It's actually cheaper and faster to get cash from an ATM than to fuss with traveler's checks. **Cirrus** (☎ 800/424-7787; www.mastercard.com/atm/) and **Plus** (☎ 800/843-7587; www.visa.com/atms) are the two most popular networks; check the back of your ATM card to see which network your bank belongs to. Use the 800 numbers to locate ATMS in your destination. Be sure to check the daily withdrawal limit before you depart.

The United States dollar is the accepted currency in Hawaii.

TRAVELER'S CHECKS

Traveler's checks are something of an anachronism from the days before the ATM made cash accessible at any time. Many banks, however, impose a fee every time a card is used at an ATM in a different city or bank. If you're withdrawing money every day, you might be better off with traveler's checks—provided that you don't mind showing identification every time you want to cash a check.

You can get traveler's checks at almost any bank. **American Express** offers denominations of $10, $20, $50, $100, $500, and $1,000. You pay a service charge ranging from 1%–4%. You can also get American Express traveler's checks over the phone by calling ☎ **800/221-7282;** by using this number, Amex gold and platinum cardholders are exempt from the 1% fee. AAA members can get checks without a fee at most AAA offices.

Visa offers traveler's checks at Citibank locations nationwide, as well as several other banks. The service charge ranges between 1.5% and 2%; checks come in denominations of $20, $50, $100, $500, and $1,000. **MasterCard** offers traveler's checks, too. Call ☎ **800/223-9920** for a location near you.

2 When to Go

The majority of visitors don't come to Hawaii when the weather's best in the islands; rather, they come when it's at its worst everywhere else. Thus, the **"high" season**—when prices are up and resorts are booked to capacity—is generally from mid-December through March or mid-April. The last 2 weeks of December, in particular, is a prime time for travel to Hawaii. If you're planning a holiday trip, make your reservations as early as possible, expect to travel with holiday crowds, and to pay top dollar for accommodations and airfare.

The best **bargains** are available in the spring (from mid-April to mid-June) and fall (from September to mid-December)—ironic, since these are the best seasons in Hawaii, in terms of reliably great weather. If you're looking to save money, or if you just want to avoid the crowds, this is the time to visit. Hotel rates tend to be significantly lower during this "off" season. Airfares also tend to be lower—sometimes substantially—and

What Things Cost in Waikiki	U.S. $
Taxi from Honolulu International Airport to Waikiki	23.00
Shuttle van from Honolulu International Airport to Waikiki	8.00
Local telephone call (on same island)	.35
Double at The Breakers (inexpensive)	91.00
Double at Doubletree Alana Waikiki (moderate)	135.00
Double at Hilton Hawaiian Village (expensive)	210.00
Double at Halekulani (very expensive)	310.00
Admission to Bishop Museum, Honolulu	14.95
Movie ticket	7.00

good packages and special deals are often available. (*Note:* If you plan to come to Hawaii between the last week in April and mid-May, be sure to book in advance your accommodations, interisland air reservations, and car rental. Waikiki is especially busy during this time because the Japanese, who are on holiday for "Golden Week," are also booking reservations.)

Because of the large number of families traveling in summer (June through August), you won't get the fantastic bargains of spring and fall. However, you'll still do much better on accommodations and airfare prices than you will in the winter months.

CLIMATE

Since Hawaii lies at the edge of the tropical zone, it technically has only two seasons, both of them warm. There's a **dry season** that corresponds to summer, and the **rainy season** generally runs during the winter from November to March. It rains every day somewhere in the islands at all times of the year, but the rainy season can cause "gray" weather and spoil your tanning opportunities. Fortunately, it seldom rains for more than 3 consecutive days.

The year-round temperature usually varies no more than 10°F, but this does depend on where you are. Oahu is like a ship in that it has a leeward and a windward side. The leeward side (the west and south, from Waianae to Honolulu and Waikiki) is usually hot and dry, while the windward side (east and north, from Haleiwa to Waimanalo) is generally cooler and moist. When you want arid, sun-baked weather, go leeward. When you want lush, often wet, junglelike weather, go windward.

Hawaii also has many microclimates, thanks to its interior valleys, coastal plains, and mountain peaks. It can be pouring rain at the University of Hawaii in Manoa, and sunny and dry in Waikiki, a 15-minute drive away.

The **best months** to be in Hawaii are April, May, September, and October, when the nearly perfect weather is even better—not too windy, not too humid, but just right. And this is the off-season: The kids are in school, and the tourists have thinned out. The state's "carrying capacity," as they say here, isn't maxed out. Hotels, restaurants, and attractions aren't as crowded, and everyone is more relaxed.

On rare occasions, the weather can be disastrous. The official hurricane season is June to November. (Remember Hurricane Iniki in September 1992? It was the most powerful Pacific storm in history, and it crushed Kauai with 225-mile-an-hour winds.) Tsunamis, huge tidal waves caused by far-off earthquakes, have swept the shores of the islands. But those are extreme exceptions. Usually one sunny day simply follows another here, each quite like the other. You have only to decide where and how to spend them.

HOLIDAYS

When Hawaii observes holidays, especially those over a long weekend, travel between the islands increases, interisland airline seats are fully booked, rental cars are at a premium, and hotels and restaurants are busier than at other times.

Federal, state, and county government offices are closed on all federal holidays: January 1 (New Year's Day); third Monday in January (Martin Luther King, Jr. Day); third Monday in February (Presidents' Day, Washington's Birthday); last Monday in May (Memorial Day); July 4 (Independence Day); first Monday in September (Labor Day); second Monday in October (Columbus Day); November 11 (Veteran's Day); fourth Thursday in November (Thanksgiving Day); and December 25 (Christmas).

State and county offices are also closed on local holidays. They include: March 26 (Prince Kuhio Day), honoring the birthday of Hawaii's first delegate to the U.S. Congress; June 11 (King Kamehameha Day), a statewide holiday commemorating Kamehameha the Great, who united the islands and ruled from 1795 to 1819; and the third Friday in August (Admission Day), which honors Hawaii's admission as the 50th state to the United States on August 21, 1959.

Other special days celebrated by many people in Hawaii that don't involve the closing of federal, state, and county offices are: Chinese New Year (in January or February), Girl's Day (March 3), Buddha's Birthday (April 8), Father Damien's Day (April 15), Boy's Day (May 5), Samoan Flag Day (in August), Aloha Festivals (September to October), and Pearl Harbor Day (December 7).

Oahu Calendar of Events

For information on sporting events, see "Calendar of Events: Sports" in chapter 7, "Fun in the Surf & Sun."

January

- **Narcissus Festival,** Honolulu. Around Chinese New Year, this cultural festival includes a queen pageant, cooking demonstrations, and cultural fair. January or February, depending on Chinese New Year. Call ☎ **808/538-6901.**

February

○ **Punahou School Carnival,** Punahou School, Honolulu. Everything you can imagine in a school carnival, from high-speed rides to homemade jellies, all benefiting scholarship funds for Hawaii's most prestigious school. Call ☎ **808/944-5711.**

March

- **St. Patrick's Day Parade,** Fort Derussy to Kapiolani Park, Waikiki. Bagpipes, bands, clowns and marching groups troop through Waikiki to celebrate St. Patty's Day on March 17. Call ☎ **808/946-8514.**
- **Prince Kuhio Celebration,** commemorates the birth of Jonah Kuhio Kalanianaole, born March 26, 1871. He might have been one of Hawaii's kings if the Hawaiian monarchy had not been overthrown. After Hawaii's annexation to the United States, Prince Kuhio was elected to Congress (1902). Ceremonies are held at the Prince Kuhio Federal Building, at Kuhio Beach in Waikiki, and other locations throughout Oahu. Check the local newspapers for details.
○ **Kamehameha Schools Song Contest,** Neal Blaisdell Center, Honolulu. For more than three-quarters of a century, Hawaii's top Hawaiian school has conducted this traditional Hawaiian chorale contest. Call ☎ **808/842-8338.**

April

- **Easter Sunday,** National Cemetery of the Pacific, Punchbowl, Honolulu. For a century, people have gathered at this famous cemetery for Easter sunrise services. Call ☎ **808/293-9788.**
- **Buddha Day,** at various Hongwanji missions throughout the island. Some Buddhist missions have a flower pageant honoring the birth of Buddha. April 6. Call ☎ **808/595-2144.**
- **Hawaiian Slack Key Concert,** Honolulu Academy of Arts, Honolulu. A great opportunity to listen to this traditional form of music. The date of the concert varies from year to year; call ☎ **808/532-8701** for details.

May

- ✪ **Annual Lei Day Celebration.** May Day is Lei Day in Hawaii, celebrated with lei-making contests, pageantry, arts and crafts, and a concert at the Waikiki Shell. May 1. Call ☎ **808/924-8934.**
- ✪ **World Fire-Knife Dance Championships & Samoan Festival,** Polynesian Cultural Center, Laie. Junior and adult fire-knife dancers from around the world converge on the center in the most amazing performance you'll ever see. Authentic Samoan food and cultural festivities. Mid-May. Call ☎ **808/293-3333.**
- **State Fair,** Aloha Stadium, Honolulu. The annual state fair is a great one, with the biggest rides and shows. Check out the livestock contests, orchid displays, food booths, and local music and hula performances. Last Saturday in May through mid-June. Call ☎ **808/488-3389.**
- **Memorial Day,** National Memorial Cemetery of the Pacific, Punchbowl, Honolulu. The Armed Forces have a ceremony recognizing those who have died for their country. Call ☎ **808/566-1430.**
- **Lantern Floating,** Keehi Lagoon. A ceremonial floating of some 700 lanterns takes place at sunset, representing an appeal for peace and harmony. Hula and music follows. Call ☎ **808/523-8802,** ext. 11.

June

- ✪ **King Kamehameha Celebration,** a state holiday with a massive floral parade, *hoolaulea* (party), and much more. First weekend in June. On Oahu, call ☎ **808/586-0333.**
- **King Kamehameha Hula Competition,** Neal Blaisdell Center, Honolulu. One of the top hula competitions with dancers from as far away as Japan. Third weekend in June. Call ☎ **808/586-0333.**
- ✪ **Taste of Honolulu,** Civic Center Grounds, Honolulu. Benefiting the Easter Seals campaign, Hawaii's premier outdoor food festival features tastings from 30 restaurants. Entertainment, beer and wine tasting, cooking demos, gourmet marketplace, and children's activities. End of June. Call ☎ **808/536-1015.**

July

- **Pacific Island Taro Festival,** Windward Community College, Kaneohe. Music, storytelling, dance, an arts-and-crafts fair, and a farmers' market help explain and celebrate the cultures and traditions of the Pacific Islands. Usually first Saturday in July. Call ☎ **808/235-7433.**
- **Fourth of July Fireworks,** Desiderio and Sills Field, Schofield Barracks, Wahiawa. A day-long celebration with entertainment, food, and games that ends with spectacular fireworks. Free and open to the public. Call ☎ **808/665-0143.**

- **Na Wahine O' Hawaii,** McCoy Pavilion, Ala Moana Park, Honolulu, Oahu. This all-female competition focuses on all aspects of the performing arts. Early July. Call ☎ **808/239-4336.**
- **Hawaii International Jazz Festival,** Sheraton Waikiki, Waikiki. Evening concerts and daily jam sessions, scholarship giveaways, the USC jazz band, along with many popular jazz and blues artists. Mid-July. Call ☎ **808/941-9974.**
- **Ukulele Festival,** Kapiolani Bandstand, Waikiki. This annual event features 400 children and special guest stars. Presented by Sheraton Hotels in Waikiki. End of July. Call ☎ **808/732-3739.**

August

- **Admissions Day.** Hawaii became the 50th state on August 21, 1959, so the state takes a holiday (all state-related facilities and the local banks are closed) on the third Friday in August.
- ✪ **Hawaiian Slack-Key Guitar Festival.** Five-hour festival held annually at a different location on Oahu, presenting the best of Hawaii's slack-key guitar players. Call ☎ **808/239-4336.**

September

- ✪ **Aloha Festivals,** various sites across Oahu. Parades and other events celebrate Hawaiian culture. Call ☎ **800/852-7690** or 808/545-1771 for a schedule of events.

October

- **Makahiki Festival,** Waimea Valley. Hawaiian games, crafts, music, and food, all in a tremendous natural setting. The Hula Kahiko Competition is a major highlight. First weekend in October. Call ☎ **808/638-8511.**

November

- **Hawaii International Film Festival,** various locations in Honolulu. A cinema festival with a cross-cultural spin, featuring filmmakers from Asia, the Pacific Islands, and the U.S. First 2 weeks in November. Call ☎ **808/528-FILM.**
- **World Invitational Hula Festival,** Waikiki Shell. Competitors from all over the world dance for the prizes. Early to mid-November. Call ☎ **808/486-3185.**

December

- **Pacific Handcrafters Guild's Christmas Faire,** Thomas Square. One of the largest and finest fairs in the state selling art and fine crafts takes place the first weekend in December, with local entertainment and food booths to liven up the atmosphere. Call ☎ **808/637-9447.**
- **Festival of Trees,** Honolulu. Downtown display of one-of-a-kind decorated trees, wreaths, and decorations to benefit Queen's Medical Center. First or second week of the month. Call ☎ **808/547-4780.**
- ✪ **First Night,** downtown Honolulu. A festival of arts and entertainment. For 12 hours, musicians, dancers, actors, jugglers, magicians, and mimes perform; food is available; and fireworks bring in the New Year. Alcohol-free. December 31. Call ☎ **808/532-3131.**

3 Health & Insurance

STAYING HEALTHY

Hawaii is one of the healthiest places in the world to visit. People who live here have a longer life expectancy than anywhere else in the U.S. (74 years for men and over

79 years for women). However, there are some hazards you should be aware of so that, in the unlikely event you encounter them, you can take the necessary steps to avoid more serious health problems.

ON LAND

INSECTS   As in any tropical climate, there are lots of bugs in Hawaii. Most of them won't harm you; however, three insects—mosquitoes, centipedes, and scorpions—do sting and can cause anything from a minor annoyance to severe swelling and pain.

Mosquitoes   There's not much you can do about mosquitoes (which are not native, but arrived in 1826 as larvae stowed away in the water barrels on the ship *Wellington* when it anchored in Lahaina), except to apply commercial repellent to keep them off you, burn mosquito punk or citronella candles to keep them out of your immediate area, or apply ointments (which you can pick up at any drugstore) after they have bitten you to stop the stinging, itching, and swelling. Most bites disappear after anywhere from a few hours to a few days.

Centipedes   These segmented insects with a jillion legs come in two varieties: the 6- to 8-inch-long brown ones, and the smaller 2- to 3-inch-long blue guys, which really pack a wallop with their sting. Centipedes are generally found in damp, wet places, like under wood piles or compost heaps. Wearing closed-toe shoes can help prevent stings if you accidentally unearth one. If stung, the reaction can range from something similar to a mild bee sting to severe pain; apply ice at once to prevent swelling and pain. See a doctor if the pain is extreme, or if you experience swelling, nausea, or any other severe reaction.

Scorpions   Rarely seen, scorpions are found in arid, warm regions; their stings can be serious. Campers in dry areas should always check their boots before putting them on, and shake out sleeping bags and bed rolls. Symptoms of a scorpion sting include shortness of breath, hives, swelling, and nausea. In the unlikely event that you're stung, apply diluted household ammonia and cold compresses to the area of the sting and seek medical help immediately.

HIKING SAFETY   In addition to taking the appropriate precautions against Hawaii's bug population (see above), hikers should always let someone know where they're headed, when they're going, and when they plan to return; too many hikers are lost in Hawaii because they don't let others know their basic plans.

Always check weather conditions with the **National Weather Service** (☎ **808/ 973-4381**) before you go out. Hike with a pal, never alone. Wear hiking boots, a sun hat, clothes to protect you from the sun and from getting scratches, and high-SPF sunscreen on all exposed areas of skin. Take water. Stay on the trail. Watch your step. It's easy to slip off precipitous trails and into steep canyons with disastrous, even fatal, results. Incapacitated hikers are often plucked to safety by Fire and Rescue squads, who must use helicopters to gain access to remote sites. Today, many experienced hikers pack a cell phone; in case of emergency, dial ☎ **911.**

IN THE OCEAN

Because many people coming to Hawaii are unfamiliar with the ocean environment, they're unaware of its potential hazards. With just a few precautions, your ocean experience can be a safe and happy one. An excellent book to get is *All Stings Considered: First Aid and Medical Treatment of Hawaii's Marine Injuries* (University of Hawaii Press, 1997), by Craig Thomas (an emergency-medicine doctor) and Susan Scott (a registered nurse). These avid water people have put together the authoritative book on first aid for Hawaii's marine injuries.

Health & Insurance   23

Warning

Never, under any circumstances, should you touch a coral head. Not only can you sustain a cut, but you can also damage a living organism that has taken decades to grow.

SHARKS   Fortunately, sharks are not a big problem in Hawaii; in fact, they're spotted so infrequently that locals look forward to seeing them. Since records have been kept, starting in 1779, there have been only about 100 shark attacks in Hawaii; 40% have been fatal. The most frequent attacks have occurred after a person fell into the ocean from the shore or from a boat; in these cases, the sharks probably attacked after the person was dead. The general rules for avoiding sharks are: Don't swim at sunrise, sunset, or where the water is murky because of stream runoff—sharks may mistake you for one of their usual meals. And don't swim where there are bloody fish in the water (sharks become aggressive around blood).

SEASICKNESS   The waters in Hawaii can be as smooth as glass to downright turbulent (in storm conditions); they usually fall somewhere in between. In general, expect rougher conditions in winter than in summer.

Some 90% of the population are prone to seasickness. If you've never been out on a boat, or if you've been seasick in the past, you might want to note the following suggestions:

- The day before you go out on the boat, avoid alcohol, caffeine, citrus and other acidic juices, and greasy, spicy, or hard-to-digest foods.
- Get a good night's sleep the night before.
- Take or use whatever seasickness prevention works best for you—medication, an acupressure wristband, ginger-root tea or capsules, or any combination— *before* you board; once you set sail, it's generally too late.
- While you're on the boat, stay as low and as near the center of the boat as possible. Avoid the fumes (especially if it's a diesel boat); stay out in the fresh air and watch the horizon. Do not read.
- If you start to feel queasy, drink clear fluids like water, and eat something bland, such as a soda cracker.

STINGS   The most common source of stings in Hawaii's waters are jellyfish, particularly Portuguese man-of-war and box jellyfish. Since the poisons they inject are very different, you need to treat each sting differently.

Portuguese Man-of-War   A bluish-purple floating bubble with a long tail, the Portuguese man-of-war causes some 6,500 stings a year on Oahu alone. Stings are painful and a nuisance but rarely harmful; fewer than one in a thousand requires medical treatment. The best prevention is to watch for these floating bubbles as you snorkel (look for the hanging tentacles below the surface). Get out of the water if anyone near you spots these jellyfish.

Reactions to stings range from mild burning and reddening to severe welts and blisters. *All Stings Considered* recommends the following treatment: First, pick off any visible tentacles with a gloved hand, a stick, or anything handy; then rinse the sting with salt or fresh water, and apply ice to prevent swelling and to help control pain.

Hawaii folklore advises using vinegar, meat tenderizer, baking soda, papain, alcohol, or even urinating on the wound. Studies have shown that these remedies could actually cause further damage. Most Portuguese man-of-war stings disappear by themselves within 15 to 20 minutes if you do nothing at all to treat them. Still, be sure to see a doctor if pain persists or a rash or other symptoms develop.

Don't Get Burned: Smart Tanning Tips

For years, the best souvenir to bring back from Hawaii was a golden tan, especially in mid-winter. Oh, the look of green-eyed envy from your friends as your bronzed glow silently told the world you'd just returned from Hawaii!

Tanning just ain't what it was in the past. Nowadays, it can kill you—especially if in your quest for a tan, you burn instead. Strong words, but supported by reality: Hawaii's Caucasian population has the highest incidence of deadly skin cancer, malignant melanoma, than anywhere else in the U.S. But none of us are safe from the sun's harmful rays: People of all skin types and races can burn when exposed to the sun too long.

To ensure that your vacation won't be ruined by a painful, throbbing sunburn (especially in your first few days in the islands), here are some helpful tips on how to tan safely and painlessly:

Wear a strong sunscreen at all times. Use a sunscreen with a sun-protection factor (SPF) of 15 or higher; people with a light complexion should use 30. The SPF rating works this way: A fair-skinned person, without any sun protection, can burn in 10 minutes in the sun; a sunscreen with an SPF of 30 gives its wearer 10 minutes of protection from the sun (the time before you burn) times 30 (the SPF), or 300 minutes (5 hours) of protection.

Apply sunscreen as soon as you get out of the shower in the morning and at least 30 minutes before you're exposed to the sun.

And use lots of it. Margaret Tucker, chief of genetic epidemiology at the National Cancer Institute, says "a little dab will not do ya." You need 1 tablespoon of lotion per limb; slather it on and rub it in. No matter what the box says—even if the sunscreen is waterproof—reapply it every 2 hours and immediately after swimming.

Read the labels. To avoid developing allergies to sunscreens, New York University dermatologist Robert Friedman suggests avoiding any sunscreen that contain *para-aminobenzoic acid* (PABA). The American Academy of Dermatology suggests looking for sunscreens with zinc oxide, talc, or titanium dioxide because these elements reduce the risk of developing skin allergies.

Wrinkle Prevention. Scientists have recently discovered that wrinkles, sagging skin, and other signs of premature aging can be caused by Ultraviolet A (UVA) rays. For years sunscreens concentrated on blocking out just Ultraviolet B (UVB) rays. The best protection from UVA rays is zinc oxide (the white goo that lifeguards wear on their noses), but other ingredients provide protection. Read the label; if your sunscreen doesn't contain one of the following, get another brand: zinc oxide, benzophenone, oxybenzone, sulisobenzone, titanium dioxide, and avobenzone (also known as Parsol 1789).

Also wear a hat and sunglasses. The hat should have a minimum 4-inch-wide brim (all the way around, to cover not only your face but also the sensitive back

Box Jellyfish   These transparent, square-shaped jellyfish are nearly impossible to see in the water. Fortunately, they seem to follow a monthly cycle: 8 to 10 days after the full moon, they appear in the waters on the leeward side of the island and hang around for about 3 days. Also, they seem to sting more in the morning hours, when they're on or near the surface. The best prevention is to get out of the water.

of your neck). Make sure your sunglasses have UV filters to protect your corneas from getting sunburned and to prevent cataracts. To avoid the irritation of sunscreen dripping into your eyes, use a waxy sunscreen stick (available just about everywhere in Hawaii) to draw half-circles above your eyebrows.

Don't rely on a T-shirt for protection. Believe it or not, that T-shirt you put over your bathing suit has a SPF of only 6. Either wear special UV-protective clothing, or lather on a high-SPF sunscreen.

Avoid being in the sun between 9am and 3pm. Seek the shade during these peak hours. Remember that a beach umbrella is not enough protection from the sun's harmful UV rays; in fact, with the reflection from the water, the sand, and even the sidewalk, some 85% of the ultraviolet rays are still bombarding you.

Protect children from the sun, and keep infants out of the sun altogether. Infants under 6 months should not be in the sun at all. Older babies need zinc oxide to protect their fragile skin, and children should be slathered with sunscreen every hour. The burns children get today predict what their future will be with skin cancer tomorrow.

If you start to turn red, **get out of the sun.** Contrary to popular belief, you don't have to turn red to tan; if your skin is red, it's burned, and that's serious. The redness from a burn may not show until 2 to 8 hours after you get out of the sun, and the full force of that burn might not appear for 24 to 36 hours. During that time, you can look forward to pain, itching, and peeling. The best **remedy** for a sunburn is to get out of the sun immediately and stay out of the sun until all the redness is gone. Aloe vera (straight from the plant or from a commercial preparation), cool compresses, cold baths, and anesthetic benzocaine may also help with the pain of sunburn.

Often, people go to tanning salons to prepare for a trip to the tropics. Laying this kind of base tan "will give you some protection, but the tropical sun is too intense, and you should still use sunscreen and a visor when in the sun in Hawaii," Dr. Craig Thomas, author of *All Stings Considered,* tells me. "However, I don't recommend using a tanning salon for a 'base coat' because fair-skinned people don't do well with ultraviolet radiation from the sun *or* the tanning salon—your skin will pay the price with aging or skin cancer. The risk of melanoma is even higher with intermittent sun exposure than it is with long-term exposure; the worst thing you can do is to go to the tropics once a year for 10 years and get burned."

If you have decided to get a head start on your tan by using a "self-tanning" lotion that dyes your skin a darker shade, remember that this does not protect you from the sun, either. You still need to generously apply a high-SPF sunscreen before you head out.

Stings range from no visible marks to red, hivelike welts and blisters. Pain (a burning sensation) lasts from 10 minutes to 8 hours. *All Stings Considered* recommends the following treatment: First, pour regular household vinegar on the sting; this might not relieve the pain, but it stops additional burning. Do not rub the area. Pick off any vinegar-soaked tentacles with a stick. For pain, apply an ice pack. Seek additional medical treatment if you experience shortness of breath, weakness, palpitations, muscle cramps, or any other severe symptoms. Again, ignore any folk remedies. Most box jellyfish stings disappear by themselves without any treatment.

PUNCTURES   Most sea-related punctures come from stepping on or brushing against the needlelike spines of **sea urchins** (known locally as *wana*). Be careful when you're in the water; don't put your foot down (even if you have booties or fins on) if you can't clearly see the bottom. Waves can push you into wana in shallow water (the wana's spines can even puncture a wet suit).

A sea-urchin sting can result in burning, aching, swelling, and discoloration (black or purple) around the area where the spines entered your skin. The best thing to do is to pull any protruding spines out. The body will absorb the spines within 24 hours to 3 weeks, or the remainder of the spines will work themselves out. Again, do not urinate or pour vinegar on the embedded spines—it doesn't help.

CUTS   All cuts occurring in the marine environment must be taken seriously because the high level of bacteria present can quickly cause the cut to become infected. The most common cuts come from **coral.** Contrary to popular belief, coral cannot grow inside your body. However, bacteria can—and very often does—grow inside a cut. The best way to prevent cuts is to wear a wet suit, gloves, and reef shoes.

The symptoms of a coral cut can range from a slight scratch to severe welts and blisters. *All Stings Considered* recommends gently pulling the edges of the skin open and removing any embedded coral or grains of sand with tweezers, or rinsing well with fresh water. Next, scrub the cut well with fresh water. Never use ocean water to clean a cut. If the wound is bleeding, press a clean cloth against the wound until it stops. If bleeding continues, or the edges of the injury are jagged or gaping, seek medical treatment.

WHAT TO DO IF YOU GET SICK AWAY FROM HOME

It can be hard to find a doctor you trust when you're in an unfamiliar place. Try to take proper precautions the week before you depart to avoid falling ill while you're away from home. Amid the last-minute frenzy that often precedes a vacation break, make an extra effort to eat and sleep well—especially if you feel an illness coming on. If you suffer from a chronic illness, consult your doctor before your departure. For conditions like epilepsy, diabetes, or heart problems, wear a **Medic Alert Identification Tag** (☎ 800/825-3785; www.medicalert.org), which immediately alerts doctors to your condition and gives them access to your records through Medic Alert's 24-hour hotline. Membership is $35, plus a $15 annual fee. If you have dental problems, a nationwide referral service known as **1-800-DENTIST** (☎ 800/336-8478) can supply the name of a nearby dentist or clinic.

Pack prescription medications in your carry-on luggage. Carry written prescriptions in generic, not brand-name form, and dispense all prescription medications from their original labeled vials. Also, bring along copies of your prescriptions in case you lose your pills or run out.

INSURANCE

There are three kinds of travel insurance: trip cancellation, medical, and lost luggage coverage. **Trip cancellation insurance** is a good idea if you have paid a large portion of your vacation expenses upfront. The other types of insurance, however, don't make much sense for most travelers.

Your insurance policies may be adequate, but before you travel, see what limitations, if any, there might be to your coverage while you are away from home. Check your auto insurance policy to see if it covers you while driving a rental car in Hawaii (where car insurance is mandated by law). Review your homeowners' policy to make sure any theft or loss (luggage, cameras, etc.) is covered, and finally, check your health insurance to ensure that medical problems will be covered. Hawaii law mandates that all employers provide health insurance coverage for employees, so most health care providers insist on health insurance. Without health insurance, you could have a problem finding a medical provider.

4 Tips for Travelers with Special Needs

FOR TRAVELERS WITH DISABILITIES

A disability shouldn't stop anyone from traveling, and travelers with disabilities are made to feel very welcome in Hawaii. There are more than 2,000 ramped curbs on Oahu alone, hotels are usually equipped with wheelchair-accessible rooms, and tour companies provide many special services. The **Hawaii Center for Independent Living,** 414 Kauwili St., Suite 102, Honolulu, HI 96817 (☎ **808/522-5400;** fax 808/586-8129; www.hawaii.gov/health/cpd_indx.htm; e-mail: cpdppp@aloha.net), can provide information and send you a copy of the *Aloha Guide to Accessibility* ($15).

HandiCabs of the Pacific (☎ **808/524-3866**) provides wheelchair taxi service and a variety of wheelchair-accommodated activities on Oahu, including sightseeing tours, luaus, and cruises. Airport pickup to a Waikiki hotel costs $37 one-way.

For disabled travelers who want to do their own driving, hand-controlled cars can be rented from **Avis** (☎ **800/331-1212**) and **Hertz** (☎ **800/654-3131**). The number of hand-controlled cars in Hawaii is limited, so they should be booked well in advance. Hawaii recognizes other states' windshield placards indicating that the car's driver is disabled. Use them to park in specially marked handicapped stalls. For wheelchair-accessible vans, contact **Accessible Vans of Hawaii,** 186 Mehani Circle, Kihei, HI 96753 (☎ **800/303-3750** or 808/879-5521; fax 808/879-0640), which has vans on Oahu.

Vision-impaired travelers who use a Seeing-Eye dog can now travel to Hawaii without the hassle of quarantine. A recent court decision ruled that visitors with Seeing-Eye dogs need only to present documentation that the dog has had rabies shots and that it is a trained Seeing-Eye dog. Previously, all dogs and cats in Hawaii had to spend 4 months in quarantine because Hawaii is rabies-free (quarantine has been reduced to 1 month, Seeing-Eye dogs exempted). For more information, contact the **Animal Quarantine Facility** (☎ **808/483-7171;** www.hawaii.gov).

FOR SENIORS

Don't be shy about asking for discounts, but always carry some kind of identification, such as a driver's license, which shows your date of birth. Also, mention that you're a senior citizen when you first make your travel reservations.

Discounts for seniors are available at almost all of Hawaii's major attractions and occasionally at hotels and restaurants. Always ask when making hotel reservations. Members of the **American Association of Retired Persons (AARP),** 601 E. St. NW, Washington, D.C. 20049 (☎ **800/424-3410** or 202/434-2277), get discounts not only on hotels, but on airfares and car rentals, too. AARP offers members a wide range of special benefits, including *Modern Maturity* magazine and a monthly newsletter.

There are some great, low-cost trips to Hawaii available for people 60 and older through **Elderhostel,** 75 Federal St., Boston, MA 02110 (☎ **617/426-7788;** www.elderhostel.org), a nonprofit group that offers travel and study programs around the world. Trips are usually unbelievably cheap and include moderate accommodations and meals in one low package price.

FOR GAY & LESBIAN TRAVELERS

Known for its acceptance of all groups, Hawaii welcomes gays and lesbians just as it does any other group. The number of gay- or lesbian-specific accommodations on the islands are limited, but you can expect to be greeted like any other traveler—with aloha.

The best travel guide for gay and lesbian travelers is the ***Rainbow Handbook Hawaii,*** written by travel writer Matthew Link. This book not only covers travel on every island, but also has information on Hawaii's gay history, gay and lesbian businesses in Hawaii, and interviews with Hawaii residents. The book is available for $14.95 by writing to P.O. Box 100, Honaunau, HI 96726 (☎ **800/260-5528**) or via the Net at www.rainbowhandbook.com/.

The **Gay and Lesbian Community Center,** 1566 Wilder Ave., Honolulu, HI 96822 (☎ **808/951-7000;** fax 808/951-7240; open Monday to Friday noon to 5pm), is a referral service for nearly every kind of gay-related service you can think of. Another Oahu-based referral service is the **Gay Community Director** (☎ **808/ 532-9000**), which can refer you to all kinds of gay-friendly places and services, from hotels to doctors to support groups; the line can also tell you where to pick up gay-oriented publications.

There are two good, biannual English-language gay guidebooks, both focused on gay men, but including information for lesbians. You can get the ***Spartacus International Gay Guide*** or ***Odysseus*** from most gay and lesbian bookstores, or order them from Giovanni's Room (☎ **215/923-2960**), or A Different Light Bookstore (☎ **800/ 343-4002** or 212/989-4850). Both lesbians and gays might want to pick up a copy of ***Gay Travel A to Z*** ($16). The **Ferrari Guides** (www.q-net.com) is yet another very good series of gay and lesbian guidebooks.

FOR FAMILIES

Hawaii is paradise for children: beaches to run on, water to splash in, unusual sights to see, and a host of new foods to taste. The larger hotels and resorts have supervised programs for children and can refer you to qualified baby-sitters. (*Note:* Hawaii state law mandates that hotels offering supervised activity programs can accept only children ages 5 to 12.) You can also contact **People Attentive to Children (PATCH),** which can refer you to baby-sitters who have taken their training courses on childcare; contact ☎ **808/839-1791.** For cribs, strollers, high chairs, playpens, infant seats, and other necessary rentals, call **Dyans Rentals** (☎ **808/591-8207**).

Several books on the market offer tips to help you travel with kids. For good general advice that's applicable to travel anywhere, get ***Family Travel*** (Lanier Publishing International) or ***How to Take Great Trips with Your Kids*** (The Harvard Common Press). Another reliable tome, with a worldwide focus, is ***Adventuring with Children*** (Foghorn Press).

FOR WOMEN

Several Web sites offer women advice on how to travel safely and happily. The **Executive Woman's Travel Network** (www.delta-air.com/womenexecs/) is the official women's travel site of Delta airlines and offers women tips on staying fit while

---

Travel Tip

When traveling with children, don't forget a deck of cards, toys, extra bottles, pacifiers, diapers, and chewing gum to help them relieve ear pressure buildup during the plane's ascent and descent.

traveling, eating well, finding special airfares, and dealing with many other travel issues. **WomanTraveler** (www.womantraveler.com/) is an excellent guide that suggests places where women can stay and eat in various destinations. The site is authored by women and includes listings of women-owned businesses, such as hotels, hostels, etc.

FOR SINGLE TRAVELERS

Many people prefer traveling alone—save for the relatively steep cost of booking a single room, which usually costs well over half the price of a double. **Travel Companion** (☎ 516/454-0880) is one of the nation's oldest roommate finders for single travelers. Register with them and find a trustworthy travel mate who will split the cost of the room with you and be around as little, or as often, as you like during the day.

Several tour organizers cater to solo travelers. **Experience Plus** (☎ 800/685-4565; fax 907/484-8489) offers an interesting selection of single-only trips. **Travel Buddies** (☎ 800/998-9099 or 604/533-2483) runs single-friendly tours with no singles supplement. **The Single Gourmet Club** (133 E. 58th St., New York, NY 10022; ☎ 212/980-8788; fax 212/980-3138) is an international social, dining, and travel club for singles, with offices in 21 cities in the United States and Canada and one in London.

You might also want to research the *Outdoor Singles Network* (P.O. Box 781, Haines, AK 99827). An established quarterly newsletter (since 1989) for outdoor-loving singles, ages 19 to 90, the network will help you find a travel companion, pen pal, or soulmate within its pages. A 1-year subscription costs $45, and your own personal ad is printed free in the next issue. Current issues are $15. Write for free information, or check out the group's Web site at www.kcd.com/bearstar/osn.html.

5 Planning an Island Wedding

Fragrant blossoms, lush vegetation, perfect sun-kissed days: Whatever your dreams, Hawaii is a great place for a wedding. Not only do the islands exude romance and beauty, but after the ceremony, you're only a few steps from the perfect honeymoon. And your family, friends, and members of your wedding party will probably be delighted—you've given all of them the perfect excuse for their own island vacations.

Couples can get married, or remarried, in historic Hawaiian churches; on the beach; under a waterfall in a rain forest; on horseback in a pasture with an ocean view; in a lush tropical garden; on a sailboat, with Diamond Head as a backdrop; on a deserted islet; underwater with a school of brilliant-colored fish for witnesses; barefoot on the beach at sunset and draped in fragrant leis; or in full regalia on formal parade from chapel to luxury hotel.

More than 20,000 marriages are performed each year in Hawaii, most of them on the island of Oahu. Nearly half (44.6%) of the couples married here are from somewhere else. This booming business has spawned more than 70 companies that can help you organize a long-distance event and stage an unforgettable wedding, Hawaiian-style or your style (see "Using a Wedding Planner," below). However, you can also plan your own island wedding, even from afar, and not spend a fortune doing it.

THE PAPERWORK

The state of Hawaii has minimal procedures for getting a marriage license. The first thing you should do is contact the **Honolulu Marriage License Office,** State Department of Health Building, 1250 Punchbowl St., Honolulu, HI 96813 (☎ 808/586-4545; open Monday through Friday from 8am to 4pm, except holidays; www.hawaii.gov). They'll mail you their brochure, *Getting Married,* and direct you to the marriage licensing agent closest to where you'll be staying in Hawaii.

And Fragrant Flowers Fill the Airport:
The Welcoming Lei

When you arrive in Hawaii, the air is fragrant with flowers. Sweet scents are everywhere, in a profusion of perfumes from gardens, street trees, and fields—and around your neck in a welcoming flower lei.

A tradition born in the Pacific and cherished by all who love Hawaii, the lei is a garland of fresh, fragrant flowers. It's given to honor guests and to celebrate birthdays, weddings, graduations, triumphs, and farewells. Bus drivers tuck fragrant blossoms behind their ears or onto their dashboards. Musicians hang leis from their microphones. The dance isn't really hula without leis, and no woman is fully dressed for evening unless she's wearing flowers.

Lei making is a tropical art form. All are fashioned by hand in a variety of traditional patterns. Some leis are sewn of hundreds of tiny blooms or shells, or bits of ferns and leaves. Some last only a few hours, but the memories last forever.

Every island has its own special flower lei. On Oahu, the choice is *ilima,* a small orange flower. On Kauai, it's the *mokihana,* a fragrant green vine and berry. Big Islanders prefer the *lehua,* a large delicate red puff. Maui likes the *lokelani,* a small rose. Molokai prefers the *kukui,* the white blossom of a candlenut tree. And Lanai's lei is made of *kaunaoa,* a bright yellow moss, while Niihau uses its abundant seashells to make leis once prized by royalty and now worth a small fortune.

Leis are available at the lei stands at the Honolulu International Airport. Other places to get creative, inexpensive leis are the half-dozen lei shops on Maunakea Street in Honolulu's Chinatown, and Flowers by Jou & T Jr., 2653 S. King St. (near University Ave.).

So pick up a lei and feel the spirit of Aloha. Welcome to Hawaii!

Upon arrival in Hawaii, the prospective bride and groom must go together to the marriage licensing agent to get a license. A license costs $25 and is good for 30 days; if you don't have the ceremony within the time allotted, you have to pay another $25 for another license. The only requirements are that both parties must be 18 years of age or older, and not more closely related than first cousins. That's it.

Contrary to some reports from the media, gay couples cannot marry in Hawaii. A few years ago, the state courts ruled that the state of Hawaii had to show a compelling reason why the state would not issue a marriage license to gay couples. Today the issue is still being debated, and until it's resolved, the state will not issue marriage licenses to same-sex couples.

PLANNING THE WEDDING
DOING IT YOURSELF

The marriage licensing agents, which range from the governor's satellite office to private individuals, are usually friendly, helpful people who can steer you to a nondenominational minister or marriage performer who's licensed by the state of Hawaii to perform the ceremony. These marriage performers are good sources of information for budget weddings. They usually know great places to have the ceremony for free or a nominal fee.

If you don't want to use a wedding planner (see below) but want to make arrangements before you arrive in Hawaii, we advise that you get a copy of the daily newspapers on the island where you want to have the wedding. People willing and qualified to conduct weddings advertise in the classifieds. They're great sources of information, as they know the best places to have the ceremony and can recommend caterers, florists, and everything else you need. On Oahu, check out the *Honolulu Advertiser,* P.O. Box 3110, Honolulu, HI 96802 (☎ **808/525-8000**), the *Honolulu Star Bulletin,* P.O. Box 3080, Honolulu, HI 96802 (☎ **808/525-8000**); and *MidWeek,* 45-525 Luluku Rd., Kaneohe, HI 96744 (☎ **808/235-5881**).

USING A WEDDING PLANNER

Wedding planners—many of whom are marriage licensing agents themselves—can arrange everything for you, from a small private outdoor affair to a full-blown formal ceremony in a tropical setting. They charge anywhere from $450 to a small fortune—it all depends on what you want. The Hawaii Visitors and Convention Bureau (see "Visitor Information & Money," above) can supply contact information on wedding coordinators.

If you want to get married at sea, call Capt. Ken Middleton, of **Tradewind Charters,** 1098 Kumukumu St., Suite E, Honolulu, HI 96825 (☎ **800/829-4899** or 808/973-0311; fax 808/396-5094; www.hinet.com/twc/twc.html) for a private wedding and reception on the ocean waves.

For a wedding and reception in Waimea Valley Adventure Park, contact the wedding coordinator, **Waimea Valley Adventure Park,** 59-88864 Kamehameha Hwy., Haleiwa, HI 96712, at ☎ **808/638-8511.**

If you want a romantic wedding in an exotic setting, such as near a waterfall, on the beach, or in a garden chapel, **AAA Above Heaven's Gate** (☎ **800/800-2WED** or 808/259-5429; www.hawaiiweddings.com), can arrange it.

Other wedding planners include **Affordable Weddings of Hawaii,** P.O. Box 26475, Honolulu, HI 96825 (☎ **800/942-4554** or 808/923-4876); or **Aloha Wedding Planners,** 1860 Ala Moana Blvd., Suite 115, Honolulu, HI 96815 (☎ **800/ 288-8309** or 808/943-2711; www.alohaweddingplanners.com).

6 Getting There

ARRIVING IN THE ISLANDS

All major American and many international carriers fly to Honolulu International Airport.

United Airlines (☎ 800/225-5825; www.ual.com) offers the most frequent service from the U.S. mainland, but **American Airlines** (☎ 800/433-7300; www.americanair.com), **Continental Airlines** (☎ 800/231-0856), **Delta Airlines** (☎ 800/221-1212; www.delta-air.com), **Hawaiian Airlines** (☎ 800/367-5320; www.hawaiianair.com), **Northwest Airlines** (☎ 800/225-2525; www.nwa.com), and **TWA** (☎ 800/221-2000; www2.twa.com) all have regular flights. TWA flies nonstop from its St. Louis hub to Honolulu. Continental offers the only daily nonstops to Honolulu from the New York area (Newark).

Based in Honolulu, **Hawaiian Airlines** (☎ 800/367-5320 or 808/537-5100) offers nonstop service on wide-body DC-10s from San Francisco, Seattle, Los Angeles, Portland, and Las Vegas. Hawaiian works with Fly AAway Vacations, the tour unit of American Airlines. For information about its package tours, phone **Hawaiian Airlines Vacations** at ☎ **800/353-5393,** or ask your travel agent.

FLYING FOR LESS: TIPS FOR GETTING THE BEST AIRFARES

Consolidators, also known as bucket shops, are a good place to find low fares. Consolidators buy seats in bulk from the airlines and then sell them back to the public at

Cyber Deals for Net Surfers

It's possible to get some great deals on airfare, hotels, and car rentals via the Internet. So go grab your mouse and start surfing before you hit the real waves in Hawaii—you could save a bundle on your trip. The Web sites we've highlighted below are worth checking out, especially since all services are free.

Air Fare

E-Savers Programs   Several major airlines, most of which serve the Hawaiian islands, offer a free e-mail service known as **E-Savers,** by which they send you their best bargain airfares on a weekly basis. Here's how it works: Once a week (usually Wednesday), subscribers get a list of discounted flights to and from various destinations, both international and domestic. Now here's the catch: These fares are available only if you leave the next Saturday (or sometimes Friday night) and return on the following Monday or Tuesday. It's really a service for the spontaneously inclined and travelers looking for a quick getaway (for Hawaii, that usually means travelers from the West Coast). But the fares are cheap, so it's worth taking a look. If you have a preference for certain airlines (in other words, the ones you fly most frequently), sign up with them first. Another caveat: You get frequent-flier miles if you purchase one of these fares, but you can't use miles to buy the ticket.

Here's a list of airlines and their Web sites, where you can not only get on the e-mailing lists, but also book flights directly:

- **American Airlines:** www.americanair.com
- **Continental Airlines:** www.flycontinental.com
- **Northwest Airlines:** www.nwa.com
- **TWA:** www.twa.com
- **US Airways:** www.usairways.com
- **United:** www.ual.com

The following sites will search for the cheapest round-trip seats:

Internet Air Fare (www.air-fare.com)   One of the best sites for searching for low airfares. The site tracks all the major carriers to Hawaii and lists not only the lowest airfare, but also includes the fares for seven other categories, including last-minute airfare and even the lowest first-class fare.

Airlines of the Web (www.itn.net/airlines)   One of the most comprehensive Internet airline information sources with a unique feature—ITN's Low Fare Ticker, which allows you to monitor fares around the clock—that's particularly useful during fare wars. Fare Mail notifies you via e-mail when a flight you're interested in dips below your personal price threshold.

AirSaver.com (www.airsaver.com)   Specializes in consolidated tickets, which sometimes can save you big bucks off the cheapest airfares. If the fares aren't low enough, you can choose to go on the e-mail list if airfares drop.

Cheap Fare Finder (www.cheapfarefinder.com)   Not only can they search the major airlines for the cheapest fares, but they can also arrange to have your ticket waiting for you at the airport.

Deals on Air, Accommodations, Car Rental & Packages

Arthur Frommer's Budget Travel (www.frommers.com)   Home of the Encyclopedia of Travel and *Arthur Frommer's Budget Travel* magazine and daily newsletter, this site offers information on 200 cities and islands around the world, and up-to-the-minute ways to save dramatically on flights, hotels, car reservations, and cruises. Book a vacation online and research your destination before you leave. Consult the message board to set up "hospitality exchanges" in other countries, to talk with other travelers who have visited a hotel you're considering, or to direct travel questions to Arthur Frommer himself. The newsletter is updated daily to keep you abreast of the latest breaking ways to save and to publicize new hot spots and best buys.

Microsoft Expedia (www.expedia.com)   The best part of this multipurpose travel site is the Fare Tracker: You fill out a form on the screen indicating that you're interested in cheap flights to Hawaii from your hometown, and once a week, they e-mail you the best airfares deals. The site's Travel Agent steers you to bargains on hotels and car rentals, and you can book everything, including flights, right online. This site is even useful once you're booked: Before you go, log on to Expedia for oodles of up-to-date travel information, including weather reports.

Travelocity (www.travelocity.com)   This is one of the best travel sites out there. In addition to its Personal Fare Watcher, which notifies you via e-mail of the lowest fares for up to five different destinations, Travelocity tracks the three lowest fares for any routes on any dates in minutes. You can book a flight right then and there, and if you need a rental car or hotel, Travelocity can find you the best deal. Click on "Last Minute Deals" for the latest travel bargains, including a link to "H.O.T Coupons" (www.hotcoupons.com), where you can print out electronic coupons for travel in the U.S. and Canada.

Epicurious Travel (travel.epicurious.com)   Another good travel site that allows you to sign up for all the airline e-mail lists at once.

Pleasant Hawaiian Holidays (pleasantholidays.com)   In the travel tour business (air, car, accommodations) for decades, Pleasant Hawaiian Holidays, one of Hawaii's largest travel companies, now offers its low-cost deals on the Web. Check out the "Surround Video" tours on the site, a 360-degree video of hotels and destinations.

The Hottest Airfares on Earth (www.etn.nl/hotfares.htm)   This site is a clearinghouse of information from low-cost ticket suppliers, tour operators, and travel agents. It publishes low airline fares, packages, and hotel deals.

Travel Shop (www.aonestoptravel.com)   Not only does this site have discounted air, accommodations, car, etc., it also has access to consolidated rates on every aspect of travel to Hawaii. It even promises to meet or beat any quote you get from a travel agent or airline.

Travelzoo.com (www.travelzoo.com)   Check out the package deals to Hawaii on this site (at press time, they were offering 7 nights on Maui with condo, car, and airfare from Los Angeles for $595).

The Unusual

TravelBids—A Travel Auction (www.travelbids.com)   An online auction, TravelBids works by you researching the airlines and hotels and getting the best deal you can. Before you pay for your travel arrangements, you pay a $5 listing fee to TravelBid and list the price for your hotel and airfare. Travel agents then bid for your business, and you choose the lowest bid. It works because some travel agents are willing to split their commission with you (giving you a 6% to 12% discount).

—Jeanette Foster

Tips for Flying in Comfort

You might find the following tips helpful when making your airline reservations. Remember, the plane ride to Hawaii is a long one!

- You'll find the most leg room in a bulkhead seat, in the front row of each airplane cabin. Consider, however, that you have to store all your carry-on luggage in the overhead bin, and you don't have the best seat in the house for the in-flight movie.

- When you check in, ask for one of the emergency-exit-row seats, which also have extra leg room. They are assigned at the airport, usually on a first-come, first-serve basis. In the unlikely event of an emergency, however, you'll be expected to open the emergency-exit door and help direct traffic.

- Ask for a seat toward the front of the plane so you're one of the first to disembark after the gangway is in place.

---

prices below even the airlines' discounted rates. Before you pay, however, ask for a confirmation number from the consolidator and then call the airline itself to confirm your seat. Be prepared to book your ticket with a different consolidator—there are many to choose from—if the airline can't confirm your reservation. Also, be aware that bucket shop tickets are usually nonrefundable or rigged with stiff cancellation penalties, often as high as 50% to 75% of the ticket price.

Reliable consolidators include **Cheap Tickets** (☎ 800/377-1000 or 212/570-1179), **TFI Tours International** (☎ 800/745-8000 or 212-736-1140), **1-800-FLY-CHEAP** (www.websrus.com/flycheap), and **1-800-FLY-4-LESS** (E-mail: fly4less@juno.com). **Travel Bargains** (☎ 800/AIR-FARE; www.1800airfare.com) was formerly owned by TWA, but now offers the deepest discounts on many other airlines with a 4-day advance purchase.

AGRICULTURAL SCREENING AT THE AIRPORTS

At Honolulu International and the neighbor-island airports, baggage and passengers bound for the mainland and other countries must be screened by agricultural officials before boarding. This takes a little time, but isn't a problem unless you happen to be carrying a football-sized local avocado home to Aunt Emma. Officials will confiscate fresh avocados, bananas, mangoes, and many other kinds of local produce for the purpose of fruit-fly control. Pineapples, coconuts, and papayas inspected and certified for export; boxed flowers; leis; and processed foods (macadamia nuts, coffee, jams, dried fruit, and the like) will pass. Call federal or state agricultural officials before leaving for the airport if you're not sure about your trophy.

MONEY-SAVING PACKAGE DEALS

Booking an all-inclusive travel package that includes some combination of airfare, accommodations, rental car, meals, airport and baggage transfers, sightseeing, and more, is often the most cost-effective way to travel to Hawaii. You can sometimes save so much money by buying all the pieces of your trip through a packager that your transpacific airfare ends up, in effect, being free.

The best place to start looking for a package deal is in the travel section of your local Sunday newspaper. Also check the ads in the back of national travel magazines such as *Travel & Leisure, National Geographic Traveler,* and *Condé Nast Traveler.* **Liberty Travel** (check your local directory, since there's not a central toll-free number), one of the biggest packagers in the Northeast, usually boasts a full-page ad in Sunday papers. You won't get much in the way of service, but you will get a good deal. At press time, Liberty was offering a 7-day/6-night package to Hawaii with accommodations at the Sheraton Moana Surfrider on Waikiki Beach for $1,029 per person, double occupancy, including round-trip airfare from New York City, all airport transfers, a double room (hotel tax included), a flower-lei greeting, and some sightseeing—not a bad deal, considering that the Moana's cheapest room officially goes for $265 a night, and round-trip airfare is at least $650 or $700 each and can run as high as $800. Of course, package prices are always in flux, but this should give you an idea of how well you can do if you book your trip as a package. **American Express Travel** (☎ **800/AXP-6898;** www.americanexpress.com/travel) can also book you a well-priced Hawaiian vacation; it advertises in many Sunday travel sections.

Hawaii is such an ideal destination for vacation packages that some packagers book Hawaiian vacations as the majority of their business. **Pleasant Hawaiian Holidays** (☎ **800/2-HAWAII** or 800/242-9244; www.pleasantholidays.com or www.2hawaii. com) is, by far, the biggest and most comprehensive packager to Hawaii. It offers an extensive, high-quality collection of 50 condos and hotels in every price range. **Sunscapes** (☎ **800/229-8376** or 425/643-1620; www.sunscapes.com) sells only Hawaii vacations, concentrating on budget and moderately priced hotels and condos.

Other reliable packagers include the airlines themselves, which often package their flights together with accommodations. **United Vacations** (☎ 800/328-6877; www.unitedvacations.com) is by far the most comprehensive airline packager to Hawaii, offering great air-inclusive and land-only deals on a surprisingly wide selection of accommodations throughout the islands. Other airlines offering good-value packages to the islands are **American Airlines Vacations** (☎ 800/321-2121; www. 2travel.com/americanair/hawaii.html), **Continental Airlines Vacations** (☎ 800/ 634-5555 or 800/301-3800; www.coolvacations.com), **Delta Dream Vacations** (☎ 800/872-7786; www.deltavacations.com), and **TWA Getaway Vacations** (☎ 800/GETAWAY or 800/438-2929; www.twa.com). If you're traveling to the islands from Canada, ask your travel agent about package deals through **Air Canada Vacations** (☎ 800/776-3000; www.aircanada.ca).

INTERISLAND FLIGHTS

If you want to see another island during your visit to Oahu, access is via airlines. Don't expect to jump a ferry between any of the Hawaiian islands. Today, everyone island-hops by plane. In fact, almost every 20 minutes of every day from just before sunrise to well after sunset (usually around 8pm), a plane takes off or lands at Honolulu International Airport on the interisland shuttle service. If you miss a flight, don't worry; they're like buses—another one will be along real soon.

Aloha Airlines (☎ **800/367-5250** or 808/484-1111; www.alohaair.com) is the state's largest provider of interisland air transport service. It offers 275 regularly scheduled daily jet flights throughout Hawaii and has one of the lowest complaint records in the airline industry. Aloha's sister company, **Island Air** (☎ **800/323-3345** or 808/484-2222), operates eight deHavilland Twin Otter turboprop aircraft and serves Hawaii's small interisland airports in West Maui, Hana (Maui), Lanai, and Molokai.

Hawaiian Airlines (☎ **800/367-5320** or 808/835-3700; www.hawaiianair.com), Hawaii's oldest interisland airline, has carried more than 100 million passengers around the state on its jets and prop planes. It's one of the world's safest airlines, never having had a fatal incident since it started flying in 1929.

7 Tips on Accommodations

Hawaii offers all kinds of accommodations, from simple rooms in resorted plantation homes and quaint cottages on the beach to luxurious oceanview condo units and opulent suites in beachfront resorts. Each has its pluses and minuses, so before you book, make sure you know what you're getting into. Below, we discuss the accommodation options available in Hawaii, how to get the best possible rate, and when you should consider using a booking agency.

TYPES OF ACCOMMODATIONS

HOTELS   In Hawaii, *hotel* can mean a wide range of options, from few or no on-site amenities to enough extras to call it a mini-resort. Generally, a hotel offers daily maid service and has a restaurant, on-site laundry facilities, a swimming pool, and a sundries/convenience-type shop (rather than the shopping arcades most resorts have these days). Top hotels also have activities desks, concierge and valet service, room service (although it may be limited), business centers, an airport shuttle, a bar and/or lounge, and maybe a few more shops. The advantage of staying in a hotel is privacy and convenience. The disadvantage is generally noise: either thin walls between rooms or loud music from a lobby lounge late into the night.

Hotels are often a short walk from the beach instead of being beachfront (but some, like the Sheraton Moana Surfrider and the New Otani in Waikiki, are right on the sand). Since they come with fewer amenities than full-fledged resorts, hotels tend to be cheaper, but not always.

RESORTS   In Hawaii, a resort offers everything a hotel offers and more. What you get varies from property to property, of course, but expect facilities, services, and amenities such as direct beach access, with beach cabanas and chairs; pools (often more than one) and a Jacuzzi; a spa and fitness center; restaurants, bars, and lounges; a 24-hour front desk; concierge, valet, and bell services; room service (often around the clock); an activities desk; tennis and golf (some of the world's best courses are at Hawaii resorts); ocean activities; a business center; kid's programs; and more.

The advantages of a resort are that you have everything you could possibly want in the way of services and things to do; the disadvantage is that the price generally reflects this. Don't be misled by a name—just because a place is called "ABC Resort" doesn't mean it actually *is* a resort. Make sure you're getting what you pay for.

CONDOS   The roominess and convenience of a condo—which is usually a fully equipped, multiple-bedroom apartment—makes it a great choice for families. Condominium properties in Hawaii are generally several apartments set in a single high-rise or a cluster of low-rise units. Condos generally have amenities such as limited maid service (ranging from daily to weekly; it may or may not be included in your rate, so be sure to ask), a swimming pool, laundry facilities (either in your unit or in a central location), and an on-site front desk or a live-in property manager. The advantages of a condo are privacy, space, and conveniences—which usually include full kitchen facilities, a washer and dryer, a private phone, and more. The downsides are the standard lack of an on-site restaurant and the density of the units (versus the privacy of a single-unit vacation rental).

Condos vary in price according to size, location, and amenities. Many of them are located on or near the beach, and they tend to be clustered in resort areas. While there are some very high-end condos, most tend to be quite affordable, especially if you're traveling in a group that's large enough to require more than one bedroom.

BED-AND-BREAKFASTS   Hawaii has a wide range of places that call themselves B&Bs, everything from a traditional B&B—several bedrooms (which may or may not share a bathroom) in a home, with breakfast served in the morning—to what is essentially a vacation rental on an owner's property that comes with fixings to make your own breakfast. Make sure that the B&B you're thinking about booking matches your own mental picture. Would you prefer conversation around a big dining-room table as you eat a hearty breakfast, or just a muffin and juice to enjoy in your own private place? Laundry facilities and a private phone are not always available at B&Bs. We've reviewed several wonderful B&Bs in chapter 5, "Accommodations." If you have to share a bathroom, we've spelled it out in the listing; otherwise, you can assume that you will have a private bath.

The advantage of a traditional B&B is its individual style and congenial atmosphere. B&Bs are great places to meet other visitors to Hawaii, and the host is generally happy to act as your own private concierge, giving you tips on where to go and what to do. In addition, they're usually an affordable way to go (although fancier ones can run $150 or more a night). The disadvantages are lack of privacy, usually a set time for breakfast, few amenities, generally no maid service, and the fact that you'll have to share the quarters beyond your bedroom with others. In addition, B&B owners usually require a minimum stay of 2 or 3 nights, and it's often a drive to the beach.

VACATION RENTALS   This is another great choice for families and for long-term stays. "Vacation rental" usually means that there's no one on the property where you're staying. The actual accommodation can range from an apartment in a condominium building to a two-room cottage on the beach to an entire fully equipped house. Generally, vacation rentals are the kind of places you can settle into and make yourself at home for awhile. They have kitchen facilities (either a complete kitchen or just a kitchenette with microwave, refrigerator, burners, and coffeemaker), on-site laundry facilities, and a phone; some also come outfitted with such extras as a TV, VCR, and stereo. The advantages of a vacation rental are complete privacy, your own kitchen (which can save you money on meals), and lots of conveniences. The disadvantages are a lack of an on-site property manager and generally no maid service; often, a minimum stay is required (sometimes as much as a week). If you book a vacation rental, be sure you have a 24-hour contact so that when the toilet won't flush or you can't figure out how to turn on the air-conditioning, you have someone to call.

A Note on Smoking: Hotels, resorts, condos, and vacation rentals generally allow smoking in the rooms (most have nonsmoking rooms, too), but the majority of the bed-and-breakfast units forbid smoking in the rooms. Be sure to check the policy of your accommodation before you book.

PRICE BARGAINING

Like the price of a car, accommodation rates can sometimes be bargained down, but it depends on the place. In general, each type of accommodation allows a different amount of latitude in bargaining on their rack (or published) rates.

The best bargaining can be had at **hotels** and **resorts.** Hotels and resorts regularly pay travel agents as much as 30% of the rate they're getting for sending clients their way; if business is slow, some hotels may give you the benefit of at least part of this commission if you book directly instead of going through an airline or travel agent. Most also have *kamaaina* or "local" rates for islanders, which they may extend to visitors during slow periods. It never hurts to ask politely for a discounted or local rate; there is also a host of special rates available for the military, seniors, members of the travel industry, families, corporate travelers, and long-term stays. Ask about package deals, where for the same price as a room, you can get a car rental or free breakfast. Hotels and resorts have packages for everyone: golfers, tennis players, families, honeymooners, and more (for more on these, see "Money-Saving Package Deals," above). We've found that it's worth the extra few cents to make a local call to the hotel; sometimes the local reservations person knows about package deals that the 800 operators are unaware of. If all else fails, try to get the hotel or resort to upgrade you to a better room for the same price as a budget room, or waive the extra fees for children or the parking fee. Persistence and asking politely can pay off.

The rates for a **bed-and-breakfast** are the hardest to bargain on. Sometimes you can be successful in bargaining down the minimum stay, or you might be able to negotiate a discount if you're staying a week or longer. Generally, however, a B&B owner has only a few rooms and has already priced the property at a competitive rate; expect to pay what's asked.

You have somewhat more leeway to negotiate on **vacation rentals** and **condos.** In addition to asking for a discount on a multi-night stay, ask if they can throw in a rental car to sweeten the deal; believe it or not, they often will.

USING A BOOKING AGENCY VS. DOING IT YOURSELF

Sometimes you can save money by making the arrangements yourself—not only can you bargain on the phone, but some accommodations might be willing to pass on a percentage of the commission they normally pay a travel agent or a booking agency.

However, if you don't have the time or money to call several places to make sure they offer the amenities you'd like and to bargain for a price you're comfortable with, then you might consider a booking agency. The time they spend on your behalf could well be worth any fees you have to pay.

The top reservations service in the state is ✪ **Hawaii's Best Bed & Breakfasts,** P.O. Box 563, Kamuela, HI 96743 (☎ **800/262-9912** or 808/885-4550; fax 808/885-0559; www.bestbnb.com). The service charges you $15 to book the first two locations and $5 for each additional location. Barbara and Susan Campbell personally select the traditional homestays, cottages, and inns throughout the islands they represent, based on each one's hospitality, distinctive charm, and attention to detail. They also book vacation rentals, hotels, and resorts. Another great statewide booking agent is **Bed & Breakfast Hawaii,** P.O. Box 449, Kapaa, HI 96746 (☎ **800/733-1632** or 808/822-7771; fax 808/822-2723; www.bandb-hawaii.com), offering a range of accommodations from vacation homes to B&Bs, starting at $65 a night.

For vacation rentals, contact **Hawaii Beachfront Vacation Homes** (☎ **808/247-3637** or 808/235-2644; www.hotspots.hawaii.com/beachrent1.html). **Hawaii Condo Exchange** (☎ **800/442-0404;** http://wwte.com/condos) acts as a consolidator for condo and vacation-rental properties.

For Foreign Visitors

3

by Jeanette Foster

The pervasiveness of American culture around the world might make you feel that you know the United States pretty well, but leaving your own country for the States—especially the unique island state of Hawaii—still requires an additional degree of planning.

1 Preparing for Your Trip

ENTRY REQUIREMENTS

Immigration laws are a hot political issue these days; the following requirements may have changed somewhat by the time you plan your trip. Check at any U.S. embassy or consulate for current information and requirements.

DOCUMENT REGULATIONS Canadian citizens can enter the United States without visas; they need only proof of residence.

The U.S. State Department has a **Visa Waiver Pilot Program** allowing citizens of certain countries to enter the United States without a visa for stays of up to 90 days. At press time, they included Andorra, Australia, Austria, Belgium, Brunei, Denmark, Finland, France, Germany, Iceland, Ireland, Italy, Japan, Liechtenstein, Luxembourg, Monaco, the Netherlands, New Zealand, Norway, San Marino, Spain, Sweden, Switzerland, and the United Kingdom. Citizens of these countries need only a valid passport and a round-trip air or cruise ticket in their possession upon arrival. If they first enter the United States, they may then visit Mexico, Canada, Bermuda, and/or the Caribbean islands and return to the United States without needing a visa. Further information is available from any U.S. embassy or consulate.

Citizens of all other countries must have (1) a valid **passport** with an expiration date at least 6 months later than the scheduled end of their visit to the United States, and (2) a **tourist visa,** which can be obtained without charge from the nearest U.S. consulate.

To get a visa, you must submit a completed application form (either in person or by mail) with a 1½-inch-square photo, and you must demonstrate binding ties to a residence abroad. Usually, you can get a visa at once or within 24 hours, but it could take longer during the summer rush from June to August. If you cannot go in person, contact the nearest U.S. embassy or consulate for directions on applying by mail. Your travel agent or airline office might also be able to supply you with visa applications and instructions. The U.S. consulate or embassy that issues your visa will determine whether you are issued a multiple- or single-entry visa and any restrictions for the length of your stay.

Travel Tip

Be sure to keep a copy of all your travel papers separate from your wallet or purse, and leave a copy with someone at home should you need it faxed in an emergency.

U.K. citizens can get up-to-date passport and visa information by calling the **U.S. Embassy Visa Information Line** at ☎ **0891/200-290** or the **London Passport Office** at ☎ **0990/210-410** (for recorded information).

Foreign driver's licenses are recognized in Hawaii, although you may want to get an international driver's license if your home license is not written in English.

MEDICAL REQUIREMENTS   Inoculations are not needed to enter the United States unless you are coming from or have stopped over in areas known to be suffering from epidemics, particularly cholera or yellow fever.

If you have a disease requiring treatment with medications containing narcotics or requiring a syringe, carry a valid signed prescription from your physician to allay suspicions that you are smuggling drugs.

CUSTOMS REQUIREMENTS   Every adult visitor may bring in the following free of duty: 1 liter of wine or hard liquor, 200 cigarettes or 100 cigars (but no cigars from Cuba) or 3 pounds of smoking tobacco, and $100 worth of gifts. These exemptions are offered to travelers who spend at least 72 hours in the United States and who have not claimed them within the preceding 6 months. It is altogether forbidden to bring into the country foodstuffs (particularly cheese, fruit, cooked meats, and canned goods) and plants (vegetables, seeds, tropical plants, and so on). Foreign tourists may bring in or take out up to $10,000 in U.S. or foreign currency with no formalities; larger sums must be declared to customs on entering and leaving.

In addition, you cannot bring fresh fruits and vegetables into Hawaii, even if you're coming from the U.S. mainland and have no need to clear customs. Every passenger is asked shortly before landing to sign a certificate declaring that he or she does not have fresh fruits and vegetables in their possession. The form also asks questions for the Hawaii Visitors and Convention Bureau about your visit, such as how long you plan to stay, which island or islands you will visit, and how many times you have been to Hawaii.

INSURANCE   The United States does not have a nationwide health system, and the cost of medical care in Hawaii is extremely high. Accordingly, we strongly advise you to secure health-insurance coverage before setting out.

You may want to take out a comprehensive travel policy that covers (for a relatively low premium) sickness or injury costs (medical, surgical, and hospital); loss or theft of your baggage; trip-cancellation costs; guarantee of bail in case you are arrested; and costs of accident, repatriation, or death. Such packages (for example, "Europe Assistance" in Europe) are sold by automobile clubs at attractive rates, as well as by insurance companies and travel agencies. U.K. travelers might call the **Association of British Insurers** (☎ **020/7600-3333**), which gives advice by phone and publishes the free *Holiday Insurance,* a guide to policy provisions and prices.

MONEY

CURRENCY   The American monetary system has a decimal base: 1 U.S. **dollar** ($1) = 100 **cents** (100¢). Dollar bills commonly come in $1 ("a buck"), $5, $10, $20, $50, and $100 denominations (the latter two are not welcome when paying for small purchases and are not accepted in taxis or movie theaters).

There are six denominations of coins: 1¢ (one cent, or a "penny"), 5¢ (five cents, or a "nickel"), 10¢ (10 cents, or a "dime"), 25¢ (25 cents, or a "quarter"), 50¢ (50 cents, or a "half-dollar"), and the rare $1 piece.

EXCHANGING CURRENCY   Exchanging foreign currency for U.S. dollars can be painless in Hawaii. Generally, the best rates of exchange are available through the bank; most major banks in Hawaii will exchange your foreign currency for U.S. dollars. In downtown Honolulu, you can also get reliable currency service at **Monyx International,** 307 Royal Hawaiian Ave. (between the Waikiki Medical Building and the Waikiki Shopping Plaza), Honolulu, HI 96815 (☎ **808/923-6626**). In Waikiki, go to **A-1 Foreign Exchange,** which has offices in the Royal Hawaiian Shopping Center, 2301 Kalakaua Ave., and in the Hyatt Regency Waikiki Tower, 2424 Kalakaua Ave. (☎ **808/922-3327**). There also are currency services at **Honolulu International Airport.** Most of the major hotels offer currency-exchange services, but generally the rate of exchange is not as good as what you get at a bank.

TRAVELER'S CHECKS   It's actually cheaper and faster to get cash at an **automated teller machine** (ATM) than to fuss with traveler's checks. As noted in "Visitor Information & Money" in chapter 2, "Planning a Trip to Oahu," Hawaii has ATMs almost everywhere. If you do bring traveler's checks, and they are denominated in U.S. dollars, they will be readily accepted at most hotels, restaurants, and large stores. Do not bring traveler's checks denominated in any currency other than U.S. dollars.

CREDIT CARDS   The method of payment most widely used is the credit card: Visa (BarclayCard in Britain), MasterCard (EuroCard in Europe, Access in Britain, Chargex in Canada), American Express, Diners Club, Discover, and Carte Blanche. You can save yourself trouble by using "plastic money" rather than cash or traveler's checks in most hotels, restaurants, and retail stores (a growing number of food and liquor stores now accept credit cards). Note that you must have a credit card to rent a car in Hawaii.

SAFETY

GENERAL   Although tourist areas are generally safe, crime is a part of life everywhere in the United States, and Hawaii—especially Waikiki—is no exception. Visitors should always stay alert. It's wise to ask the island tourist office if you're in doubt about which neighborhoods are safe. Avoid deserted areas, especially at night. Don't go into any city park at night unless there's an event that attracts crowds—for example, the Waikiki Shell concerts in Kapiolani Park. Generally speaking, you can feel safe in areas where there are many people and open establishments.

Avoid carrying valuables with you on the street, and don't display expensive cameras or electronic equipment. Hold onto your pocketbook, and place your billfold in an inside pocket. In theaters, restaurants, and other public places, keep your possessions in sight.

Recently, there have been a series of purse-snatching incidents on Oahu. Thieves in slow-moving cars or on foot have snatched handbags from female pedestrians (in some instances, dragging women who refuse to let go of their pocketbooks down the street). The Honolulu police department advises women to carry their purses on the shoulder away from the street or, better yet, to wear the strap across the chest instead of on one shoulder. Women with clutch bags should hold their bags close to their chest.

Remember, too, that hotels are open to the public; in a large hotel, security might not be able to screen everyone entering. Always lock your room door—don't assume that once inside your hotel, you are automatically safe and no longer need to be aware of your surroundings.

DRIVING   Safety while driving is particularly important. Question your rental agency about personal safety, or ask for a brochure of traveler safety tips when you pick up your car. Get written directions or a map with the route marked in red from the agency showing you how to get to your destination.

Recently, more crime has involved burglary of tourist rental cars in hotel parking structures and at beach parking lots. Park in well-lighted and well-traveled areas if possible. If you leave your rental car unlocked and empty of your valuables, you are probably safer than locking your car with valuables in plain view. Never leave any packages or valuables in sight. If someone attempts to rob you or steal your car, do not try to resist the thief/carjacker—report the incident to the police department immediately.

For more information on driving rules and getting around by car in Hawaii, see "Getting Around" in chapter 4.

2 Getting to & Around the United States

Airlines serving Hawaii from other than the U.S. mainland include **Air Canada** (☎ 800/776-3000; www.aircanada.ca); **Canadian Airlines** (☎ 800/426-7000; www.cdnair.ca); **Canada 3000** (☎ 888/CAN-3000; www.canada3000.com); **Air New Zealand** (☎ 0800/737-000 in Auckland, 64-3/379-5200 in Christchurch, 800/926-7255 in the U.S.), which runs 40 flights per week between Auckland and Hawaii; **Qantas** (☎ 800/227-4500 in the U.S., 008/177-767 in Australia), which flies between Sydney and Honolulu daily (plus additional flights 4 days a week); **Japan Air Lines** (☎ 800/525-3663 in the U.S., 03/5489-1111 in Tokyo); **All Nippon Airways** (ANA) (☎ 800/235-9262 in the U.S., 03/5489-1212 in Tokyo); **China Airlines** (☎ 800/227-5118 in the U.S., 02/715-1212 in Taipei); **Garuda Indonesian** (☎ 800/342-7832 in the U.S., 251-2235 in Jakarta); **Korean Airlines** (☎ 800/223-1155 on the East Coast, 800/421-8200 on the West Coast, 800/438-5000 from Hawaii, 02/656-2000 in Seoul); and **Philippine Airlines** (☎ 800/435-9725 in the U.S., 631/816-6691 in Manila).

Travelers coming from Europe can take advantage of the **APEX** (Advance Purchase Excursion) fares offered by all major U.S. and European carriers. Aside from these, attractive values are offered by **Icelandair** (☎ **800/223-5500** in the U.S., 354/5050-100 in Reykjavik, 020/7388-5599 in London; www.icelandair.is) on flights from Luxembourg to New York, and by **Virgin Atlantic Airways** (☎ **800/862-8621** in the U.S., 0293/747-747 in Britain; www.fly.virgin.com) from London to New York/Newark. You can then catch a connecting domestic flight to Honolulu.

Some large American airlines—such as **TWA, American Airlines, Northwest, United,** and **Delta**—offer travelers on transatlantic or transpacific flights special discount tickets under the name **Visit USA,** allowing travel between any U.S. destinations at reduced rates. They're not on sale in the United States and must, therefore, be purchased before you leave your foreign point of departure. This system is the best, easiest, and fastest way to see the United States at a low cost. You should get information well in advance from your travel agent or the office of the airline concerned, since the conditions attached to these discount tickets can change without advance notice.

Money-Saving Tip

The **ETN (European Travel Network)** operates a Web site offering discounts on international airfares to the United States, as well as on accommodations, car rentals, and tours; point your Internet browser to **www.discount-tickets.com.**

The visitor arriving by air should cultivate patience and resignation before setting foot on U.S. soil. Getting through immigration control may take as long as 2 hours on some days, especially summer weekends. Add the time it takes to clear customs, and you'll see that you should make a very generous allowance for delay in planning connections between international and domestic flights—an average of 2 to 3 hours at least.

For further information about travel to Hawaii, see "Getting There" in chapter 2.

Fast Facts: For the Foreign Traveler

Automobile Organizations   Auto clubs supply maps, suggested routes, guide-books, accident and bail-bond insurance, and emergency road service. The major auto club in the United States, with 955 offices nationwide, is the **American Automobile Association** (AAA; often called "triple A"). Members of some foreign auto clubs have reciprocal arrangements with the AAA and enjoy its services at no charge. If you belong to an auto club, inquire about AAA reciprocity before you leave. The AAA can give you an **International Driving Permit** validating your foreign license. You might be able to join the AAA even if you are not a member of a reciprocal club. To inquire, call ☎ **800/736-2886.**

Oahu's local AAA office is at 1270 Ala Moana Blvd., Honolulu 96814 (☎ **808/593-2221**). Some car-rental agencies now provide automobile club–type services, so you should inquire about their availability when you rent your car.

Business Hours   See "Fast Facts: Oahu" in chapter 4, "Getting to Know Oahu."

Climate   See "When to Go" in chapter 2.

Electricity   Hawaii, like the U.S mainland and Canada, uses 110–120 volts, 60 cycles, compared to the 220–240 volts, 50 cycles used in most of Europe and in other areas of the world, including Australia and New Zealand. In addition to a 100-volt transformer, small appliances of non-American manufacture, such as hair dryers or shavers, require a plug adapter with two flat, parallel pins.

Embassies & Consulates   All embassies are located in the national capital, Washington, D.C. Some consulates are located in major cities, and most nations have a mission to the United Nations in New York City. Listed here are the embassies and some consulates of the major English-speaking countries. Travelers from other countries can find telephone numbers for their embassies and consulates by calling directory information for Washington, D.C. (☎ **202/ 555-1212**).

The embassy of **Australia** is at 1601 Massachusetts Ave. NW, Washington, DC 20036 (☎ **202/797-3000**). There is also an Australian consulate in Hawaii at 1000 Bishop St., Penthouse Suite, Honolulu, HI 96813 (☎ 808/524-5050).

The embassy of **Canada** is at 501 Pennsylvania Ave. NW, Washington, DC 20001 (☎ **202/682-1740**). Canadian consulates are also at 1251 Avenue of the Americas, New York, NY 10020 (☎ 212/768-2400), and at 550 S. Hope St., 9th floor, Los Angeles, CA 90071 (☎ 213/346-2700).

The embassy of the **Republic of Ireland** is at 2234 Massachusetts Ave. NW, Washington, DC 20008 (☎ **202/462-3939**). There's a consulate office in San Francisco at 44 Montgomery St., Suite 3830, San Francisco, CA 94104 (☎ 415/ 392-4214).

The embassy of **New Zealand** is at 37 Observatory Circle NW, Washington, DC 20008 (☎ **202/328-4800**). The only New Zealand consulate in the United States is at 12400 Wilshire Blvd., Los Angeles, CA 90025 (☎ **310/207-1605**).

The embassy of the **United Kingdom** is at 3100 Massachusetts Ave. NW, Washington, DC 20008 (☎ **202/462-1340**). British consulates are at 845 Third Ave., New York, NY 10022 (☎ 212/745-0200), and 11766 Wilshire Blvd., Suite 400, Los Angeles, CA 90025 (☎ 310/477-3322).

The embassy of **Japan** is at 2520 Massachusetts Ave. NW, Washington, DC 20008 (☎ **202/939-6700**). The consulate general of Japan is located at 1742 Nuuanu Ave., Honolulu, HI 96817 (☎ 808/536-2226). There are several other consulates, including one in New York at 299 Park Ave., New York, NY 10171 (☎ 212/371-8222).

Emergencies   Call ☎ **911** to report a fire, call the police, or get an ambulance.

Gasoline (Petrol)   One U.S. gallon equals 3.8 liters, and 1.2 U.S. gallons equals 1 Imperial gallon. You'll notice there are several grades (and price levels) of gasoline available at most gas stations. And you'll also notice that their names change from company to company. The ones with the highest octane are the most expensive, but most rental cars take the least expensive "regular" gas, with an octane rating of 87.

Holidays   See "When to Go" in chapter 2.

Languages   English is the official language. Major Hawaii hotels may have multilingual employees, and most Honolulu and Waikiki shops have multilingual staffs who speak English, Japanese, Korean, and several dialects of the Philippines. Unless your language is very obscure, they can usually supply a translator on request. See "Life & Language" in the appendix "Honolulu & Oahu in Depth" for information about the Hawaiian language.

Legal Aid   The ordinary tourist will probably never become involved with the American legal system. If you are pulled over for a minor infraction (for example, driving faster than the speed limit), never attempt to pay the fine directly to a police officer; you could wind up arrested on the much more serious charge of attempted bribery. Pay fines by mail or directly into the hands of the clerk of the court. If accused of a more serious offense, it's wise to say and do nothing before consulting a lawyer (you have a right to both remain silent and to consult an attorney under the U.S. Constitution). Under U.S. law, an arrested person is allowed one telephone call to a party of his or her choice; call your embassy or consulate.

Mail   Mailboxes are generally found at intersections, are blue with a blue-and-white eagle logo, and carry the inscription U.S. POSTAL SERVICE. If your mail is addressed to a U.S. destination, don't forget to add the five-digit postal code, or ZIP code, after the two-letter abbreviation of the state to which the mail is addressed. The abbreviation for Hawaii is HI.

International airmail rates are 60¢ for half-ounce letters (40¢ for letters going to Mexico and 46¢ for letters to Canada) and 50¢ for postcards (35¢ to Mexico and 40¢ to Canada). All domestic first-class mail goes from Hawaii to the U.S. mainland by air.

Taxes   The United States has no VAT (value-added tax) or other indirect taxes at a national level. Every state, and each city in it, has the right to levy its own local tax on all purchases, including hotel and restaurant checks, airline tickets, and so on. In Hawaii, sales tax is 4%; there's also a 7.25% hotel-room tax, so the total tax on your hotel bill will be 11.25%.

Telephone & Fax   The telephone system in the United States is run by private corporations, so rates, particularly for long-distance service and operator-assisted calls, can vary widely—especially on calls made from public telephones. Local calls—that is, calls to other locations on the island you're on—made from public phones in Hawaii cost 35¢. The international country code is 1, just as it is for the rest of the United States and Canada.

Generally, hotel surcharges on long-distance and local calls are astronomical. You are usually better off using a **public pay telephone,** which you will find clearly marked in most public buildings and private establishments as well as on the street.

Most **long-distance and international calls** can be dialed directly from any phone. For calls to Canada and other parts of the United States, dial 1, followed by the area code and the seven-digit number. For international calls, dial 011, followed by the country code, city code, and telephone number of the person you want to call.

In Hawaii, interisland phone calls are considered long-distance and often are as costly as calling the U.S. mainland.

For **reversed-charge or collect calls,** and for **person-to-person calls,** dial 0 (zero, not the letter "O"), followed by the area code and number you want; an operator then comes on the line, and you should specify that you are calling collect, person-to-person, or both. If your operator-assisted call is international, ask for the overseas operator.

Note that all phone numbers with the area code 800 or 888 are toll-free.

For **local directory assistance** ("information"), dial 411; for **long-distance information,** dial 1, then the appropriate area code and 555-1212.

Fax facilities are widely available and can be found in most hotels and many other establishments. Try **Mail Boxes, Etc.** (check the local Yellow Pages) or any photocopying shop.

Telephone Directory   There are two kinds of telephone directories in the United States. The general directory is the so-called **White Pages,** in which private and business subscribers are listed in alphabetical order. The inside front cover lists the emergency numbers for police, fire, and ambulance, and other vital numbers (like the Coast Guard, poison-control center, crime-victims' hotline, and so on). The first few pages are devoted to community-service numbers, including a guide to long-distance and international calling, complete with country codes and area codes.

The second directory, printed on yellow paper (hence its name, **Yellow Pages**), lists all local services, businesses, and industries by type of activity, with an index at the front. The listings cover not only such obvious items as automobile repairs by make of car, or drugstores (pharmacies), often by geographical location, but also restaurants by type of cuisine and geographical location, bookstores by special subject and/or language, places of worship by religious denomination, and other information that the tourist might otherwise not readily find. The Yellow Pages include detailed maps, postal ZIP codes, and a calendar of events.

Time   See "Fast Facts: Oahu" in chapter 4.

Tipping   It's part of the American way of life to tip, on the principle that you must expect to pay for any service you get. Many personnel receive little direct salary and must depend on tips for their income. In fact, the U.S. government imposes income taxes on service personnel based on an estimate of how much they should have earned in tips relative to their employer's total receipts. In other words, they might have to pay taxes on a tip you didn't give them!

Here are some tipping guidelines:

In **hotels,** tip bellhops at least $1 per piece of luggage ($2 to $3 if you have a lot of luggage), and tip the housekeeping staff $1 per person, per day. Tip the doorman or concierge only if he or she has given you some specific service (for example, calling a cab for you or finding difficult-to-get theater tickets). Tip the valet-parking attendant $1 every time you get your car.

In **restaurants, bars, and nightclubs,** tip service staff 15% to 20% of the check, tip bartenders 10% to 15%, and tip valet-parking attendants $1 per vehicle. Tip the doorman only if you were provided with some specific service (such as calling a cab for you). Tipping is not expected in cafeterias and fast-food restaurants.

Tip **cab drivers** 15% of the fare.

As for **other service personnel,** tip skycaps at airports at least $1 per piece ($2 to $3 if you have a lot of luggage), and tip hairdressers and barbers 15% to 20%.

Tipping ushers at movies and theaters and gas-station attendants is not expected.

Toilets   Foreign visitors often complain that public toilets are hard to find in most U.S. cities. True, there are none on the streets, but visitors can usually find one in a bar, fast-food outlet, restaurant, hotel, museum, department store, or service station—and it will probably be clean (although the last-mentioned sometimes leaves much to be desired). Note, however, a growing practice in some restaurants and bars of displaying a notice that "toilets are for the use of patrons only." You can ignore this sign, or better yet, avoid arguments by paying for a cup of coffee or soft drink, which will qualify you as a patron. The cleanliness of toilets at parks and beaches is more open to question.

Getting to Know Oahu

4

by Jeanette Foster

Oahu—just letting the name roll off your tongue is a bit like blowing smoke rings as the round vowels line up one after another. Oahu is not the biggest island in the Hawaiian chain (the Big Island of Hawaii holds that distinction) or the oldest (Kauai wins by a few million years), but it certainly is the best known. The business and financial center of the state, Oahu is also the population center with nearly 875,000 residents, 75% of the total state population.

Actually, it is a relatively small island, measuring 26 miles long and some 44 miles across at its widest, totaling 608 square miles of land, with 112 miles of coastline. From outer space, Oahu looks somewhat like a frayed Indian arrowhead with two mountain ridges shoring up each side: the 4,000-foot Waianae Mountains on the leeward (western) coast and the 3,000-foot Koolau Mountains on the windward (eastern) side. At night you can see the lights of suburban Oahu pouring down and out of the mountain valleys and reaching toward the shoreline.

In the minds of many, Oahu and its most famous city, Honolulu, are synonymous. In fact, some people think the name of the island is Honolulu, a misnomer further compounded by the islandwide county calling itself the "City and County of Honolulu." The population of Honolulu is 377,059, the largest urban area not only on Oahu but in the entire state. Honolulu's equally well-known neighbor, Waikiki, a mere 500 acres of land (and 133 acres of that is Kapiolani Park), has a resident population of some 19,768 with an additional 83,400 tourists visiting on an average day.

To help you navigate around the nearly one million people on this 608-square-mile island, we have provided information in this chapter to give you a feel for the lay of the land. We've also made some recommendations for what to see if your time is limited, and offered logistical advice for getting around the island. Finally, we've provided some handy facts and phone numbers to make your trip as hassle-free as possible.

1 Arriving

Honolulu International Airport sits on the south shore of Oahu, west of downtown Honolulu and Waikiki, near Pearl Harbor. All major American and many international carriers fly to Honolulu from the mainland: **United Airlines** (☎ 800/225-5825; www.ual.com) offers

Oahu

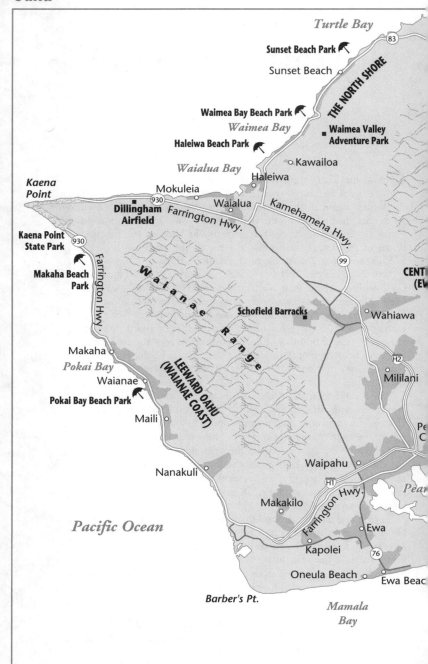

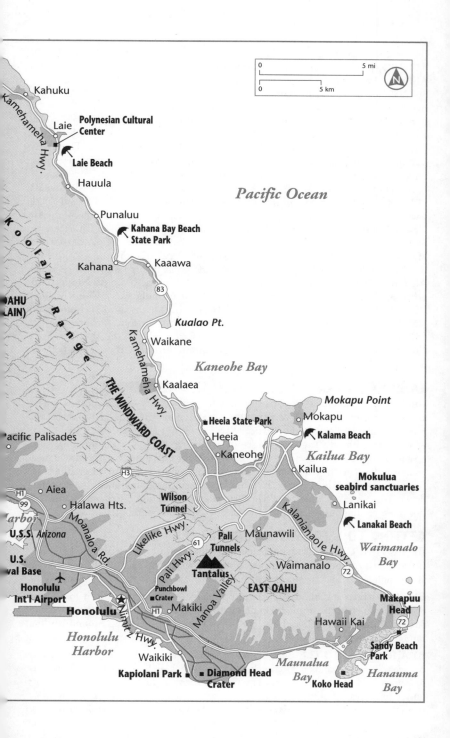

the most frequent service from the U.S. mainland, but **American Airlines** (☎ 800/433-7300; www.americanair.com), **Continental Airlines** (☎ 800/231-0856), **Delta Airlines** (☎ 800/221-1212; www.delta-air.com), **Hawaiian Airlines** (☎ 800/367-5320; www.hawaiianair.com), **Northwest Airlines** (☎ 800/225-2525; www.nwa.com), and **TWA** (☎ 800/221-2000; www2.twa.com) all have regular flights.

Based in Honolulu, **Hawaiian Airlines** (☎ **800/367-5320** or 808/537-5100; www.hawaiianair.com) offers nonstop service on wide-body DC-10s from San Francisco, Seattle, Los Angeles, Portland, and Las Vegas. Hawaiian works with Fly AAway Vacations, the tour unit of American Airlines. For information about its package tours, phone Hawaiian Airlines Vacations at ☎ **800/353-5393,** or ask your travel agent.

Airlines serving Honolulu from other than the U.S. mainland include **Air Canada** (☎ 800/776-3000; www.aircanada.ca); **Canadian Airlines** (☎ 800/426-7000; www.cdnair.ca); **Canada 3000** (☎ 888/CAN-3000; www.canada3000.com); **Air New Zealand** (☎ 0800/737-000 in Auckland, 64-3/379-5200 in Christchurch, 800/926-7255 in the U.S.), which runs 40 flights per week between Auckland and Hawaii; **Qantas** (☎ 008/177-767 in Australia, 800/227-4500 in the U.S.), which flies between Sydney and Honolulu daily (plus additional flights 4 days a week); **Japan Air Lines** (☎ 03/5489-1111 in Tokyo, 800/525-3663 in the U.S.); **All Nippon Airways (ANA)** ☎ 03/5489-1212 in Tokyo, 800/235-9262 in the U.S.); **China Airlines** (☎ 02/715-1212 in Taipei, 800/227-5118 in the U.S.); **Garuda Indonesian** (☎ 251-2235 in Jakarta, 800/342-7832 in the U.S.); **Korean Airlines** (☎ 02/656-2000 in Seoul, 800/223-1155 on the East Coast, 800/421-8200 on the West Coast, 800/438-5000 from Hawaii); and **Philippine Airlines** (☎ 631/816-6691 in Manila, 800/435-9725 in the U.S.).

LANDING AT HONOLULU INTERNATIONAL AIRPORT

Landing in Honolulu is like arriving in a foreign country—the airport is full of exciting strangers from every corner of the world. On any given day, it's probably the most cosmopolitan spot in the Pacific.

While the airport is large and constantly expanding, the layout is quite simple and easy to navigate. You can walk or take the **Wiki-Wiki Bus,** a free airport shuttle, from your arrival gate to the main terminal and baggage claim, which is on the ground level. After collecting your bags, exit to the palm-lined street, where uniformed attendants flag down taxis, Waikiki shuttles, and rental car vans; they can also direct you to **TheBUS** (for transportation information, see "Getting To & From the Airport," below).

GETTING TO & FROM THE AIRPORT

BY RENTAL CAR   All major rental companies have cars available at Honolulu International Airport (see "Getting Around," below). Rental agency vans pick you up at the middle curbside outside baggage claim and take you to their off-site lot.

BY TAXI   Taxis are abundant at the airport; an attendant will be happy to flag one down for you. Taxi fare from Honolulu International to downtown Honolulu is about $16; to Waikiki, about $23. If you need to call a taxi, see "Getting Around," below, for a list of cab companies.

BY AIRPORT SHUTTLE   Shuttle vans operate 24 hours a day every day of the year between the airport and all 350 hotels and condos in Waikiki. At a rate of $8 one-way to Waikiki and $13 round-trip, it's a much better bargain than taking a taxi—if there's only one or two of you. If you're in a group of three or more, it's probably more cost-efficient to grab a cab. **Trans-Hawaiian Services** (☎ 800/533-8765 or 808/566-7000) serves the airport with passenger vans every 20 to 30 minutes, depending on traffic. Children small enough to sit on your lap ride for free. No reservation is necessary, but do book ahead for hotel pickup for a departing flight. Look for attendants in red shirts that say SHUTTLE VEHICLE; pickup is at the middle curb outside baggage claim. You can board with two pieces of luggage and a carry-on at no extra charge; surfboards and bicycles are prohibited for safety reasons. Backpacks are okay. Tips are welcome.

BY TheBUS   TheBUS is by far the cheapest way to get to Waikiki—but you've got to be traveling light to use it. Bus nos. 19 and 20 (Waikiki Beach and Hotels) run from the airport to downtown Honolulu and Waikiki. The first bus from Waikiki to the airport is at 4:50am on weekdays and 5:25am on weekends; the last bus departs the airport for Waikiki at 11:45pm on weekdays, 11:25pm on weekends. There are two bus stops on the main terminal's upper level; a third is on the second level of the Inter-Island terminal.

You can board TheBUS with a carry-on or small suitcase as long as it fits under the seat and doesn't disrupt other passengers; otherwise, you'll have to take a shuttle or taxi. The approximate travel time to Waikiki is an hour. The one-way fare is $1, 50¢ for students (exact change only). For information on routes and schedules, call TheBUS at ☎ **808/848-5555.**

2 Orienting Yourself: The Lay of the Land

VISITOR INFORMATION

The Hawaii Visitors and Convention Bureau (HVCB) is at 2270 Kalakaua Ave., 7th floor, Suite 801, Honolulu, HI 96815 (☎ **800/GO-HAWAII** or 808/923-1811), and on the Net at www.gohawaii.com. The bureau supplies free brochures, maps, accommodation guides, and *Islands of Aloha,* the official HVCB magazine. **Oahu Visitors Bureau,** 1001 Bishop St., Pauahi Tower, Suite 47, Honolulu, HI 96813 (☎ **800/ OAHU-678** or 808/524-0722; www.visit-oahu.com) distributes a free 64-page visitors booklet.

A number of free publications, including *This Week* and *Guide to Oahu,* are packed with money-saving coupons offering discounts on dining, shops, and activities around the island; look for them on the visitors' publication racks at the airport and around town.

The Island in Brief

Honolulu   America's 11th largest city looks like any other big metropolitan center with tall buildings. In fact, some cynics refer to it as "Los Angeles West." But within Honolulu's boundaries you'll find rainforests, deep canyons, valleys and waterfalls, a nearly mile-high mountain range, coral reefs, and gold-sand beaches. The city proper—where most of Honolulu's 850,000 residents live—is approximately 12 miles wide and 26 miles long, running east–west roughly between Diamond Head and Pearl Harbor (you'll see Pearl Harbor from the left side of your airplane on your final approach into Honolulu International). It extends over seven hills laced by seven streams that run to Mamala Bay.

Up close, Honolulu becomes exceedingly complex: Downtown, street vendors sell papayas from a truck along skyscraper-lined concrete canyons, where professional women wear muumuus and carry briefcases. Joggers and BMWs rush by the United States's only palace. Burly bus drivers sport fragrant white ginger flowers on their dashboards, and Methodist churches look like Asian temples. Doctors and dope dealers share surfing spots, and the entire social spectrum spreads mats edge to edge on a lawn to hear folksy Hawaiian music and watch hula under the stars. Tokyo teenagers sun on

Honolulu's Neighborhoods in Brief

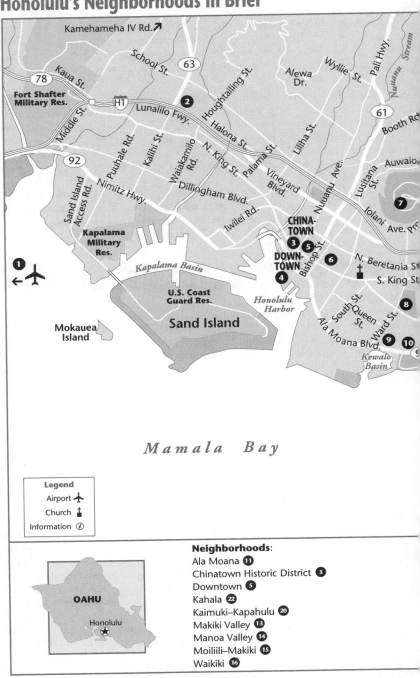

Kamehameha IV Rd.

School St.

63

Alewa Dr.

Wyllie St.

Pali Hwy.

Nuuanu Stream

78

Kaua St.

Fort Shafter Military Res.

H1

Lunalilo Fwy.

Houghtailing St.

Halona St.

Liliha St.

2

61

Booth Rd.

Middle St.

92

Puuhale Rd.

Kalihi St.

Waiakamilo Rd.

N. King St.

Palama St.

Vineyard Blvd.

Nuuanu Ave.

Lusitana St.

Auwaio

Sand Island Access Rd.

Nimitz Hwy.

Dillingham Blvd.

Iolani Ave.

7

Iwilei Rd.

CHINA-TOWN

3 **5**

Bishop St.

N. Beretania St.

Kapalama Military Res.

Kapalama Basin

DOWN-TOWN

4

6

S. King St.

1

✈
←

U.S. Coast Guard Res.

Honolulu Harbor

8

South St.

Queen St.

Ward St.

Mokauea Island

Sand Island

Ala Moana Blvd.

9 **10**

Kewalo Basin

M a m a l a   B a y

Legend

Airport ✈
Church ✝
Information ⓘ

OAHU

Honolulu ★

Neighborhoods:
Ala Moana **11**
Chinatown Historic District **3**
Downtown **5**
Kahala **22**
Kaimuki–Kapahulu **20**
Makiki Valley **13**
Manoa Valley **14**
Moiliili–Makiki **15**
Waikiki **16**

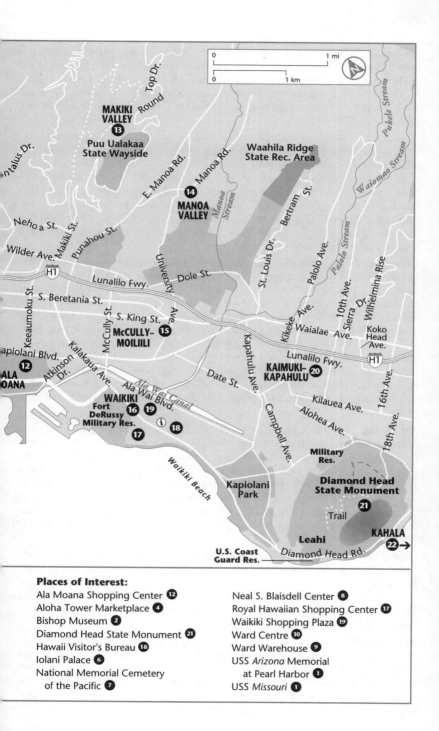

Places of Interest:

Ala Moana Shopping Center **12**
Aloha Tower Marketplace **4**
Bishop Museum **2**
Diamond Head State Monument **21**
Hawaii Visitor's Bureau **18**
Iolani Palace **6**
National Memorial Cemetery
   of the Pacific **7**

Neal S. Blaisdell Center **8**
Royal Hawaiian Shopping Center **17**
Waikiki Shopping Plaza **19**
Ward Centre **10**
Ward Warehouse **9**
USS *Arizona* Memorial
   at Pearl Harbor **1**
USS *Missouri* **1**

the beach in bikinis while their older Hawaiian cousins carry parasols for shade, and waiters, if asked, will stand and recite their 14 cultural antecedents in a tradition as old as Polynesia. What is this place? The third world's American capital, mankind's hope for the future, or just the stuff between the airport and the beach at Waikiki? Watch out while you find out; some cities tug at your heart, but Honolulu is a whole love affair.

Downtown   Now a tiny cluster of high-rise offices west of Waikiki, downtown Honolulu is the financial, business, and government center of Hawaii. Fort Street runs inland from the iconic 1926-vintage Aloha Tower, once the tallest building on Oahu.

The history of Hawaii can be read architecturally downtown—Italianate Monarchy–style buildings stand next to New England mission houses and the 1920s buildings of the "Big Five" cartel. There's a Carnegie-built Mediterranean-style library, a Spanish-style City Hall, a Julia Morgan YWCA, and a State Capitol, which looks like a volcano, designed by John Carl Warnecke. And there's the gingerbread palace that became a prison for Hawaii's last queen.

Chinatown Historic District   In Chinatown, on the edge of downtown, you can buy thousand-year-old duck eggs or fresh flower leis, find an ancient potion, get a $3 haircut, play pool in a 1930s bar, get treated by an acupuncturist, buy fresh Chinese *manapua,* eat Vietnamese *pho,* or browse Oahu Market, where 17 vendors sell fish, ducks, spices, fresh fruits, and vegetables under a tin roof. Founded in 1860 by Chinese immigrants, it's the oldest Chinatown in America and still one of Honolulu's liveliest neighborhoods. A quaint village of tin-roofed sheds, brightly painted shops, and often crowded streets, this historic 15-block district is a nonstop pageant of people, sights, sounds, smells, and tastes—not all Chinese, now that Southeast Asians, including many Vietnamese, share the old storefronts. Go on Saturday morning when everyone shops in Chinatown for fresh goods like ginger root, fern fronds, and hogs' heads.

Ala Moana   The name of a great beach as well as a famous shopping center, Ala Moana is the retail and transportation hub of Honolulu, a place where you can both shop and suntan in one afternoon. All bus routes lead to the open-air Ala Moana Shopping Center, a modern mall across the street from Ala Moana Beach, a wonderful family playground. This 50-acre, 200-shop emporium attracts 56 million customers a year; people fly up here from Tahiti just to buy their Christmas gifts. Every European designer from Armani to Vuitton has a shop here, and Neiman Marcus's huge department store anchors the mammoth shopping center. It's Honolulu's answer to Beverly Hills's Rodeo Drive.

Manoa Valley   First inhabited by white settlers, the Manoa Valley above Waikiki still has vintage *kamaaina* (native-born) homes; Lyon Arboretum, one of Hawaii's premier botanical gardens; Manoa Falls; and the 320-acre campus of the University of Hawaii, where 50,000 students hit the books when they're not on the beach. At the university's East-West Center, a major Pacific Rim education and research center, scholars work together to find solutions to third-world problems.

TO THE EAST: Kahala   Just beyond Diamond Head, you'll find one of Oahu's top-drawer neighborhoods, where the grandiose estates of world-class millionaires line the beach. In between the gated mansions are narrow sand alleys that lead to the thin, gnarly beach that fronts the mansions. The only hotel here is the newly opened—and very pricey—Mandarin Oriental.

Waikiki   When King Kalakaua played in Waikiki, it was "a hamlet of plain cottages . . . its excitements caused by the activity of insect tribes and the occasional fall of a coconut."

The Merrie Monarch, who gave his name to Waikiki's main street, would love the scene today. It's where all the action is. Waikiki is an urban beach backed by 175 high-rise hotels with more than 33,000 guest rooms, all in a 1½-square-mile beach zone. The beach district boasts 279 drinking establishments, 240 restaurants, 90 hotels, and 4 churches. Waikiki is honeymooners and sun seekers, bikinis and bare buns, a round-the-clock beach party every day of the year. And it's all because of a thin crescent of imported sand.

Some say Waikiki is past its prime and that everybody goes to Maui now, but Waikiki is the very incarnation of Yogi Berra's comment about Toots Shor's famous New York restaurant: "Nobody goes there anymore. It's too crowded."

EAST OAHU   Well beyond Waikiki and past Kahala lie the suburban bedroom communities of Aina Haina, Niu Valley, Kuliouou, Hawaii Kai, Portlock, and Kalama Valley, all linked by Kalanianaole Highway and each chock-a-block with homes, condos, fast-food joints, and shopping malls. It looks like southern California on a good day. You'll find yourself in this area if you're splurging on lunch or dinner at Roy's (the original and still outstanding Hawaii Regional restaurant) in Hawaii Kai; visiting Hanauma Bay for some great snorkeling; heading to Sandy Beach to watch daredevil surfers risk their necks; or just enjoying the natural splendor of the lovely coastline, which might include a hike to Makapuu Lighthouse.

THE WINDWARD COAST   For years, travel writers—hoping, no doubt, to keep a great secret—portrayed Oahu's northeastern side as wet, windy, and unappealing to visitors. Well, the secret's out. The Windward Coast looks like the South Pacific of the travel posters: green and lush, backed by the awesome cliffs of the Koolau Range, with plenty of sun, cool trade winds, and miles of empty coral-sand beaches fronted by bays and reefs. This is Oahu in its natural state, a place of beauty not yet violated by high-rise hotels—but you will find plenty of beach cottages (some for rent) and B&Bs in little villages on big beaches.

Kailua   The biggest little beach town in Hawaii, Kailua sits at the foot of the green Koolau Mountains, on a great bay with two of Hawaii's best beaches. The town itself is a low-rise cluster of timeworn shops and homes. Kailua has become the bed-and-breakfast capital of Hawaii; it's an affordable alternative to Waikiki, with rooms and vacation rentals from $50 a day and up. It's a funky little town full of fun restaurants like Buzz's (where President Clinton ate when he came to town), the publike Kailua Beach Grill, and Brent's, an authentic New York–style deli. With the prevailing trade winds whipping up a cooling breeze, Kailua attracts windsurfers from around the world.

Kaneohe   Helter-skelter suburbia sprawls around the edges of Kaneohe Bay, one of the most scenic bays in all the Pacific. After you clear the trafficky maze of Kaneohe, you return to Oahu's more natural state. This great bay beckons to you, and you can get to it from Heeia Boat Harbor on snorkeling or fishing charters and visit Ahu o Laka ("the altar of Laka," a canoe-sailing god), the sandbar that appears and disappears in the middle of the bay. From out there, you get a panoramic view of the Koolau Range.

Kualoa/Laie   The upper northeast shore is one of the most sacred places on Oahu. It's an early Hawaiian landing spot where even kings dipped their sails, the cliffs hold ancient burial sites, and ghosts still march in the night.

Sheer cliffs stab this sea coast fringed by coral reef. Old fishponds are tucked along the two-lane coast road that weaves around beautiful Kahana Bay and by empty gold-sand beaches in towns with too many vowels, like Kaaawa. Thousands "explore" the South Pacific at the Polynesian Cultural Center, in Laie, a Mormon settlement with its own Tabernacle Choir of sweet Samoan harmony.

THE NORTH SHORE Only 28 miles from downtown Honolulu, the little beach town of Haleiwa and the surrounding shoreline seems like a separate paradise; once some people get the roar of the surf in their head, they never leave. They come to see the big waves roll up on world-famous beaches like Sunset Beach and Banzai Pipeline, go deep-sea fishing, visit the island's biggest heiau, explore Oahu's Waimea Falls, shop and eat shave ice in artsy Haleiwa town, and stay in affordable beachfront cottages on the edge of the roaring Pacific.

CENTRAL OAHU: The Ewa Plain Flanked by the Koolau and Waianae mountain ranges, the hot, sun-baked Ewa Plain runs up and down the center of Oahu. Once covered with the sandalwood forests that were hacked down for the China trade, and later the sugarcane and pineapple backbone of Hawaii, Ewa today sports a new crop: suburban homes stretching to the sea. But let your eye wander west to the Waianae Range and Mount Kaala, the highest summit on Oahu at 4,020 feet. Up there in the misty rainforest, native birds thrive in the hummocky bog.

Hawaiian chiefs once fought on the Ewa Plain for supremacy over Oahu. In 1928, the U.S. Army pitched a tent camp on the plain. It became Schofield Barracks, which author James Jones called "the most beautiful army post in the world." Hollywood filmed Jones's *From Here to Eternity* here, the film that launched Frank Sinatra's comeback.

LEEWARD OAHU: The Waianae Coast The west coast of Oahu is a hot and dry place of spectacular natural beauty: big beaches, steep cliffs, and wildness. The rustic villages of Nanakuli, Waianae, and Makaha are the last stands of native Hawaiians. This side of Oahu is seldom visited, except by surfers bound for Yokohama Bay and anyone else who wants to see needle-nose Kaena Point (the island's westernmost outpost) and a coastal wilderness park under a 768-foot peak named for the endangered Hawaiian owl.

3 Oahu in a Nutshell: Suggested Itineraries for 1 to 5 Days

If You Have 1 Day

No question—drive around the island of Oahu. If you don't have a car, take TheBUS 52 or 55 (see the "By Bus" section below). If you do have a car, take off across the middle of Oahu and go to Haleiwa for breakfast. Spend the morning stopping at as many beaches as you have time for. Wander into the Polynesian Cultural Center in the early afternoon. Drive along the windward side for a late afternoon dip at Lanikai Beach. Head back to Honolulu and Waikiki as the sun is setting, and plan on dinner at Roy's in Hawaii Kai to finish your perfect day.

If You Have 2 Days

Spend the first day driving around the island (see above). On the second day, get up early and go to the USS *Arizona* Memorial at Pearl Harbor (get there early, as the lines get longer as the day goes on); be sure to check out the USS *Bowfin* submarine next door. In the afternoon, hit either Waikiki Beach or Hanauma Bay for snorkeling and swimming. Head for Waikiki at sunset for sweet Hawaiian music and a night on the town.

If You Have 3 Days

See above for the first 2 days. On day 3, put on your walking shoes and explore Honolulu: downtown (take in the cultural sites from the Iolani Palace to the Mission Museum House), Chinatown (where the smells will compel you to stop for lunch), and the Waterfront area. In the afternoon, check out the Waikiki Aquarium. Take in a luau in the evening.

⊛ Frommer's Favorite Honolulu & Oahu Experiences

Snorkeling Hanauma Bay. It has a reputation of being too crowded, but for clear, warm water and an abundance of fish that are so friendly they'll eat out of your hand, there's no place like Hanauma Bay. The best thing about this underwater park is that anyone can join the fun. Just wade in and look down to see the kaleidoscope of fish that call Hawaii's waters home. Go early to avoid the crush.

Climbing Diamond Head. The hike to the summit of this 760-foot-high volcanic crater takes about 45 minutes, but the reward is a breathtaking 360-degree view—with Waikiki, Honolulu, and the Pacific Ocean at your feet. This one's for everyone, especially kids.

Watching the North Shore Waves. Humongous. Totally awesome. No other words describe the monster winter waves of Oahu's North Shore. You've seen it on TV, in the opening shot of "Hawaii Five-0": blue-green water in a perfect tube. But see it in person for the full effect. It snarls out of the Pacific like a tsunami and roars like a 30-foot-high freight train before smashing almost at your feet in foam. The surfers who take them on will keep you spellbound for hours.

Exploring Oahu's Rainforests. In the misty sunbeams, colorful birds flit among giant ferns and hanging vines, and towering tropical trees form a thick canopy that shelters all below in cool shadows. This emerald world is a true Eden. For the full experience, try Manoa Falls Trail, a walk of about a mile that ends at a freshwater pool and waterfall.

Wearing an Aloha Shirt. Aloha shirts are one of the best things about tropical Honolulu. They're light, colorful, and fun. You don't have to button them or tuck them in. Some think only tourists wear them; it's not true. In Honolulu, the aloha-shirt capital of the world, men wear bright floral-print shirts to work every day. Invitations to many of Honolulu's exclusive social engagements specify "aloha attire."

If You Have 5 Days or More

See above for the first 3 days. On day 4, you might want to consider driving to Southeast Oahu and going to Sea Life Park in the morning, with a quick swim at one of the many beaches lining the coast. In the afternoon, explore Kailua and Kaneohe: Wander through Heeia State Park, check out the replica of the 900-year-old Byodo-In in the Valley of the Temples, bike or horseback ride in Senator Fong's Plantation and Gardens, or take windsurfing lessons at Kailua Beach.

The next day, return to the North Shore, spending time at all the activities at Waimea Valley, stopping to watch the surfers during the winter, or snorkeling the incredible reefs in the summer.

4 Getting Around

BY CAR

Oahu residents own 600,000 registered vehicles, but they have only 1,500 miles of mostly two-lane roads. That's 400 cars for every mile, a fact that becomes abundantly clear during morning and evening rush hours. You can avoid the gridlock by driving between 9am and 3pm or after 6pm.

State law mandates that all passengers in a car must wear a seat belt. The law is enforced with vigilance and the fine is quite stiff—so buckle up.

CAR RENTALS   All the major car-rental firms have agencies on Oahu, at the airport and in Waikiki, including **Alamo** (☎ 800/327-9633), **Avis** (☎ 800/321-3712), **Budget** (☎ 800/935-6878), **Enterprise** (☎ 800/325-8007), **Hertz** (☎ 800/654-3011), **National** (☎ 800/227-7368), **Payless** (☎ 800/729-5377), **Sears** (☎ 800/527-0770), and **Thrifty** (☎ 800/367-2277).

Most of the local, "Rent-A-Wreck"–type car rental companies have gone by the wayside on Oahu (even Tropical Rent-a-Car has closed); however, one reliable, affordable, and accessible company remains: **Tradewinds,** 2875-A Koapaka St., Honolulu, HI 96819 (☎ **888/388-7368** or 808/834-1465; e-mail: Rent-a-Car@gte.net), a small, family-run company with a fleet of some 300 cars. Depending on the time of year, daily rentals are at least $5 less than what the national chains charge; weekly and monthly rentals at Tradewinds offer super savings; and collision coverage is also cheaper—$9 per day versus $14 to $20. It's best to book in advance. When you arrive at Honolulu airport, get your luggage, go to the courtesy phones for car rentals, and push the button for Tradewinds—they'll send a van to pick you up.

MOTORCYCLE RENTALS   If your dream is to go screaming down the highway on the back of a big Harley Hog, here's your chance; rent a motorcycle. **Island Motorcycle,** 512-B Atkinson Dr. at Kapiolani Boulevard, Honolulu, HI 96814 (☎ **808/957-0517**), has Harley Heritage, Heritage Classic, Fat Boy, and Bad Boy cycles starting at $98 for 4 hours, $138 for 8 hours, and $188 for 24 hours (insurance is included in the price). In Waikiki try **Thrifty's,** 1778 Ala Moana Blvd., Discovery Bay Plaza, Honolulu, HI 96815 (☎ **808/971-2660**), which has brand-new Harley Fat Boys, Wide Glides, and Heritages starting at $149 a day (includes helmet), or **Coconut Cruisers,** 2301 Kalakaua Ave., across the street from the International Market Place, Honolulu, HI 96815 (☎ **808/924-1644**), which has a range of bikes from $135 to $220 a day. You must have a valid motorcycle license to rent a bike.

Main Streets & Highways

Navigating around Oahu is actually easy; there are only a few roads that circle the perimeter of the island and a handful that cut across the island.

TO & FROM THE AIRPORT   The main thoroughfare that runs from the airport to Honolulu and Waikiki is the H-1 Freeway. The H-1 also runs in the opposite direction to Pearl Harbor and Ewa. The artery that runs from the airport to Honolulu and Waikiki is Nimitz Highway (which has stoplights). In downtown Honolulu, Nimitz Highway becomes Ala Moana Boulevard.

HONOLULU   The myriad of one-way streets in Honolulu can be confusing and frustrating. If you want to travel in the Diamond Head direction, King Street is one-way going toward Diamond Head. Beretania Street is one-way in the opposite, or Ewa, direction. In the mauka and makai direction: Punchbowl and Bishop streets run toward the ocean (makai), and Alakea and Bethel streets run toward the mountains (mauka).

WAIKIKI   There are three parallel main streets in Waikiki: Kalakaua Avenue (which is one-way going toward Diamond Head and eventually fronts Waikiki Beach), Kuhio Avenue (1 block mauka of Kalakaua Avenue, which has two-way traffic), and Ala Wai Boulevard (which fronts the Ala Wai Canal and runs one-way in the Ewa direction).

AROUND OAHU   From Waikiki, HI. 72 (Kalanianaole Hwy.) takes you around Makapuu Point into Kailua and Kaneohe. From Kailua and Kaneohe, HI. 83 (Kamehameha Hwy.) takes you around the North Shore to Haleiwa, where it is still called the Kamehameha Highway, but the number of the highway changes to 99, and then cuts through mid-Oahu past Schofield Barracks and Wahiawa, and swings out to Pearl

Finding Your Way Around, Oahu Style

Local residents give directions a bit differently than what mainlanders are used to. Seldom will you hear east, west, north, and south; instead, islanders refer to directions as either **makai** (*ma*-kae), meaning toward the sea, or **mauka** (*mow*-kah), toward the mountains. In Honolulu, people use **"Diamond Head"** as a direction referring to the east (in the direction of the world-famous crater called Diamond Head), and **"Ewa"** as a direction referring to the west (in the direction of the town called Ewa, on the other side of Pearl Harbor).

So if you ask a local for directions, this is what you're likely to hear: "Drive 2 blocks makai (toward the sea), then turn Diamond Head (east) at the stoplight. Go 1 block, and turn mauka (toward the mountains). It's on the Ewa (western) side of the street."

City. On the leeward coast, H-1 Freeway becomes two-lane Hi. 93 (Farrington Hwy.); after Makaha, the number changes to Hi. 930, but it is still called Farrington Highway all the way out to Kaena Point. Although you cannot drive around Kaena Point, Farrington Highway (still called Hi. 930) picks up on the north side of the point and goes through Mokuleia and Waialua.

ACROSS OAHU   Highways that cut across the island are Hi. 99 (see above), the Likelike Highway (also called Hi. 63, which goes from Honolulu to Kaneohe), and the Pali Highway (also called Hi. 61, which goes from Honolulu to Kailua). The H-3 Freeway, which starts at Pearl Harbor, is the fastest way to get to Kaneohe and Kailua.

STREET MAPS

One of the best general maps of the island is the *Map of Oahu,* cartography by James A. Bier, published by the University of Hawaii Press, available at bookstores or by writing the Marketing Department, University of Hawaii Press, 2840 Kolowalu St., Honolulu, HI 96822 (☎ **808/956-8255**). For a more specific street map, the best one we have found is *TMK Maps: Oahu Streets and Condos,* published by Hawaii TMK Service, Inc., 222 S. Vineyard St., Suite 401, Honolulu, HI 96813 (☎ **808/ 533-4601**).

BY BUS

One of the best deals anywhere, **TheBUS** (☎ **808/848-5555,** or 808/296-1818 for recorded information) will take you around the whole island for $1. In fact, on a daily basis, more than 260,000 people use the system's 68 lines and 4,000 bus stops. TheBUS goes almost everywhere almost all the time. The most popular route is no. 8 (Waikiki/Ala Moana), which shuttles people between Waikiki and Ala Moana Center every 10 minutes or so (the ride is 15 to 20 minutes). The no. 19 (Airport/Hickam), no. 20 (Airport/Halawa Gate), no. 47 (Waipahu), and no. 58 (Waikiki/Ala Moana) also cover the same stretch. Waikiki service begins daily at 5am and runs until midnight; buses run about every 15 minutes during the day and every 30 minutes in the evening.

The Circle Island–North Shore route is no. 52 (Wahiawa/Circle Island); it leaves from Ala Moana Shopping Center every 30 minutes and takes about 4½ hours to circle the island. The Circle Island–South Shore route is no. 55 (Kaneohe/Circle Island) and also leaves Ala Moana every half hour and takes about 3 to 4½ hours to circle the island.

TheBus

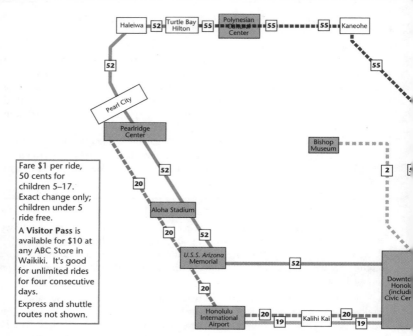

Fare $1 per ride, 50 cents for children 5–17. Exact change only; children under 5 ride free.

A **Visitor Pass** is available for $10 at any ABC Store in Waikiki. It's good for unlimited rides for four consecutive days.

Express and shuttle routes not shown.

Common Bus Routes:

Ala Moana Shopping Center: Take bus #19 & #20 AIRPORT. Return via #19 WAIKIKI, or cross Ala Moana Blvd. for #20.

Bishop Museum: Take #2 SCHOOL STREET get off at Kapalama St., cross School St., walk down Bernice St. Return to School St. and take #2 WAIKIKI.

Byodo-In Temple: Take bus #2 to Hotel-Alakea St. (TRF) to #55 KANEOHE-KAHALUU. Get off at Valley of the Temple cemetery. Also #19 and #20 AIRPORT to King-Alakea St., (TRF) on Alakea St. to #55 KANEOHE-KAHALUU.

Circle Island: Take a Bus to ALA MOANA CENTER (TRF) to #52 WAHIAWA CIRCLE ISLAND or #55 KANEOHE CIRCLE ISLAND. This is a four-hour bus ride.

Chinatown or Downtown: Take any #2 bus going out of Waikiki, to Hotel St. Return take #2 WAIKIKI on Hotel St., or #19 or #20 on King St.

The Contemporary Museum & Punchbowl (National Cemetery of the Pacific): Take #2 bus (TRF) at Alapai St. to #15 MAKIKI-PACIFIC HGTS. Return, take #15 and get off at King St., area (TRF) #2 WAIKIKI.

Diamond Head Crater: #22 HAWAII KAI-SEA LIFE PARK to the crater. Take a flashlight. Return to the same area and take #22 WAIKIKI.

Dole Plantation: Take bus to ALA MOANA CENTER (TRF) to #52 WAHIAWA CIRCLE ISLAND.

Foster Botanic Gardens: Take #2 bus to Hotel-Riviera St. Walk to Vineyard Blvd. Return to Hotel St. Take #2 WAIKIKI, or take #4 NUUANU and get off at Nuuanu-Vineyard. Cross Nuuanu Ave. and walk one block to the gardens.

Aloha Tower Marketplace & Hawaii Maritime Center: Take #19-#20 AIRPORT and get off at Alakea–Ala Moana. Cross the Street to the Aloha Tower.

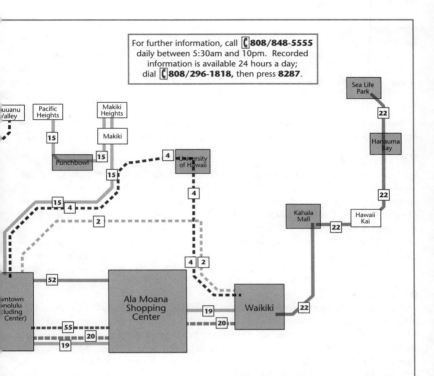

For further information, call ☎ **808/848-5555** daily between 5:30am and 10pm. Recorded information is available 24 hours a day; dial ☎ **808/296-1818,** then press **8287**.

Honolulu Zoo: Take any bus on Kuhio Ave. going DIAMOND HEAD direction to Kapahulu Ave.

Iolani Palace: also **State Capitol, Honolulu Hale, Kawaihao Church, Mission Houses, Queen's Hospital, King Kamehameha Statue, State Judiciary Bldg.,** take any #2 bus and get off at Punchbowl and Beretania St. Walk to King St. Return #2 WAIKIKI on King St.

Kahala Mall: #22 HAWAII KAI–SEA LIFE PARK to Kilauea Ave. Return #22 WAIKIKI.

Pearl Harbor (*Arizona* Memorial): Open Daily 8ᴀᴍ to 3ᴘᴍ. Free. Take #20 AIRPORT. Get off across from Memorial, or take a bus to Ala Moana Center (TRF) to #52.

Polynesian Cultural Center: Take a bus to ALA MOANA CENTER (TRF) to #55 KANEOHE CIRCLE ISLAND. Bus ride takes two hours one way. PCC opens at 12:30ᴘᴍ. Closed on Sundays.

Queen Emma's Summer Home: Take #4 NUUANU and it will take you there, or board a bus to ALA MOANA CENTER (TRF) to #55 KANEOHE.

Sea Life Park: #22 HAWAII KAI-SEA LIFE PARK. #22 will stop at Hanauma Bay enroute to the park.

University of Hawaii: Take #4 NUUANU. The bus will go to the University enroute to Nuuanu.

Waimea Valley & Adventure Park: Take a bus to ALA MOANA CENTER (TRF) to #52 WAHIAWA CIRCLE ISLAND or #55 KANEOHE CIRCLE ISLAND.

Warning

Recently, visitors waiting for a bus along the North Shore have been attacked and robbed in broad daylight. You might want to consider splurging on a rental car to visit the North Shore.

You can buy a **Visitors Pass** for $10 at any ABC store in Waikiki (ABC stores are literally everywhere in Waikiki). It's good for unlimited rides anywhere on Oahu for 4 days.

BY TROLLEY

It's fun to ride the 34-seat, open-air, motorized **Waikiki Trolley** (☎ **800/824-8804** or 808/596-2199), which looks like a San Francisco cable car. It loops around Waikiki and downtown Honolulu, stopping every 40 minutes at 12 key places: Hilton Hawaiian Village, Iolani Palace, Wo Fat's in Chinatown, the State Capitol, King Kamehameha's Statue, the Mission House Museum, Aloha Tower, Honolulu Academy of Arts, Hawaii Maritime Museum, Ward Centre, Fisherman's Wharf, and Restaurant Row. A 1-day pass at $17 for adults, $5 for children under 12, allows you to jump on and off all day long. Five-day passes cost $30 for adults, $10 for children under 12.

BY TAXI

Oahu's major cab companies offer islandwide, 24-hour radio-dispatched service, with multilingual drivers, air-conditioned cars, limos, vans, and vehicles equipped with wheelchair lifts. Fares are standard for all taxi firms; from the airport, expect to pay about $23 (plus tip) to Waikiki, about $16.50 to downtown, about $35 to Kailua, about $35 to Hawaii Kai, and about $75 to the North Shore. Try **Aloha State Cab** (☎ 808/847-3566), **Charley's Taxi & Tours** (☎ 808/531-1333), **City Taxi** (☎ 808/524-2121), **Royal Taxi & Tour** (☎ 808/944-5513), **Sida Taxi & Tours** (☎ 808/836-0011), **Star Taxi** (☎ 808/942-7827), or **TheCab** (☎ 808/422-2222). **Coast Taxi** (☎ 808/261-3755) serves Windward Oahu; **Hawaii Kai Hui/Koko Head Taxi** (☎ 808/396-6633) serves East Honolulu/Southeast Oahu.

There is a discount taxi service, offering a fixed-price fare of $15 (up to five passengers) to Waikiki, with no additional charge for baggage, from **Star Taxi** (☎ **800/671-2999** or 808/366-0594). You must book it in advance.

Fast Facts: Oahu

American Express The Honolulu office, at 1440 Kapiolani Blvd., Suite 104 (☎ **808/946-7741**), is open Monday to Friday 8am to 5pm. There's also an office at Hilton Hawaiian Village, 2005 Kalia Rd. (☎ **808/947-2607** or 808/951-0644), and one at the Hyatt Regency Waikiki, 2424 Kalakaua Ave. (☎ **808/926-5441**); both offer financial services daily from 8am to 8pm..

Area Code All of the Hawaiian Islands, including Oahu, are in the **808** area code.

Business Hours Most offices open at 8am and close by 5pm. The morning commute usually runs from 6am to 8am, and the evening rush is from 4pm to 6pm. Many people work at two or three jobs and drive their children to and from private schools, which creates extra traffic. Bank hours are Monday to Thursday from 8:30am to 3pm, Fridays from 8:30am to 6pm. Some banks open on Saturdays. Shopping centers open Monday to Friday from 10am to 9pm, Saturdays from 10am to 5:30pm, and Sundays from noon to 5pm or 6pm.

Dentists   If you need dental attention while you're on Oahu, contact the **Hawaii Dental Association** (☎ **808/536-2135**).

Doctors   **Straub Doctors on Call,** 2222 Kalakaua Ave. (at Lewers St.), Honolulu, HI 96815 (☎ **808/971-6000**), can dispatch a van if you need help getting to the main clinic, or to any of their additional clinics at the Royal Hawaiian Hotel, Hyatt Regency Waikiki, Hawaiian Regent Hotel, Hilton Hawaiian Village, Kahala Mandarin Oriental, and Ihilani Resort and Spa.

Electricity   Like the rest of the United States, Hawaii's electric power is 110 volts, 60 cycles.

Emergencies   Call ☎ **911** for police, fire, and ambulance.

Hospitals   Hospitals offering 24-hour emergency care include **Queens Medical Center,** 1301 Punchbowl St. (☎ 808/538-9011); **Kuakini Medical Center,** 347 Kuakini St. (☎ 808/536-2236); **Straub Clinic and Hospital,** 888 S. King St. (☎ 808/522-4000); **Moanalua Medical Center,** 3288 Moanalua Rd. (☎ 808/834-5333); **Kapiolani Medical Center for Women and Children,** 1319 Punahou St. (☎ 808/973-8511); and **Kapiolani Medical Center at Pali Momi,** 98–1079 Moanalua Rd. (☎ 808/486-6000). In Central Oahu, go to **Wahiawa General Hospital,** 128 Lehua St. (☎ 808/621-8411). On the windward side, go to **Castle Medical Center,** 640 Ulukahiki St., Kailua (☎ 808/263-5500).

Legal Aid   Call the **Legal Aid Society of Hawaii,** 1108 Nuuanu Ave., Honolulu HI 96817 (☎ **808/536-4302**).

Liquor Laws   The legal drinking age in Hawaii is 21.

Newspapers   *The Honolulu Advertiser* and *Honolulu Star-Bulletin* are Oahu's daily papers. *Midweek, Pacific Business News,* and *Honolulu Weekly* are weekly papers. *Honolulu Weekly,* available free at restaurants, clubs, shops, bookstores, and newspaper racks around Oahu, is the best source for what's going on around town. It features discriminating restaurant reviews and an informed critique of the nightclub scene, plus a weekly Calendar of Events that lists concerts, theater and dance performances, gallery and museum shows, workshops, children's events, hikes and walks, and often neighboring island events, too.

Poison Control Center   It's located at 1319 Punahou St. (☎ **808/941-4411**).

Post Office   To find the location nearest you, call ☎ **800/275-8777.** The downtown office is in the old U.S. Post Office, Customs, and Court House Building at 335 Merchant St. (across from the Iolani Palace and next to the Kamehameha Statue; TheBUS: 2). Referred to as the "old Federal Building," this building was designated as a Historic Customs House in 1977. Other convenient locations include the Waikiki Post Office, 330 Saratoga Ave. (Diamond Head side of Fort DeRussy; TheBUS: 19 or 20), and the Ala Moana Shopping Center branch (TheBUS: 8, 19, or 20).

Radio & TV   Honolulu has a score of radio stations that broadcast in English, Hawaiian, Japanese, and Filipino throughout the islands. The most popular are KCCN (1420 AM), which features Hawaiian music; KHPR (88.1 or 90.7 FM), the National Public Radio station; KGU (760 AM), for news and talk radio; KUMU (94.7 FM), for easy listening; and KSSK (590 AM), the pop-music station and the top morning-drive disc-jockeys.

All major Hawaiian islands are equipped with cable TV and get major mainland network broadcast programs, which local stations delay by several hours so they appear as "prime time" in Hawaii's time zone. This includes sports events, so fans who want to follow their teams "live" should seek out establishments with satellite dishes. CNN is the prime source of 24-hour news.

Safety   Although Hawaii is generally a safe tourist destination, visitors have been crime victims, so stay alert. The most common crime against tourists is rental car break-ins. Never leave any valuables in your car, not even in your trunk. Thieves can be in and out of your trunk faster than you can open it with your own keys. Be leery of high-risk areas, such as beaches and resort areas. Also, never carry large amounts of cash in Waikiki and other tourist zones. Stay in well-lighted areas after dark. Don't hike on deserted trails alone.

Smoking   It's against the law to smoke in public buildings, including the airports, grocery stores, retail shops, movie theaters, banks, and all government buildings and facilities. Hotels have nonsmoking rooms available, restaurants have nonsmoking sections, and car-rental agencies have nonsmoking cars. Most bed-and-breakfasts prohibit smoking inside their buildings.

Taxes   Hawaii's sales tax is 4%. Hotel occupancy tax is 7%, and hoteliers are allowed by the state to tack on an additional .0042% excise tax. Thus, expect taxes of about 11.42% to be added to every hotel bill.

Telephone   Hawaii's telephone system operates like any other state's. Long-distance calls can be directly dialed to the islands from the U.S. mainland and from most foreign countries. The international country code is 1, the same as for the rest of the United States and for Canada. Local calls costs 35¢ at a pay phone (if you can find one). Interisland calls are billed at the same rate as long distance. Hotels add a surcharge on local, interisland, mainland, and international calls.

Time   For the time, call ☎ **808/983-3211.** Hawaii standard time is in effect year-round. Hawaii is 2 hours behind Pacific standard time and 5 hours behind eastern standard time. In other words, when it's noon in Hawaii, it's 2pm in California and 5pm in New York during standard time on the mainland. There's no daylight saving time here, so when daylight saving time is in effect on the mainland (Apr through Oct), Hawaii is 3 hours behind the West Coast and 6 hours behind the East Coast—so in summer, when it's noon in Hawaii, it's 3pm in California and 6pm in New York.

Hawaii is east of the international dateline, putting it in the same day as the U.S. mainland and Canada, and a day behind Australia, New Zealand, and Asia.

Transit Info   For information on TheBUS, call ☎ **808/848-5555;** www.thebus.org.

Weather Reports   For National Weather Service recorded forecasts for Honolulu, call ☎ **808/973-4380;** for marine reports, call ☎ **808/973-4382;** for surf reports, call ☎ **808/973-4383.**

Accommodations

5

by Jeanette Foster

The island of Oahu, while not the biggest in the Hawaiian chain, offers the widest choices in accommodations. (See "Tips on Accommodations" in chapter 2.) You can stay in near-palatial surroundings where kings, heads of state, billionaires, and rock stars have spent the night, or in a quaint bed-and-breakfast on the North Shore where the rolling surf lulls you to sleep at night. You can opt for the bright lights and action of Waikiki, the quiet comforts of Kahala, or the rural calm of the windward side. Oahu has the perfect place for everyone.

WAIKIKI   Some five million tourists visit Oahu every year, and nine out of ten of them choose accommodations in Waikiki. This is where the action is: fast food to fine dining, nightlife including everything from the sweet sounds of Hawaiian melodies to spicy dance music, shopping from bargains to brand names, and every ocean activity you can imagine. Staying here puts you in the heart of it all, but be aware that Waikiki is an on-the-go city with traffic noise 24 hours a day, has its share of crime, and is almost always crowded.

HONOLULU & NEIGHBORHOODS   The city of Honolulu encompasses a fairly large area and houses the majority of Oahu's population. Downtown Honolulu is relatively small, occupying only a handful of blocks. The financial, government, and corporate headquarters of businesses are found here. Other neighborhoods range from the quiet suburbs of Hawaii Kai to the old *kamaaina* neighborhoods like Manoa. With the exception of staying in the heart of downtown, these neighborhoods are generally quieter than Waikiki, more residential, yet within minutes of beaches, shopping, and all the activities Oahu has to offer.

WINDWARD   On the opposite side of the island from Waikiki, the windward side is where the trade winds blow, rain squalls support lush, tropical vegetation, and subdivisions dot the landscape. The communities of Kailua and Kaneohe dominate here. Numerous bed-and-breakfasts (ranging from oceanfront estates to tiny cottages on quiet residential streets) abound. This is the place for "island" experiences— you'll enjoy ocean activities, explore the surrounding rural areas, and still be within a 15-minute drive from Waikiki and Honolulu.

NORTH SHORE   Here's the Hawaii of Hollywood: giant waves, surfers galore, tropical jungles, waterfalls, and mysterious Hawaiian temples. If you're looking for a quieter vacation, closer to nature, filled

Waikiki Accommodations

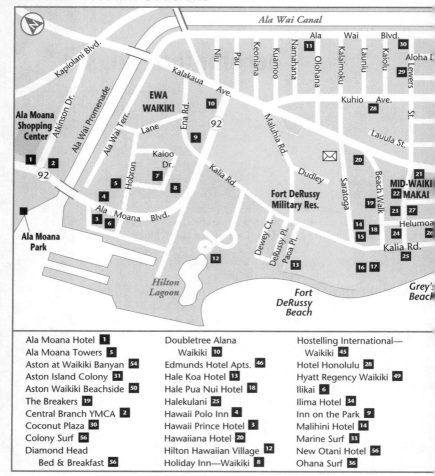

Ala Wai Canal

Ala Moana Shopping Center

Ala Moana Park

Hilton Lagoon

EWA WAIKIKI

Fort DeRussy Military Res.

Fort DeRussy Beach

MID-WAIKIKI MAKAI

Grey's Beach

Ala Moana Hotel **1**	Doubletree Alana Waikiki **10**	Hostelling International— Waikiki **45**
Ala Moana Towers **5**	Edmunds Hotel Apts. **46**	Hotel Honolulu **28**
Aston at Waikiki Banyan **54**	Hale Koa Hotel **13**	Hyatt Regency Waikiki **49**
Aston Island Colony **31**	Hale Pua Nui Hotel **18**	Ilikai **6**
Aston Waikiki Beachside **50**	Halekulani **25**	Ilima Hotel **34**
The Breakers **19**	Hawaii Polo Inn **4**	Inn on the Park **9**
Central Branch YMCA **2**	Hawaii Prince Hotel **3**	Malihini Hotel **14**
Coconut Plaza **30**	Hawaiiana Hotel **20**	Marine Surf **33**
Colony Surf **56**	Hilton Hawaiian Village **12**	New Otani Hotel **56**
Diamond Head Bed & Breakfast **56**	Holiday Inn—Waikiki **8**	Ohana Surf **36**

with swimming, snorkeling, diving, surfing, or just plain hanging out on some of the world's most beautiful beaches, the North Shore is your place. With many of the advantages of the city (restaurants, shopping, and cultural activities), but with the quiet of country living, the North Shore offers an alternative place to spend your vacation. Bed-and-breakfasts are the most common accommodations, but there are first-class and inexpensive options to consider. Be forewarned: It's nearly an hour's drive from the North Shore to Honolulu and Waikiki.

LEEWARD   A new frontier for Oahu visitors. Currently, there is only one exquisite resort in this beach-lined rural section of Oahu, but more are planned. Here's a chance to escape and be far, far away from the hustle and bustle of Waikiki. This is the sunny side of the island, with little rain and lots of sandy beaches. People who love to play golf, enjoy the ocean, and explore cultural activities will have plenty to do. However,

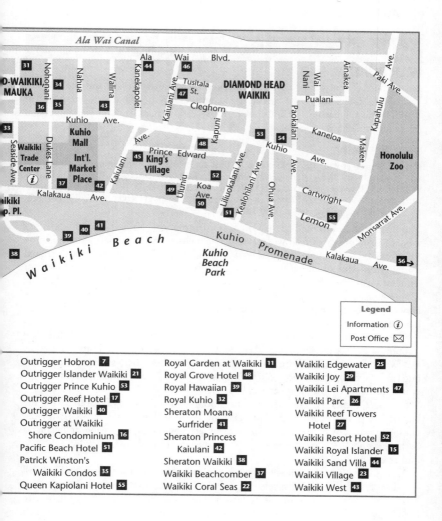

Outrigger Hobron **7**
Outrigger Islander Waikiki **21**
Outrigger Prince Kuhio **53**
Outrigger Reef Hotel **17**
Outrigger Waikiki **40**
Outrigger at Waikiki
    Shore Condominium **16**
Pacific Beach Hotel **51**
Patrick Winston's
    Waikiki Condos **35**
Queen Kapiolani Hotel **55**

Royal Garden at Waikiki **11**
Royal Grove Hotel **48**
Royal Hawaiian **39**
Royal Kuhio **32**
Sheraton Moana
    Surfrider **41**
Sheraton Princess
    Kaiulani **42**
Sheraton Waikiki **38**
Waikiki Beachcomber **37**
Waikiki Coral Seas **22**

Waikiki Edgewater **25**
Waikiki Joy **29**
Waikiki Lei Apartments **47**
Waikiki Parc **26**
Waikiki Reef Towers
    Hotel **27**
Waikiki Resort Hotel **52**
Waikiki Royal Islander **15**
Waikiki Sand Villa **44**
Waikiki Village **23**
Waikiki West **43**

outside the Ko Olina Resort area, there is little in the way of fine dining or interesting shopping.

Before you reach for the phone to reserve a place, consider when you will be traveling to Hawaii. Hawaii has two seasons—high and low. The **highest season** is mid-December to March. This is the time of year when rooms are always booked and rates are at the top end. The second "high" season is June to September, when rates are high, but bookings are somewhat easier. The **low season,** with fewer tourists, cheaper rates—and sometimes, even "deals" on rooms—is April to June and September to mid-December.

The last word on rates is Hawaii's hotel and room tax: Be sure to add 11.42% to all the listed rates to get a true picture of your bill. Don't forget to include parking, which, at Waikiki hotels, can quickly add up.

1 Waikiki

WAIKIKI, EWA END

All the hotels listed below are located between Ala Wai Boulevard and the Ala Wai Yacht Harbor, and between Ala Wai Terrace in the Ewa direction (or western side of Waikiki) and Olohana Street and Fort DeRussy Park in the Diamond Head direction (or eastern side of Waikiki).

VERY EXPENSIVE

Hawaii Prince Hotel. 100 Holomoana St. (just across Ala Wai Canal Bridge, on the ocean side of Ala Moana Blvd.), Honolulu, HI 96815. ☎ **800/321-OAHU** or 808/956-1111. Fax 808/946-0811. www.westin.com. 521 units. A/C TV TEL. $240–$390 double; from $500 suite. Extra person $40; children 17 or under stay free using existing bedding. AE, CB, DC, JCB, MC, V. Valet parking $12; self-parking $8. TheBUS: 19 or 20.

The first hotel at the entrance to Waikiki is this striking $150-million, twin–33-story modern structure: high-tech with a view. The high-ceilinged lobby is a mass of pink Italian marble with English slate accents; a grand piano sits in the midst of the raised seating area, where high tea is served every afternoon; and a glass-encased elevator with views of Honolulu whisks you upward. Renovated in 1997, the comfortably appointed rooms are basically the same—they all face the Ala Wai Yacht Harbor, have floor-to-ceiling sliding-glass windows, in-room safes, and hair dryers in the bathroom—but the higher the floor, the higher the price.

The service here is impeccable: No detail is ignored, no request is too small. The location is perfect for shopping—Ala Moana Center is just a 10-minute walk away, and Waikiki's beaches are just a 5-minute walk away (both are also accessible via the hotel shuttle bus). In addition, the Prince has its own 27-hole golf club in Ewa Beach (with shuttle service to the greens, of course).

Dining/Diversions: The Prince Court, located on the third floor overlooking the harbor, offers casual bistro-like fare. Hakone Japanese Restaurant serves traditional cuisine prepared by master chefs, while casual Japanese dining is available at Takanawa Sushi Bar and Restaurant. The outdoor Promenade Deck is the place for cafe-style dining and tropical drinks.

Amenities: Nightly turndown service that includes a bedtime sweet and a small booklet of short stories, concierge desk, room service, complimentary newspaper, baby-sitting services, hot towels (*oshibori*) upon arrival, fitness room, full-service beauty shop. For an additional $40 a night, guests on the Hokulea Floor get such extras as a snack-filled welcome basket, a coffeemaker, tea service, a toothbrush and razor, logo bathrobes, and a CD player. A business floor can handle any business request, from computers to secretarial services.

EXPENSIVE

Ilikai. 1777 Ala Moana Blvd. (ocean side of Ala Moana Blvd., at Hobron Lane), Honolulu, HI 96815. ☎ **800/367-8434** or 808/949-3811. Fax 808/947-0892. www.nikkohotels.com. 852 units. A/C TV TEL. $210–$315 double; $515–$880 suite. Rates include continental breakfast. Extra person $30. AE, CB, DC, DISC, JCB, MC, V. Parking $10. TheBUS: 19 or 20.

This hotel has almost everything: excellent location, ocean views, huge rooms with spacious lanais, and all the activities, restaurants, and shops you can imagine. There is only one thing that stands in the way of the Ilikai being one of the best Waikiki hotels—the attitude of the staff. They appear distracted, uninterested in guests' problems, and, in some cases, just too busy to bother. We hope that management can correct this problem, because the property is beautiful and the rooms are extraordinarily spacious, with wall-mounted hair dryers, in-room safes, and large lanais overlooking the ocean and the mountains. Some of the top rooms have whirlpool spas in the bathroom, desktop fax machines, and a mini-library of bestsellers for purchase. There are great deals for seniors, and good family packages that include rooms with a full kitchen, a mid-size car, and free parking.

Dining/Diversions: Much of the Ilikai's excitement is in its restaurants and nightclubs. Its casual restaurant, Canoes, looks out over the Ala Wai Yacht Harbor, and is perfect for moderately priced, open-air family-style dining; it also offers a fabulous Sunday brunch.

Amenities: Complimentary continental breakfast; Next Club for business travelers; business class floors with in-room fax, modem capability, and office supplies; daily newspaper; no telephone access fees; voicemail; express checkouts; 24-hour medical services; shopping arcade. Waikiki's most complete tennis resort with six newly resurfaced Plexipave courts overlooking Waikiki and the yacht marina, full-time tennis staff, pro services, tennis clinics, a sports and fitness center, swimming in two pools and a nearby blue lagoon, plus sailing, surfing, and scuba diving.

MODERATE

○ **Doubletree Alana Waikiki.** 1956 Ala Moana Blvd. (on the Ewa side, between Ena Rd. and Kalakaua Ave.), Honolulu, HI 96815. ☎ **800/367-6070** or 808/941-7275. Fax 808/949-0996. www.doubletreehotels.com. 313 units. TV TEL. $135–$215 double; from $250 suite. Extra person $25; children 18 or younger stay free. AE, CB, DC, DISC, JCB, MC, V. Parking $9. TheBUS: 19 or 20.

In 1997, the Doubletree chain (known for giving guests a freshly baked chocolate-chip cookie every night) took charge of this boutique hotel, a welcome oasis of beauty, comfort, and service. The elegant second-floor lobby and other public areas feature original Picasso ceramics, and the interior designer gave the rooms a more homey feel than what you usually find in other hotels. The result is comfortable rooms that are so inviting, you may want to curl up with a good book—if it weren't for the fact that Waikiki Beach is just a walk away. Amenities include two-line telephones, voicemail, computer-fax outlets, and coffee/tea makers. The bathrooms are compact, but outfitted with everything you need, including a phone.

A good percentage of the guests are business travelers who expect top-drawer service, and the Alana Waikiki delivers. The staff is attentive to details and willing to go to any length to make you happy. Two restaurants offer superb Pacific-Rim cuisine, and full hotel amenities range from concierge and room service to a well-outfitted business center, a fitness center with sauna and massage (in-room massage service also available), a 24-hour reading room with international newspapers and magazines, and a heated pool.

Holiday Inn—Waikiki. 1830 Ala Moana Blvd. (between Hobron Lane and Kalia Rd.), Honolulu, HI 96815. ☎ **888/9WAIKIKI** or 808/955-1111. Fax 808/947-1799. www.holiday-inn-waikiki.com. 199 units. A/C TV TEL. $117–$130 double. Extra person $15; children 19 and under stay for free using existing bedding. AE, CB, DC, DISC, JCB, MC, V. Parking $6. TheBUS: 19 or 20.

Holiday Inn—with its dependable quality, amenities, and service—spent some $6 million to totally renovate the former Hawaii Dynasty Hotel. Just 2 blocks from the beach, 2 blocks from Ala Moana Shopping Center, and a 7-minute walk from the Convention Center, it's well placed for anyone's vacation. All the rooms, which have a modern Japanese look, come with either a king or two double beds, voicemail, computer jacks, coffeemaker with complimentary coffee, safe, and fridge. The property sits back from the street, so noise is at a minimum. The staff is unbelievably friendly.

✪ **The Royal Garden at Waikiki.** 440 Olohana St. (between Kuhio Ave. and Ala Wai Blvd.). ☎ **800/367-5666** or 808/943-0202. Fax 808/946-8777. www.royalgardens.com. 220 units. A/C TV TEL. $130–$180 double; $325 one-bedroom double; $600 two-bedroom (sleeps up to 4). Packages galore. Extra person $25; children under 12 stay free. AE, DC, DISC, JCB, MC, V. Parking $7. TheBUS: 19 or 20.

Deals, deals, deals—that's what you'll find at this elegant boutique hotel, tucked away on a quiet, tree-lined side street. There's a deal for everyone: Room/car packages start at $135 (that's a $130 standard room, plus a car for only $5 extra); a family plan gives you a second room at half the rack rate; and the Young-at-Heart Package allows seniors to book rooms starting at $91 (plus a 10% discount at Royal Garden restaurants). You won't believe what you get for your money: The 25-story hotel has a lobby filled with European marble and chandeliers, and plush rooms featuring a pantry kitchenette (refrigerator, wet bar, coffeemaker), marble bathroom, lots of closet space, and a lanai; voicemail and computer/fax hookups are welcome amenities. Facilities include two restaurants—Cascada, serving country-French cuisine, and Shizu, serving Japanese specialties—two freshwater pools (one with cascading waterfall), two Jacuzzis, two saunas, and a fitness center. There's also complimentary shuttle service to Kapiolani Park, Ala Moana Shopping Center, Royal Hawaiian Shopping Center, and Duty Free Shoppers. The beach is a few blocks away, but at these prices, it's worth the hike.

INEXPENSIVE

✪ **Ala Moana Towers.** 1700 Ala Moana Blvd. (between Hobron Lane and Ala Wai Canal), Honolulu, HI 96815. ☎ **800/OUTRIGGER** or 808/942-7722. Fax 808/943-7272 or 800/622-4852. www.outrigger.com. 163 units. A/C TV TEL. $100–$120 double with kitchenette; $175 one-bedroom suite for 4. Extra person $15. AE, CB, DC, DISC, JCB, MC. V. Parking $8. TheBUS: 19 or 20.

This skyscraper complex, which sits back from busy Ala Moana Boulevard, is just 4 blocks from the beach and close to Ala Moana Shopping Center, the Hawaii Convention Center, and the highlights of Waikiki. The rooms were renovated in 1995; views are stunning from the upper floors. The studio-type doubles with kitchenettes are in the 40-story Tower, whose glass elevators offer breathtaking views (but with 40 floors and only two elevators, the wait for an elevator can challenge your patience); each has a dishwasher, refrigerator, stove, coffeemaker, microwave, and cooking utensils. The one-bedroom condo-style units are in the 16-story Annex; they have a separate bedroom, living room, lanai, and kitchen with a four-burner stove, oven, refrigerator, and cooking utensils. (Mobility-impaired travelers should book in the Tower, as you have to climb a flight of stairs to reach the elevator in the Annex).

The property boasts a pool, spa, sauna, tennis courts, and laundry facilities; however, there are no restaurants on the property, but several are within walking distance. *Hot tip for views:* In the Tower, the best views are from floors 21 and above; ask for a room facing Ewa (west) for spectacular sunset views. In the Annex, the best views are from floors five and above, which overlook the Ala Wai Yacht Harbor and Ala Moana Beach Park.

Inn on the Park. 1920 Ala Moana Blvd. (at Kalia Rd.), Honolulu, HI 96815. ☎ **800/367-5004** or 808/946-8355. Fax 800/477-2329 or 808/946-4839. 238 units. A/C TV TEL. High season $103–$119 double, $129 deluxe studio with kitchenette; low season $92–$108 double, $119 deluxe studio with kitchenette. Extra person $17. AE, CB, DC, JCB, MC, V. Parking $8. TheBUS: 19 or 20.

Built in 1979, this well-positioned hotel is just across the street from Fort DeRussy and a couple of blocks from the beach. The rooms are minuscule, so don't expect to squeeze more than two in; families might want to look elsewhere or rent two rooms. Even the lanais are small—there's barely room for a chair. Most rooms have refrigerators; the studios have kitchenettes with a cooktop, toaster, and coffeemaker. The 5th-floor pool

What to Do If Your Dream Hotel Turns Out to Be a Nightmare

Don't panic! Even if you've booked into a small B&B and you absolutely hate both the bedrooms once you've seen them, usually the host wants to make you happy and may even get on the phone and book you at another place that suits you better. Hotels, resorts, and condominiums are generally easier to deal with, since they have numerous units to offer and can probably satisfy your requests by moving you to another room.

Here are some tips on how to avoid getting a room you dislike or how to complain if you've checked in and can't stand your room:

- Find out beforehand exactly what the accommodation is offering you: the cost, the minimum stay, the included amenities. Ask if there's any penalty fee for leaving early. Read the small print in the contract—especially the information on cancellation fees.

- Discuss ahead of time with the B&B, vacation rental, condominium agent, or booking agency what their cancellation policy is if the accommodation doesn't meet your expectations. Get this policy in writing (so there are no misunderstandings later).

- When you arrive, if the room you're given doesn't meet your expectations, notify the front desk, rental agent, or booking agency immediately.

- Approach the management in a calm, reasonable manner. Voice your complaint clearly and suggest a solution. Be reasonable and be willing to compromise. Do not make threats or leave. If you leave, it may be harder to get your deposit returned.

- If all else fails, when you get home, write your credit-card company or any association the accommodation may be a member of (such as the Hawaii Visitors and Convention Bureau, a resort association, or an island association). In the letter, state the name of the accommodation, the name you registered under, the date of the complaint, the exact nature of the complaint, and why the issue was not resolved to your satisfaction. And be sure to let us know if you have a problem with a place we've recommended in this book!

has a grand view of Fort DeRussy and the Waikiki skyline. There's a moped rental shop and an Italian restaurant in the lobby. If you don't mind the size of the rooms—you're in Hawaii, so how much time are you going to spend in your room, anyway?—the price here can't be beat.

MID-WAIKIKI, MAKAI

All the hotels listed below are between Kalakaua Avenue and the ocean, and between Fort DeRussy in the Ewa direction and Kaiulani Street in the Diamond Head direction.

VERY EXPENSIVE

✪ **Halekulani.** 2199 Kalia Rd. (at the ocean end of Lewers St.), Honolulu, HI 96815. ☎ **800/367-2343** or 808/923-2311. Fax 808/926-8004. www.halekulani.com. 456 units. A/C MINIBAR TV TEL. $310–$520 double; from $700 suite. Extra person $125; 1 child under 17 stays free using existing bedding; maximum 3 people per room. AE, CB, DC, JCB, MC, V. Parking $10. TheBUS: 19 or 20.

Family-Friendly Hotels

If you're traveling with the kids, you'll be welcomed with open arms by many of Oahu's resorts, condos, and B&Bs. Our favorite family-friendly accommodations on the island are listed below. If you're looking for a hotel that has supervised activities for your youngster, you might want to consider the **Sheraton Moana Surfrider,** which has a great children's program. If you're looking for a more moderately priced option, look at the **Aston Pacific Monarch** in Waikiki and **Backpacker Vacation Inn** on the North Shore, all of which love to accommodate kids and their well-behaved parents.

Waikiki Hotels

Halekulani *(see p. 71)*   Halekulani has a complimentary program for children ages 6 to 11 during the summer from early June to mid-August and at Christmas from December 18 to December 30. Daily programs include crafts, games, sightseeing, and excursions. This is a complimentary service for hotel guests; the only charges are for lunch and admission to excursions. Parents will like the "Heavenly Summer Program," which allows them to pay $295 for a second room, no matter what the cost of the first room (available to U.S. and Canadian residents only).

Hilton Hawaiian Village *(see p. 75)*   The Rainbow Express is the Hilton's year-round, 7 days a week program of activities for children ages 5 to 12. The program has a wide range of educational and fun activities, such as Hawaiiana arts and crafts, environmental nature walks, wildlife feeding, shell hunting, fishing, peeking at sea creatures at the Waikiki Aquarium, roaming through the Honolulu Zoo, and exploring the world with a computer.

Ilima Hotel *(see p. 84)*   When the Teruya brothers, who own a local supermarket chain, built this high-rise condo-hotel, they designed it with families in mind. The units are large, and all have full-size kitchens. Although there are no formal supervised children's program, there is free HBO, Disney Channel, and Super Nintendo video games in each room. The coin-operated laundry is a big help. The beach and International Market Place are both just a short walk away, and TheBUS stop is just outside. It's very popular with neighboring-island families.

Outrigger Hotels *(see p. 76)*   This chain of affordable hotels offers something for everyone, including "Malama Na Keiki" (Care for the Children). Based at the Outrigger on the Beach, the program is staffed by professional childcare counselors, and is open to children ages 5 and up, whose parents are staying at any of the 20 Outrigger properties in Waikiki. Children can enroll in half-day ($20) or full-day ($30 including lunch and a snack) programs with games, arts and crafts, beach walks, shoreline fishing, and excursions around Waikiki. Parents have the

For the ultimate heavenly Hawaii vacation, this is the place. In fact, Halekulani translates as "House Befitting Heaven"—an apt description of this luxury resort, which is spread over five acres of prime Waikiki beachfront in five buildings connected by open courtyards and lush, tropical gardens. The elegant atmosphere envelops you as soon as you step into the terrazzo and wood-lined lobby. You are immediately greeted and escorted to your rooms, where registration is handled in comfort and privacy.

option of taking a free pager while children are enrolled in the program. Transportation to the Outrigger on the Beach is provided. Reservations are necessary; call ☎ **808/923-3111.**

Royal Kuhio *(see p. 83)* If you have active kids, this is the place for you. The 7th-floor recreation area has volleyball and basketball courts, billiards, shuffleboard, an exercise room, and even a putting green. Located across the street from the International Market Place and 2 blocks from the beach, the Royal Kuhio has one-bedroom apartments (with sofa sleeper in the living room) with full kitchens. Rates allow up to four people in a unit, and will sleep five for an extra charge of $15 for the rollaway or crib.

Sheraton Waikiki *(see p. 77)* During the summer (from mid-June to mid-August), the Keiki Aloha Sunshine Club offers activities consisting of boogie boarding, kite-flying, catamaran sailing, a photo contest, and nightly movies for children ages 5 to 12. Also, on arrival, the kids are greeted with a complimentary candy lei.

Outside Waikiki
Kahala Mandarin Oriental Hawaii *(see p. 94)* The Keiki Club is the year-round activity program for children ages 5 to 12. Children dance the hula, make leis, design sand sculptures, construct origami figures, make puppets and put on puppet shows, strum ukuleles, produce shell art, make fish prints, listen to Hawaiian folk tales and legends, play Hawaiian games, participate in the beach Olympics, and a host of other activities.

North Shore
Hilton Turtle Bay Resort *(see p. 96)* This resort offers a year-round program called the Turtle Keiki Program for children ages 5 to 12. Activities include Hawaiian-style arts and crafts, coconut painting, sand sculpturing, swimming, various games, sports, movies, and storytelling.

Leeward
Ihilani Resort & Spa *(see p. 98)* The Keiki Beachcomber Club, available every day of the year, has its own facility for children from 4 to 12 years. Outdoor activities include kite-flying, tide pool exploration, snorkeling, golf, tennis, swimming, aerobics, and international games like *les boules* (similar to bocce ball), Indian kick ball, and *tinikling* (a bamboo dance from the Philippines). Hawaiian cultural activities feature lei making and hula dancing. There's a state-of-the-art computer learning center (complete with Sega Genesis, CD-ROM, and Super Nintendo) and a host of other activities.

There are so many things that set this luxury hotel apart from the others, the most important being the rooms: About 90% face the ocean, and they're big (averaging about 620 square feet) with a separate sitting area and a large, furnished lanai. The bathroom features a deep-soaking tub, a separate glassed-in shower, and a marble basin. Other luxuries include a refrigerator, three phones, a safe, and luxurious bathrobes.

Dining/Diversions: Facilities are superb: Indo-Pacific Orchids; the oceanside main dining room; the award-winning neoclassic French La Mer (see chapter 6, "Dining");

and ✪ **House Without a Key,** surely one of the world's most romantic spots for sunset cocktails, light meals, and Hawaiian entertainment.

Amenities: Twice-daily maid and turndown service, complimentary daily newspaper, and free local phone calls. Concierge desk, business and secretarial services, fitness room, running sessions and aerobic workouts, in-room massage, magnificent oceanside swimming pool, and easy access to a superb stretch of Waikiki Beach.

✪ **Royal Hawaiian.** 2259 Kalakaua Ave. (at Royal Hawaiian Ave., on the ocean side of the Royal Hawaiian Shopping Center), Honolulu, HI 96815. ☎ **800/325-3535** or 808/923-7311. Fax 808/924-7098. www.sheraton.com. 527 units. A/C MINIBAR TV TEL. $305–$590 double; from $800 suite. Extra person $50. Ask about Sheraton's Sure Saver rates, which could mean as much as 32% in savings. AE, MC, V. Valet parking $18; self-parking at Sheraton Waikiki $9. TheBUS: 19 or 20.

A shocking-pink oasis hidden away among blooming gardens in the concrete jungle that is Waikiki, the Royal Hawaiian is known around the world as a symbol of luxury. Built by Matson steamship lines and inspired by popular silent-screen star Rudolph Valentino (*The Sheik*), the Spanish-Moorish "Pink Palace" opened on February 1, 1927, on the same spot where Queen Kaahumanu had her summer palace—one of the best stretches of Waikiki Beach.

Entry into the hotel is past the lush gardens, with their spectacular banyan tree, into the black terrazzo-marble lobby, which features handwoven pink carpets and giant floral arrangements. Every guest room is enchanting, but our hearts were won over by those in the Historic Wing, which feature carved wooden doors, four-poster canopy beds, flowered wallpaper, and period furniture. But even if you stay in one of the more modern rooms, you'll find that historic touches abound, from a traditional lei greeting and freshly baked banana bread (made from the hotel's original 1927 recipe) upon arrival to Hawaiian craft displays—Hawaiian quilts, leis, weaving, and more—by local artists every Monday, Wednesday, and Friday.

Dining/Diversions: There are two dining rooms to choose from (the Surf Room is known for its elaborate seafood buffets), plus the casual Beach Club, which features an oceanfront patio that's a great place to start your day. The ✪ **Mai Tai Bar** is one of the most popular places in Waikiki for the namesake drink, which is reputed to have originated here. The Royal Hawaiian Luau, done in the grand style, is held on Monday nights.

Amenities: 24-hour room service, daily newspaper, multilingual concierge desk, 24-hour medical service, baby-sitting, valet service, business center, hospitality suite for early arrivals and late check-outs, shops, salon, freshwater pool, beach accessories from deck chairs to umbrellas, preferential tee-off times at Makaha Resort and Golf Club.

✪ **Sheraton Moana Surfrider Hotel.** 2365 Kalakaua Ave. (ocean side of the street, across from Kaiulani St.), Honolulu, HI 96815. ☎ **800/325-3535** or 808/922-3111. Fax 808/923-0308. www.moana-surfrider.com. 793 units. A/C MINIBAR TV TEL. $265–$495 double; suites from $900. Extra person and rollaway bed $40; children under 18 stay free using existing bedding. Inquire about Sure Saver rates, which could mean as much as 32% in savings. AE, CB, DC, MC, V. Valet parking $15; self-parking at sister property $9. TheBUS: 19 or 20.

Step back in time to old Hawaii at Waikiki's first hotel, which was originally built in 1901. Considered an innovation in the travel industry, the Moana featured a private bathroom and a telephone in each guest room—an unheard-of luxury at the turn of the century. The first guests thought the rooms were a bit "pricey" ($1.50 a night), but worth it. The prices may have gone up since then, but yesteryear lives on at this grand hotel: Entry is through the original colonial porte-cochère, past the highly polished front porch dotted with rocking chairs, and into the perfectly restored lobby with detailed millwork and intricate plasterwork. At check-in, you'll be greeted with a lei, a glass of fruit juice, and a welcoming smile. This hotel has not only class, but charm, too. Time seems to slow down here—the female employees even wear traditional Victorian-era muumuus—and the aloha spirit that pervades this hotel is infectious.

The hotel, which is listed in the National Register of Historic Places, consists of three wings: the original (and totally restored) Banyan Wing, the Diamond Wing, and the Tower Wing. It's hard to get a bad room here: The majority of the rooms have ocean views, and they all come with such amenities as refrigerators, irons and ironing boards, hair dryers, bedside controls, plush robes, safes, and voicemail. We're especially taken with the Banyan Wing rooms; what they lack in size and amenities—they're on the smallish side and don't have lanais—they make up for in style; even the fixtures in the smallish bathrooms are modern-day replicas of 19th-century hardware.

Dining/Diversions: Even if you do not stay here, you must drop by the Banyan Veranda, an old-fashioned porch turned into a courtly open-air dining area, where elegant meals, snacks and "high tea" are served. Great place to sip a cocktail and watch the sun sink into the Pacific Ocean. Other restaurants include the Ship's Tavern, which serves continental cuisine for dinner only in a formal atmosphere. Casual meals can be found at the Beachside Café, and a fabulous brunch is served on Sunday at the Grand Salon.

Amenities: The best reason to stay here is the beautiful stretch of Waikiki beach just steps from your room. Also available: 24-hour room service; concierge service; and historical tours of the grand old property. What the Sheraton Moana Surfrider does not have on-site, it shares with sister Sheraton Hotels, just minutes away, like the free children's program at the Sheraton Waikiki Hotel; privileges at Sheraton Waikiki's health club; and the business center at the Royal Hawaiian.

EXPENSIVE

✪ **Hilton Hawaiian Village.** 2005 Kalia Rd. (at Ala Moana Blvd.), Honolulu, HI 96815. ☎ **800/HILTONS** or 808/949-4321. Fax 808/947-7898. www.hilton.com. 2,910 units. A/C MINIBAR TV TEL. $210–$375 double; $240–$405 Alii Tower double; from $370 suite. Extra person $30; children 18 and under stay free. AE, CB, DISC, ER, JCB, MC, V. Valet parking $14; self-parking $9. TheBUS: 19 or 20.

This is Waikiki's biggest resort, so big it even has its own post office. Nearly 3,000 rooms spread over 20 acres of property that include tropical gardens dotted with exotic wildlife (flamingoes, peacocks, even tropical penguins!), award-winning restaurants, 100 different shops, a secluded lagoon, three swimming pools, two mini-golf courses, and a gorgeous stretch of Waikiki Beach.

Like everything else in the village—which really is a mini-city unto itself—there's a wide choice of accommodations housed in four towers (Rainbow, Tapa, Diamond Head, and Alii) that range from simply lovely to ultra-deluxe. All the rooms are large and beautifully furnished; if you can afford it, we highly recommend the ones in the Alii Tower. Located right on the ocean, the 348 amenity-laden rooms and suites offer all the royal treatment that the name implies, including in-room registration, an exclusive health club and swimming pool, and the full attention of a multilingual staff. Each room has a fully stocked refreshment center, in-room coffee services, no fewer than three phones (one of which is PC-compatible), and even a mini-TV on the bathroom vanity. But if you go with one of the more affordable towers, you'll still be happy. It's a great place to stay with the kids.

Dining/Diversions: Both the Golden Dragon (excellent Cantonese and Szechwan cuisine in exquisite Asian-style surroundings) and the romantic Bali By the Sea (see chapter 6, "Dining"), with ocean views and gourmet cuisine, are named among Honolulu's best restaurants year after year. Other restaurants include a couple of casual cafes (one with a "fitness-first" menu), a steak-and-seafood joint, a sushi bar, and a branch of Benihana. Illusionist John Hirokawa and "The Magic of Polynesia" are featured at the Hilton Dome. There is also a handful of bars and lounges—including the beachfront Hau Tree Bar—many featuring nightly entertainment.

Amenities: Multilingual concierge; same-day laundry; in-room fax and computer hookups in many rooms; year-round children's program (one of Waikiki's best); free fitness classes, Hawaiiana instruction, and walking tours for adults; on-site Atlantis Submarine rides; in-room massage; room service. There are also a business center, a fitness center, three pools, and tons of shops.

✪ **Outrigger Reef Hotel.** 2169 Kalia Rd. (ocean side of Kalia Rd., Ewa side of the Halekulani Hotel, and across the street from Beach Walk), Honolulu, HI 96815. ☎ **800/OUTRIGGER** or 808/923-3111. Fax 800/622-4852. www.outrigger.com. 930 units. A/C TV TEL. $160–$325 double; $190–$355 Voyagers Club; $350–$1,000 suite. Extra person $25. Children under 17 free in parents' room with existing bedding. Seniors 50 and older 20% off, AARP members 25% off. Ask about room-and-breakfast packages. Free rent-a-car when booking at rack rates. AE, CB, DC, DISC, JCB, MC, V. Parking $10. TheBUS: 19 or 20.

Location, location, location! This Outrigger is right on Waikiki Beach, across from Ft. DeRussy, with beautifully appointed rooms, excellent service, and a myriad of activities, shops, and restaurants. This is a big hotel with three towers (5, 10, and 17 floors each) and a megalobby connecting them. Off the lobby is an enormous swimming pool, with some 300 chaise longues surrounding it, three whirlpool spas, and food and cocktail service within hailing distance. Throughout the lobby are enough shops to qualify as a mini–shopping mall. And, of course, beautiful Waikiki Beach is in the backyard.

The rooms have the usual well-designed, well-appointed Outrigger furnishings and decorations with great views and plenty of extra room to have a couple of kids bedding down. Rooms include refrigerators, blackout drapes, coffeemakers, safes, and irons and ironing boards. Coin-operated laundry facilities are available, as is a hospitality room for early check-ins or late checkouts. Nonsmoking and handicapped-accessible rooms are also available.

Dining/Diversions: At poolside is the Chief's Hut for casual, family dining for breakfast, lunch, and dinner. At oceanside you'll find The Shorebird Beach Broiler, an immensely popular spot offering buffet breakfasts and broil-your-own dinners. The Shorebird Prime Rib & Pasta Company is open for dinner only. The Aloha Lobby features Hawaiian entertainment. The Shorebird Beach Bar also has live entertainment, and the Pool Terrace is a poolside sports bar with a big-screen TV.

Amenities: Many beach services, including catamaran sailing, canoe rides, and surfboard lessons; room service; fitness center; and concierge desk. It also offers one of the largest freshwater swimming pools in Waikiki and a business center with state-of-the-art equipment and the assistance of a full-time secretary.

✪ **Outrigger Waikiki.** 2335 Kalakaua Ave. (on the ocean, between the Royal Hawaiian Shopping Center and the Sheraton Moana Surfrider), Honolulu, HI 96815. ☎ **800/OUTRIGGER** or 808/923-0711. Fax 800/622-4852. www.outrigger.com. E-mail: reservations@outrigger.com. 530 units. A/C TV TEL. $175–$350 double; $290–$530 Voyager Club rooms and suites; $530 suite. Extra person $25; children 17 and under stay free using existing bedding. Seniors 50 and older get 20% discount, AARP members 25% discount; free rental car when booking at rack rates; ask about other package deals. AE, CB, DC, DISC, JCB, MC, V. Parking $10. TheBUS: 19 or 20.

The same value and quality we've come to expect in every Outrigger is definitely in evidence here, only multiplied by a factor of 10. Even the standard rooms in this 16-story oceanfront hotel are large and comfortable, and $175 a day on Waikiki Beach is definitely a deal (even if it doesn't get you an oceanview room). The prime beachfront location and loads of facilities help make this one of the chain's most attractive properties.

White columns dominate the airy atmosphere of the second-floor lobby, which is outfitted with tropical plants, rattan furniture, and big, bold artwork. The newly renovated rooms are big and comfortable, all with huge closets, roomy bathrooms, and plenty of amenities (refrigerator, iron, hair dryer, safe, coffeemaker), plus a spacious lanai; room prices are entirely dependent on the view. Rooms on the top four floors are part of the Voyager Club, where guests have the use of the private lounge serving continental breakfast and complimentary pupus in the evening.

Dining/Diversions: The beachfront Duke's Canoe Club serves great island-style seafood and steaks, complemented by Hawaiian entertainment and an extended menu of tropical cocktails (see chapter 6, "Dining"); Monterey Bay Canners and Chuck's Steakhouse are both popular places for seafood and steaks. Other choices include a "Cheers"-like pub and deli, a casual healthy-foods place, and a snack shop on the beach. The talented Society of Seven singers perform in the showroom.

Amenities: Room service (7am to 9:45pm), concierge, ATM, coin-op laundry, salon, lots of shops, Doctors on Call medical clinic, business center, hospitality room for early check-ins and late check-outs, an 800-square-foot fitness center, beautifully landscaped pool area with Jacuzzi, easy access to a prime stretch of Waikiki Beach.

Outrigger at Waikiki Shore Condominium. 2161 Kalia Rd. (on the ocean at Saratoga Rd., across the street from Fort DeRussy), Honolulu, HI 96815. ☎ **800/OUTRIGGER.** Fax 800/622-4852. www.outrigger.com. 168 units. A/C TV TEL. $170–$185 studio double; $235–$265 one-bedroom apt (sleeps up to 4); $335–$500 two-bedroom apt (up to 6). Ask about Outrigger package deals including free car rental, bed-and-breakfast, and Voyagers Club. AE, CB, DC, DISC, JCB, MC, V. Parking $10. TheBUS: 19 or 20.

As soon as you arrive, you'll see why everyone wants to stay here: the location (right on Waikiki beach) and the view (a spectacular panoramic vista of the entire shoreline from Diamond Head to Honolulu). The apartments—which are privately owned and decorated and then rented out through Outrigger—range in size from studio to two-bedroom. Each has a fully equipped kitchen, a big lanai, a spacious sitting area, washer/dryer, and those fabulous views. There are full-time residents who live in this complex, so it tends to be quiet, and entry to the units is through a locked gate and keyed elevators, so security is tight. The building sits on an excellent beach, close to restaurants and shopping. As you might expect, reservations are hard to get; book *way* in advance.

Amenities: Because this establishment is part of the Outrigger chain, guests have full access to the Outrigger Reef (located right next door), including its pool, exercise room, and business center. Daily maid service, a few on-site shops, and plenty of assistance from the front desk give this condominium stay all the benefits of hotel service with the roominess of your own apartment.

Sheraton Waikiki. 2255 Kalakaua Ave. (at Royal Hawaiian Ave., on the ocean side of the Royal Hawaiian Shopping Center and west of the Royal Hawaiian), Honolulu, HI 96815. ☎ **800/325-3535** or 808/922-4422. Fax 808/923-8785. www.sheraton.com. 1,982 units. A/C MINIBAR TV TEL. $155 Sheraton Manor Hotel double; $250–$465 Waikiki double; from $650 suite. Extra person $40. Ask about Sheraton's Sure Saver rates, which can mean as much as 32% in savings. AE, CB, DC, DISC, JCB, MC, V. Valet parking $13; self-parking $9. TheBUS: 19 or 20.

The Sheraton chain owns a substantial portion of Waikiki (three hotels on the beach and one across the street), and this is by far the largest of the four—1,852 rooms housed in two 30-story towers. This place is big, big, big; the bank of 11 elevators gives you a feel for the sheer size of the place. The lobby is immense and filled with shops, travel desks, and people. Not surprisingly, this hotel hosts numerous conventions; if you're not comfortable with crowds and conventioneers, book elsewhere. However, size does have its advantages: The Sheraton has everything from free kids' programs to historical walks for mom and dad.

It's hard to get a bad room here. There's a saying on the Waikiki strip that lots of hotels have great views of the Sheraton, but Sheraton guests have views of the beach and Diamond Head all to themselves; a whopping 1,200 rooms have some sort of ocean view, and 650 rooms overlook Diamond Head. The rooms are large, with big lanais to take in those magnificent views; other amenities include minibars (if you want to store your own food and drinks, call housekeeping to clear it out), safes, and coffeemakers.

For the budget-conscious, the Sheraton Manor Hotel occupies a separate adjacent wing and offers all the services and beachfront of the main hotel. The views aren't the best—overlooking the porte-cochère—and the air-conditioned rooms are small (two people, max) and modestly appointed (no lanai).

Dining/Diversions: Restaurants range from the open-air Ocean Terrace for casual buffet meals to the glamorous Hanohano Room for gourmet dining in a spectacular setting (take the glass elevator just for the view). There's a nightclub for dancing, drinks, and entertainment, and the pool area features snack counters and a bar.

Amenities: Sheraton is the "king" of amenities, with 24-hour room service, concierge, coin-operated laundry, 20 shops, multilingual staff, business center, fitness center, and two freshwater pools—including one of the biggest and sunniest pools along the Waikiki beachfront. Free kids' programs include a candy lei on arrival, plus activities ranging from catamaran sailing to nightly movies; activities for those over 12 include free cooking demonstrations, Hawaiian arts and crafts, complimentary fun runs, aerobics classes, and a historic walk of Waikiki. You "play and charge" at Waikiki's other Sheraton hotels as well as at the Makaha Golf Club's golf and tennis facilities.

Waikiki Parc. 2233 Helumoa Rd. (at Lewers St.), Honolulu, HI 96815. ☎ **800/422-0450** or 808/921-7272. Fax 808/923-1336. www.waikikiparchotel.com. 298 units. A/C MINIBAR TV TEL. $175–$270 double. Extra person $30; children 14 and under stay free. Ask about room/car, bed-and-breakfast, and 50%-off second-room packages. AE, CB, DC, JCB, MC, V. Valet parking $9. TheBUS: 19 or 20.

Located just 100 yards from the beach, this hotel is for people who want the elegance, grace, and style of the Halekulani, but just can't quite afford its rates. Tucked just behind the Halekulani and owned and operated by the same company, the Waikiki Parc offers beautifully appointed rooms at affordable prices. The compact guest rooms all have lanais with ocean, mountain, or city views; ceramic-tile floors with plush carpeting; and a conversation area with a writing desk and rattan couch and chair. Nice extras include a refrigerator, minibar, two phones, a safe, and adjustable floor-to-ceiling shutters for those who want to sleep in.

The Parc features the same level of service that has made the Halekulani famous. On a recent visit, we asked room service for a few items that were not exactly on the menu; they not only happily complied, but the manager checked back later to make sure we got what we wanted. We requested an out-of-town newspaper one day; the bellman said he would deliver it to our room every day, no problem. We called the valet desk and asked directions to get to an out-of-the-way location; when we picked up our car, the valet desk handed us a map with the route highlighted in yellow.

Dining/Diversions: Two excellent restaurants: With its garden-terrace atmosphere, the Parc Cafe serves fabulous buffet-style meals featuring island specialties (see chapter 6, "Dining"), while Kacho, one of Hawaii's few Kyoto-style restaurants, is a charming oasis for devotees of sushi and Japanese seafood dishes.

Amenities: Concierge desk, twice-daily maid service, secretarial and other business services, wheelchair accessibility to all public areas, room service, freshwater pool on the eighth-floor recreation deck, and a great stretch of Waikiki Beach nearby.

MODERATE

✪ **Hawaiiana Hotel.** 260 Beach Walk (near Kalakaua Ave.), Honolulu, HI 96815. ☎ **800/ 535-0085** or 808/923-3811. Fax 808/926-5728. www.marcrestors.com. 95 units (some with shower only). A/C TV TEL. $85–$190 double. Extra person $15. AE, DC, DISC, JCB, MC, V. Parking $8. TheBUS: 19 or 20.

"The spirit of old Hawaii"—the hotel's slogan says it all. The lush tropical flowers and carved tiki at the entrance on tiny Beach Walk set the tone for this intimate low-rise hotel. From the moment you arrive, you're embraced by aloha spirit: At check-in, you're given a pineapple; every morning, complimentary Kona coffee and tropical juice are served poolside; and at checkout, flower leis are presented to female guests as a fragrant reminder of their time at the Hawaiiana. The concrete hollow-tiled rooms feature a kitchenette (small refrigerator, two-burner hot plate, toaster oven, and cof-feemaker), two beds (a double and a single), TV, phone, and a view of the gardens and swimming pool. There's complimentary use of the washers and dryers. Hawaiian entertainment is featured every week. The hotel is about a block from the beach and within walking distance of Waikiki shopping and nightlife.

Outrigger Islander Waikiki. 270 Lewers St. (entry on ocean, Ewa side of Lewers St. at Kalakaua Ave.), Honolulu, HI 96815. ☎ **800/OUTRIGGER** or 808/923-7621. Fax 800/ 622-4852. www.outrigger.com. 287 units. A/C TV TEL. $125–$150 double; $165–$170 studio. Extra person $15; children 17 and under stay free when using existing bedding. Seniors 50 and older 20% discount, AARP members 25% discount. Ask about room-and-breakfast packages. Free rent-a-car when booking at rack rates. Parking $8. TheBUS: 19 or 20.

If you're looking for a moderately priced hotel in the midst of Waikiki, here's your place—Waikiki's newest hotel. In 1997, the Outrigger chain completely gutted the old Pleasant Holiday Isle Hotel, and then dropped more than $7 million for renovations to bring the property up to Outrigger standards. The location on Lewers and Kalakaua is fabulous: just across the street from the Royal Hawaiian Shopping Center, and 1 block to the beach. An escalator takes you up to the glass-encased lobby, with the pool at one end and shops and a Starbuck's Cafe at the other.

The rooms, which are all interconnected, range in size from 240 to 342 square feet, and have been refurbished in Berber carpets, with Italian tile entryways, blond island-style furniture, and matching wallpaper and artwork by Hawaiian artists. All rooms have small semicircular balconies, either a king or two double beds, coffeemakers, safes, hair dryers, and irons and ironing boards. Also available are rooms with bath-tubs, nonsmoking rooms, and wheelchair-accessible rooms.

INEXPENSIVE

The Breakers. 250 Beach Walk (between Kalakaua Ave. and Kalia Rd.), Honolulu, HI 96815. ☎ **800/426-0494** or 808/923-3181. Fax 808/923-7174. www.breakers-hawaii.com. 64 units (with shower only). A/C TV TEL. $91–$97 double. Extra person $8. AE, DC, MC, V. Lim-ited free parking; $6–$8 across the street. TheBUS: 19 or 20.

A little gem in the midst of high-rise Waikiki, The Breakers is full of old-fashioned Hawaiian aloha—and it's only steps from Waikiki Beach. This two-story hotel has a friendly staff and a loyal following, with more than 70% returning for another stay. Its six buildings are set around a pool and a tropical garden with brilliant red and yellow hibiscus; wooden jalousies and shoji doors enhance the tropical ambience. The tastefully decorated, slightly oversized rooms come with a lanai and a kitchenette with two-burner stove, toaster oven, and fridge. The poolside bar and grill serves cocktails and heavy pupus. Every Wednesday and Friday, you're invited to a formal Japanese tea ceremony from 10am to noon.

✪ **Waikiki Coral Seas.** 250 Lewers St. (between Kalakaua Ave. and Helumoa St.), Honolulu, HI 96815. ☎ **800/OUTRIGGER** or 808/923-3881. Fax 800/622-4852 or 808/922-2330. www.outrigger.com. 109 units (with shower only). A/C TV TEL. $90 double; $100 double with kitchenette; $130 one-bedroom with kitchenette (rates for up to 4). Extra person $15. AE, CB, DC, DISC, JCB, MC, V. Parking $8. TheBUS: 19 or 20.

In the heart of Waikiki, on a busy little street lined with several other Outriggers, you'll find this small, clean hotel. It's a great bargain at $90 a night. The rooms are small, but comfortable, with two double beds, a desk, TV, phone, and safe; rooms with kitchenettes come with refrigerator, microwave, sink, and cooking utensils. No grand ocean views here, but the hotel's location can't be beat—just a few minute's stroll to Waikiki Beach. If you get a room overlooking Lewers Street, you can sit on your semiprivate lanai and watch humanity parade by; Lewers may be noisy, but it's the best free show in town. The hotel has several restaurants, including a moderately priced steak-and-seafood house, an all-you-can-eat buffet, and a Chinese place. There's no pool, but you're welcome to use the one at the Waikiki Village next door.

Waikiki Edgewater. 2168 Kalia Rd. (at Beach Walk), Honolulu, HI 96815. ☎ **800/OUTRIGGER** or 808/922-6424. Fax 808/924-6354 or 800/622-4852. www.outrigger.com. 184 units. A/C TV TEL. $90–$100 double; $100 double with kitchenette; $145 one-bedroom with kitchenette (rates for up to 4). Extra person $15. AE, CB, DC, DISC, JCB, MC, V. Parking $8. TheBUS: 19 or 20.

Although this one is closer to the beach, we don't think it's as nice as the other Outriggers on Lewers Street, nor does it have the amenities they offer (no coffeemakers). The Edgewater is an older building with small rooms, renovated in 1993, and tiny lanais. Still, as in all Outrigger hotels, the rooms are tastefully decorated and come with TV, phone, and safe; those with kitchenettes have an oven, three-burner stove, sink, fridge, and cooking utensils. The hotel shares a swimming pool with the adjacent Waikiki Tower. There's a shortage of elevators; only two for seven floors and 184 rooms can cause long, long waits. Stay here for the location—all you have to do is cross the street and walk behind the Waikiki Reef Towers to get to the beach. It's also convenient to restaurants, nightlife, and shopping, but with four on-site restaurants, ranging from a deli to Italian seafood, you can even stay in for dinner.

Waikiki Reef Towers. 227 Lewers St. (near Helumoa Rd.), Honolulu, HI 96815. ☎ **800/OUTRIGGER** or 808/924-8844. Fax 808/924-6042 or 800/622-4852. www.outrigger. com. 479 units. A/C TV TEL. $105–$115 double; $120 double with kitchenette; $135 studio with kitchenette (for up to 4); $145 one-bedroom with kitchenette (for up to 4). Extra person $15. AE, CB, DC, DISC, JCB, MC, V. Parking $8. TheBUS: 19 or 20.

This is a great deal for families: Four of you can easily stay here for $135 or $145, with the advantage of a kitchenette to keep dining costs down. The Reef is one of the Outrigger's larger hotels, consisting of two 13-story towers. The rooms—renovated in 1994 and 1995—are larger than those at some nearby Outriggers, and come with a few more amenities than those in the chain's lower-priced hotels. The lanais, however, are very small. The kitchenettes come with microwave or stove/oven and fridge (toasters are available on request). The huge lobby is filled with shops, and four restaurants, from Cajun to coffee shop, are on hand; you'll also find an activities desk and a cocktail lounge. The Polynesian Showroom features some of Hawaii's top entertainers. You can order room service from the Waikiki Broiler; baby-sitting is available. There's also an on-site pool.

✪ **Waikiki Royal Islander.** 2164 Kalia Rd. (at Saratoga Rd.), Honolulu, HI 9
OUTRIGGER or 808/922-1961. Fax 808/923-4632 or 800/622-4852. www
101 units (with showers only). A/C TV TEL. $90–$115 double; $125 oceanview suite triple; $140 one-bedroom suite triple (3 people is tight) with kitchenette. $15 extra person. AE, CB, DC, DISC, JCB, MC, V. Parking $8. TheBUS: 19 or 20.

This is about as close as you can get to the beach and still pay budget prices: The sand is just across the street and through the beach access walkway. The elegant lobby of this boutique hotel gives it the look of a luxury hotel. The rooms, renovated in '92, are small (comfortable for two people, but really tight for three), but decorated in the tasteful Outrigger fashion. You can request coffeemakers from housekeeping or just bop down to the lobby in the morning, where coffee awaits. Since the Royal Islander is such a small hotel, it shares some services, such as a swimming pool and spill-over parking, with the beachfront Waikiki Reef Towers across the street. Dozens of restaurants are within a 5-minute walk.

Waikiki Village. 240 Lewers St. (near Helumoa Rd.), Honolulu, HI 96815. ☎ **800/OUTRIGGER** or 808/923-3881. Fax 808/922-2330 or 800/622-4852. www.outrigger.com. 441 units (with showers only). A/C TV TEL. $115–$145 double; $120–$150 double with kitchenette; $140–$150 triple studio with kitchenette. Extra person $15. AE, CB, DC, DISC, JCB, MC, V. Parking $8. TheBUS: 19 or 20.

Another recommendable Outrigger on Lewers Street is the Waikiki Village. This one is less than 2 blocks from the beach and in the midst of Waikiki's restaurant, shopping, and nightlife scene. The Village is considered a moderate Outrigger hotel: The rooms are small but cozy and were recently renovated (repainted, new bedspread, curtains, carpet). There are no in-room coffeemakers, but you can get your morning cup at the breakfast-only coffee shop. The pool sits in the middle of the open-air lobby, which makes for interesting people-watching as you work on your tan. Families of three might consider the studio kitchenettes, which come with microwave and refrigerator, as the hotel rooms sleep only two. *Helpful hint:* If you prefer a king bed, request one when reserving your room, as the hotel has a limited number of them.

A HOTEL FOR MILITARY PERSONNEL

Hale Koa Hotel. 2055 Kalia Rd. (across from Ft. DeRussy, between Dewey Way and Saratoga Rd.), Honolulu, HI 96815. ☎ **800/367-6027** or 808/955-0555. Fax 800/HALE-FAX. www.halekoa.com. 814 units. A/C TV TEL. $56–$88 standard double; $63–$97 moderate double; $68–$105 garden view double; $73–$112 partial oceanview double; $84–$130 oceanview double; $83–$121 deluxe oceanview double; $95–$140 oceanfront double; $101–$157 deluxe oceanfront double. Rates include continental breakfast and orientation the morning after check-in. Extra person $10. AE, DC, DISC, MC, V. Parking $3. TheBUS: 19 or 20.

We wish we could stay here, but we're not allowed. This is an exclusive hotel for active-duty and retired military and their families. It's a first-class hotel, right on Waikiki Beach, with the grassy lawns of Fort DeRussy on the other side. The price structure, which depends on military rank (lower ranks get cheaper rates), is 50% to 75% less than what comparable Waikiki hotels charge. The facilities here include three swimming pools, 66 landscaped acres with picnic tables and barbecues, health club, Jacuzzi, sauna, jogging trails, four lighted tennis courts, racquetball courts, volleyball courts, four restaurants, and lounges. The only drawback is that the hotel is always booked; some guests reserve up to a year in advance.

MID-WAIKIKI, MAUKA

These mid-Waikiki hotels, on the mountain side of Kalakaua Avenue, are a little farther away from the beach than those listed above. They're all between Kalakaua

Avenue and Ala Wai Boulevard, and between Kalaimoku Street in the Ewa direction and Kaiulani Street in the Diamond Head direction.

EXPENSIVE

Sheraton Princess Kaiulani Hotel. 120 Kaiulani Ave. (at Kalakaua Ave., across the street from the Sheraton Moana Surfrider), Honolulu, HI 96815. ☎ **800/325-3535** or 808/ 922-5811. Fax 808/923-9912. www.sheraton.com. 1,150 units. A/C TV TEL. $160–$305 double; from $500 suite. Extra person $40; children under 18 free in parents' room with existing bedding. Inquire about Sheraton's "Sure Saver" rates, available at different times of the year, which could mean as much as 32% in savings. AE, CB, DC, JCB, MC, V. Parking $8. TheBUS: 19 or 20.

Portraits of the hotel's namesake, Princess Kaiulani, heir to the throne who died in 1899 at the age of 24, fill the large open-air lobby. Her regal, youthful face looks out on the site that was once her royal estate. A huge swimming pool sits behind a row of restaurants and shops facing Kalakaua Avenue. The open-air lobby connects the three buildings of the Princess Kaiulani: the 11-story original hotel that opened in 1955, and the 11-story Kaiulani wing and the 29-story Ainahau Tower that both opened in 1960.

The rooms have been recently renovated, and double-insulated doors with sound-proofing have been added. We wish every hotel in noisy Waikiki had this feature. The soundproofing really works: You can't hear the blaring sirens or the sound of garbage cans being emptied at 3am. Other amenities include lanais, coffeemakers, safes, refrig-erators, hair dryers, and irons and ironing boards.

Dining/Diversions: Pikake Terrace offers casual dining in a poolside garden; Lotus Moon features Mandarin cuisine from northern China; Momoyama specializes in Japanese dishes; and Minute Chef is an international food court with everything from burgers to stir-fry. The Polynesian Revue features nightly shows on the dances, songs, culture, and drama of Polynesia.

Amenities: Multilingual staff and Keiki Aloha Club, a free kids' program available daily.

Waikiki Beachcomber. 2300 Kalakaua Ave. (at Duke's Lane), Honolulu, HI 96815. ☎ **800/ 622-4646** or 808/922-4646. Fax 808/923-4889. www.waikikibeachcomber.com. 500 units. A/C TV TEL. High season $180–$215 double, from $315 suites; low season $170–$205 double, from $295 suites. Extra person $22. Room/car packages from $140; 2-night minimum for packages. AE, CB, DC, JCB, MC, V. Parking $7. TheBUS: 19 or 20.

The room/car package makes this stylish Waikiki hotel a real deal. Another plus is the great location: a block from Waikiki Beach, just across the street from the upscale Royal Hawaiian Shopping Center, and next door to bargain shopping at the International Market Place. All 500 rooms were upgraded in 1996 with Berber carpets, new beds, TV armoires (allowing more drawer space), contemporary furniture, handheld showers, con-venient hot pots for making coffee or tea, and a state-of-the-art voice-message system.

The Beachcomber is Waikiki's only hotel with its own rooftop vegetable farm—yes, a farm in Waikiki. This urban hydroponics project has been so successful that it's now a two-level, 3,000-square-foot garden with a variety of lettuces, gourmet cucumbers, cherry tomatoes, and a host of herbs. Want to sample the goods? The hotel's Hibiscus Cafe features the hydroponic produce. Another reason to stay here: It's the home of the legendary "Don 'Tiny Bubbles' Ho Show."

MODERATE

Aston Island Colony Hotel. 445 Seaside Ave. (at Ala Wai Blvd.), Honolulu, HI 96815. ☎ **800/92-ASTON** or 808/923-2345. Fax 808/921-7105 or 808/922-8785. www.aston-hotels.com. 347 units. A/C TV TEL. $110–$135 double; $115–$145 studio with kitchenette;

$160–$205 one-bedroom suite with kitchen. Extra person $18. AE, CB, DC, DISC, JCB, MC, V. Parking $8. TheBUS: 19 or 20.

This elegant hotel combines the spaciousness of a condominium property with the amenities of a hotel. All units have refrigerators, coffeemakers, air-conditioning, private lanais, and daily maid service, and can sleep up to four. The studio units have kitchenettes, and the one bedrooms—which can sleep up to five—have full kitchens. The views are spectacular: Choose the jagged mountains and lush valleys, famous Diamond Head, or the sparkling Pacific Ocean. The only caveat is the miniscule bathrooms. Our bathroom was so small that the door didn't clear the toilet; it doesn't sound like a big deal, but it was annoying to have to maneuver around a tiny bathroom with a door that opened only partway. The tub/shower combo was also cramped (I had to shower with my elbows close to my sides to avoid hitting the walls).

The hotel features a pool, sun deck, restaurant, jet spa, and sauna. Access via car (always tricky on Waikiki's one-way streets) is very convenient from Ala Wai Boulevard.

✪ **Royal Kuhio.** 2240 Kuhio Ave. (between Royal Hawaiian Ave. and Seaside Ave.), c/o Paradise Mgmt., 50 S. Beretania St., Suite C207, Honolulu, HI 96813. ☎ **800/367-5205** or 808/538-7145. Fax 808/533-4621. E-mail: pmehi@gte.net. 389 units. A/C TV TEL. $95–$120 apt for 4. Extra person $15. AE, MC, V. Free parking. TheBUS: 19 or 20.

Families take note: This is one of the best deals in Waikiki. All the units in this high-rise condo are privately owned and individually decorated and furnished, and some are owner-occupied. Paradise Management is one of several companies handling apartments here, but its units—and its rates—are among the best. All have full kitchens, separate bedrooms, living area with TV and phones, and lanais. The complex has a pool, exercise room, sauna, self-service laundromat, sundeck, volleyball, billiards, basketball court, shuffleboard, and putting green. It's 2 blocks to Waikiki Beach, and everything else Waikiki has to offer is within walking distance. This is one of the few places in Waikiki where parking is free. *Hot tips:* Ask for a corner unit (they're the nicest), and if you plan to go in February, be sure to book a year in advance (it's the condo's busiest month).

✪ **Waikiki Joy.** 320 Lewers St. (at Kuhio Ave.), Honolulu, HI 96815. ☎ **800/92-ASTON** or 808/923-2300. Fax 808/924-4010. www.aston-hotels.com. 94 units. A/C TV TEL. $155–$190 double; $180–$195 club suite; $215–$230 junior suite with kitchen (sleeps up to 4); $265–$280 one-bedroom executive suite with kitchen (up to 3). Rates include continental breakfast. Extra person $18. Ask about the Island Hopper rates, which give you 25% off if you stay 7 or more consecutive nights with Aston. Valet parking $10. AE, CB, DC, DISC, JCB, MC, V. Parking $10. TheBUS: 19 or 20.

This is one hotel that truly deserves its name. An oasis right in the heart of busy Waikiki, this hidden jewel offers not only outstanding personal service, but also a Bose entertainment system and a Jacuzzi in every room! The Italian marble–accented open-air lobby and the tropical veranda—with swimming pool, sauna, and furnished deck—set the scene for the beautifully decorated guest rooms. The doubles have a marble entry, a refrigerator, a safe, and a lanai wide enough for you to sit and enjoy the views. The suites are even more luxurious: Club suites have either a king bed or two doubles, a refrigerator, microwave, coffeemaker, and wet bar. Executive suites have two double beds and a kitchen with a microwave and full refrigerator; the executive king suites add a separate living room and bedroom. Every room comes with voicemail, as well as fax and modem hookups. Still, there are a couple of downsides: The beach is 4 or 5 blocks away (a 10- to 15-minute walk), and there's a sandwich/coffee shop on-site, but the food's nothing to brag about.

INEXPENSIVE

❂ **Coconut Plaza.** 450 Lewers St. (at Ala Wai Blvd.), Honolulu, HI 96815. ☎ **800/882-9696** or 808/923-8828. Fax 808/923-3473. www.coconutplaza.com. 80 units. A/C TV TEL. $85 double; $100–$125 double with kitchenette; $175 suite with kitchenette. Rates include continental breakfast. Extra person $12. AE, CB, DC, JCB, MC, V. Parking $9. TheBUS: 19 or 20.

This small hotel is an island of integrity in a sea of tourist schlock. A self-proclaimed "studio apartment boutique hotel," Coconut Plaza offers a few perks that are rare in Waikiki: complimentary continental breakfast and the kind of personalized service that only a small hotel can offer. The recently renovated hotel has a tropical plantation feel, with big, airy rooms, terra-cotta tile, and lots of greenery. The island-style rooms have been recently redecorated in rattan and earth tones; all have a private lanai, ceramic tile bathroom, and daily maid service. The majority of the rooms have kitchenettes—with a mini-fridge, microwave, counter-top range, coffeemaker, and a complete set of cooking utensils—and most have views of the Ala Wai Canal and the mountains. There's an outdoor pool, a sun deck, exercise equipment, and a tour desk on the property; Ala Wai Golf Course is just across the canal, and the beach is 4 blocks away.

❂ **Ilima Hotel.** 445 Nohonani St. (near Ala Wai Blvd.), Honolulu, HI 96815. ☎ **800/367-5172** or 808/923-1877. Fax 808/924-8371. www.ilima.com. 99 units. A/C TV TEL. $95–$125 studio double; $140–$165 one-bedroom (up to 4); $185–$240 two-bedroom for 4 (sleeps up to 6); $267–$279 three-bedroom for 6; $295 three-bedroom penthouse (up to 6). Extra person $8. Discounted rates available for seniors. AE, CB, DC, DISC, JCB, MC, V. Limited free parking, or $8 parking across the street. TheBUS: 19 or 20.

The Teruya Brothers, owners of Hawaii's Times Supermarket, wanted to offer comfortable accommodations that Hawaii residents could afford, and they've succeeded with the Ilima. One of Hawaii's small, well-located condo-style hotels, the 17-story pale-pink Ilima (named for the native orange flower used in royal leis) offers value for your money. Rooms are huge condominium-size, the location (2 blocks to Waikiki Beach, near the International Marketplace and the Royal Hawaiian Shopping Center) is great, and prices are low. A tasteful koa-wood lobby lined with works by Hawaiian artists greets you upon arrival. There's a 24-hour front desk—a rarity at these prices and in this neighborhood—daily maid service, free local phone calls (a nice plus), and a full kitchen in every unit; all the couches fold out into beds, making this a particularly good deal for families (children 17 and younger stay free with existing bedding). Some of the beds are waveless water beds. There's a heated pool, three sundecks, a sauna, and an Italian restaurant on-site. Sorry, no ocean views—what you get is great value instead.

Marine Surf Waikiki Hotel. 364 Seaside Ave. (at Kuhio Ave.), Honolulu, HI 96815. ☎ **888/456-SURF** or 808/923-0277. Fax 808/926-5915. 110 units. A/C TV TEL. $80–$105 double; $150–$175 one-bedroom penthouse suite double. Extra person $10. CB, DC, DISC, MC, V. Parking $5. TheBUS: 19 or 20.

Located in the heart of Waikiki, this high-rise has privately owned condo units and spacious studio apartments for rent. Each one has a complete kitchen (refrigerator, stove/oven, toaster, coffee pot, and utensils), phone, two extra-long double beds, TV, and a small lanai. *Hot tip:* The best views are from floors 17 to 22, but the better the view, the higher the price. The hotel is a half-block from Kuhio Mall and the International Market Place, and just about 1½ blocks from the beach. Facilities include tour desk, pool, coin-operated laundry on every floor, and an Italian restaurant in the lobby.

Ohana Surf. 2280 Kuhio Ave. (at Nohonani St.), Honolulu, HI 96815. ☎ **800/OUTRIGGER** or 808/922-5777. Fax 808/921-3677 or 800/622-4852. www.outrigger.com. 251 units (with showers only). A/C TV TEL. $90–$100 double with kitchenette; $125 triple studio with kitchenette. Extra person $15. AE, CB, DC, DISC, JCB, MC, V. Parking $8. TheBUS: 19 or 20.

The Outrigger chain makes sure it has a hotel to suit every budget and every need; this one has recently renovated kitchenettes (in 1998)—with a two-burner stove, oven, refrigerator, coffeemaker, and cooking utensils—in every room. The guest rooms, pool deck, and lobby went through extensive renovations in 1995, and the rooms were outfitted with new bedspreads, chairs, lampshades, refurbished furniture, new TVs, and new fridges. The Surf is centrally located, across the street from the Kuhio Mall and 2 blocks from the beach; restaurants and nightlife are also within walking distance. There's an activity desk on-site.

Waikiki West. 2330 Kuhio Ave. (between Nahua and Walina sts.), Honolulu, HI 96815. ☎ **800/OUTRIGGER** or 808/922-5022. Fax 808/924-6414 or 800/622-4852. www.outrigger.com. 663 units (with shower only). A/C TV TEL. $105–$115 double; $110–$120 double with kitchenette; $215–$235 one-bedroom with kitchenette (up to 6); $150 one-bedroom suite with kitchenette (up to 3); $255 two-bedroom with kitchenette (up to 6). Extra person $15. AE, CB, DC, DISC, JCB, MC, V. Parking $8. TheBUS: 19 or 20.

On the upside, this Outrigger hotel has lots of guest services and facilities, including lounge, pool, laundry, kitchenettes, room service, lots of shops (including a pharmacy), and two restaurants (Chili's and a Patisserie bakery/deli). The downside: It's located on a very busy and noisy part of Kuhio Avenue. The rooms (redone in 1995) all have refrigerators and coffeemakers; the units with kitchenettes have a two-burner stove/oven and cooking utensils, too. Waikiki Beach is 2 blocks away, and restaurants, shopping, and nightlife are all within a 5- to 10-minute walk. International Market Place is across the street.

A GAY-FRIENDLY HOTEL

Hotel Honolulu. 376 Kaiolu St. (near Kuhio Ave., across from the metered parking lot), Honolulu, HI 96815. ☎ **800/426-2776** or 808/926-2766. Fax 808/922-3326. www.lava.net/~hotelhnl. 24 units (with shower only). Low season $69–$115 double; high season $79–$119 double. Extra person $10. 4-night minimum during Christmas season. AE, CB, DC, DISC, JCB, MC, V. Parking $5. TheBUS: 19 or 20.

This old 1940s low-rise apartment complex was renovated into a hotel in 1983, and has truly become an "oasis in time." The three-story building is a tribute to the art-deco age, but it's outfitted with modern conveniences. You enter through an atrium with carefully tended tropical plants, including a beautiful orchid collection, and singing birds. The hotel offers two types of accommodations in the main building: deluxe studios (with sitting area and queen bed) and one-bedroom suites (with living room with sofa sleeper). All rooms have kitchenettes and lanais. Each suite has a different theme: safari, art deco, bamboo, Rangoon, Hollywood, samurai, Norma Jean, and so on.

The Bamboo Lanai building is a two-story wing for budget travelers with standard studios with queen bed, small kitchenettes (with stove and refrigerator), and lanai. *Warning:* There is a hot nightclub with loud music until 1:30am behind these rooms.

Although the hotel caters to gay men and women, everyone is welcome. On-site amenities include complimentary coffee in the lobby all day, complimentary use of beach mats and towels, and use of the rooftop garden sun deck, which is great for working on your tan, or for an evening barbecue and cocktails. From the hotel, it's about a 7-minute walk to the beach and about 2 minutes to Honolulu's top gay clubs. Airport pick-up is also available for $25 round-trip.

WAIKIKI, DIAMOND HEAD END

You'll find all these hotels between Ala Wai Boulevard and the ocean, and between Kaiulani Street (1 block to Diamond Head from the International Marketplace) in the Ewa direction and the world-famous Diamond Head itself.

VERY EXPENSIVE

Hyatt Regency Waikiki. 2424 Kalakaua Ave. (at Kaiulani St., across the street from the beach), Honolulu, HI 96815. ☎ **800/233-1234** or 808/923-1234. Fax 808/923-7839. www. hyattwaikiki.com. 1,241 units. A/C MINIBAR TV TEL. $240–$400 double; $400–$465 Regency Club double; from $550 suite. Extra person $30 ($50 Regency Club); children under 19 stay free using existing bedding. AE, CB, DC, DISC, JCB, MC, V. Valet parking $12; self-parking $10. TheBUS: 19 or 20.

Located across the street from the Diamond Head end of Waikiki Beach, this is one of Oahu's largest hotels: It has two 40-story towers and covers nearly an entire city block. Some will find this Goliath of a hotel too big and impersonal. The huge second-floor lobby is decorated in koa and wraps around an atrium that rises *40 floors* up from the ground level. Smoking is allowed in the lobby, and despite the size, it can get pretty cloudy in there at times.

The guest rooms are roomy, and a $10-million investment refurbished them in 1996. Every room has a coffeemaker, but the coffee isn't free—even though you're paying at least $240 a night, expect to pay $3 extra for a package of coffee. Other amenities, such as hair dryers, bathrobes, irons and ironing boards, are complimentary. The deluxe oceanview rooms overlooking Waikiki Beach are fabulous, but can be noisy (traffic on Kalakaua is constant). For a few dollars more (well, actually more than a few dollars), you can upgrade to the Regency Club floors, where the rooms are nicer (and the coffee is free). The upgrade also entitles you to an expedited check-in and entry to the Regency Club—which serves complimentary continental breakfast, pupus in the afternoon, and concierge service all day—and a private rooftop sundeck and Jacuzzi.

Dining/Diversions: Four restaurants and five cocktail lounges, including an indoor-outdoor grill overlooking the ocean; a Japanese restaurant; a steak-and-seafood house; Harry's Bar, featuring Hawaiian and Polynesian entertainment; Ciao Mein for creative Chinese and Italian cuisine served family-style (see chapter 6, "Dining"); the Texas Rock 'N Roll Sushi Bar, a combination of country western/rock club serving Tex-Mex cuisine and sushi; and an elegant poolside bar.

Amenities: Multilingual concierge, business services (including typing, personal-computer rental, stock news, notary public), pool, baby-sitting, Camp Hyatt program for kids, room service (6am–11pm), valet service, travel desks (airline-ticket counter, American Express, Budget, Hertz), doctor's office, bank, and more than 60 shops.

EXPENSIVE

✪ **Aston Waikiki Beachside Hotel.** 2452 Kalakaua Ave. (between Uluniu and Liliuokalani aves.), Honolulu, HI 96815. ☎ **800/922-7866** or 808/931-2100. Fax 808/922-2129. www.aston-hotels.com. 79 units. A/C TV TEL. $180–$325 double; $295–$375 junior suite. Rates include continental breakfast. No more than 2 adults per room. Seniors 50 and older get 25% off rates and 7th night free, depending on availability. Ask about the Island Hopper rates, which give you 25% off if you stay 7 or more consecutive nights with Aston. AE, CB, DC, DISC, JCB, MC, V. Parking $9.50 at nearby hotel. TheBUS: 19 or 20.

There's an atmosphere of elegance and charm throughout this luxury boutique hotel, which is right across the street from Waikiki Beach. You step off busy Kalakaua Avenue into a marble-filled lobby with classical music wafting in the background, sprays of flowers everywhere, and a soothing Italian fountain. The staff is attentive to every detail. The rooms are tiny, but tastefully decorated with works of art and antiques (including hand-painted Oriental screens and 18th-century furniture). Each has its own air-conditioning system, refrigerator, complimentary safe and daily newspaper, and two phones.

Dining/Diversions: No on-site restaurant, but a complimentary continental breakfast is served daily in the lobby. A three-course tea service (with a variety of teas, sandwiches, desserts, etc.), using antique china, is presented in the lobby and courtyard on Saturday and Sunday afternoons.

Amenities: Concierge, twice-daily maid service, morning newspaper, same-day laundry and dry cleaning.

✪ **Colony Surf.** 2885 Kalakaua Ave. (on the ocean side between the Waikiki Aquarium and Outrigger Canoe Club), Honolulu, HI 96815. ☎ **888/924-SURF** or 808/924-3111. Fax 808/923-2249. www.colonysurf.com. 72 units. A/C TV TEL. West Building (studios with full kitchens) $195–$445 studio; East Building hotel rooms $225–$295 double; penthouse from $2,000. Rates include complimentary breakfast. AE, DC, DISC, JCB, MC, V. Valet parking $8. TheBUS: 19 or 20.

This elegant, two-building condominium, fronting its own white-sand beach in the quieter Diamond Head area, has been totally renovated. The West Building is the Colony Surf condominium, where rental units are mixed with full-time residential apartments. The units are all large (1,000 square feet); studios come complete with a kitchen and double beds or one giant king bed, large bathrooms, and views of Waikiki or Diamond Head that are worth every penny you pay. No air-conditioning in the studios, but the ceiling fans move the ocean breeze through the condo units. The East Building is back off the beach. The hotel lobby looks more like an elegant living room, and you'll feel like you've entered a luxurious private world. Check-in takes place in the privacy of your room, which is furnished with handmade teak furniture from Bali. In addition to the large balconies with great views of Diamond Head, there are many touches in every room that establish this hotel as a truly relaxing place—from Hawaiian music CDs to a masseuse on request.

If you're craving peace and quiet away from the Waikiki crowds, but want to be close enough (about a 10-minute walk) to enjoy the shops and restaurants, this is a perfect location. The surrounding buildings are mainly residential condos; Kapiolani Park is across the street, and the Waikiki Aquarium is just a few steps away. Both buildings have access to the small, private beach (with great swimming) in front of the Colony Surf; complimentary beach chairs and towels are available.

Dining/Diversions: Chef David Paul Johnson has brought his award-winning American cuisine from Maui to the East Building at David Paul's Diamond Head Grill (see chapter 6, "Dining"). In the West Building you'll find Michel's Restaurant, award-winning French cuisine served in an elegant oceanfront setting.

Amenities: Wonderful complimentary breakfast prepared by the staff of David Paul's Diamond Head Grill served daily, CD player and Hawaiian-music CDs, daily newspaper, complimentary overnight shoeshine, daily maid service, and complimentary beach equipment.

Pacific Beach Hotel. 2490 Kalakaua Ave. (at Liliuokalani St., across the street from the beach), Honolulu, HI 96815. ☎ **800/367-6060** or 808/922-1233. Fax 808/922-8061. www.pacificbeachhotel.com. 830 units. A/C TV TEL. $180–$285 double; $500–$1500 suite. Extra person $25; children under 18 free with existing bedding. AE, CB, DC, DISC, JCB, MC, V. Parking $7. TheBUS: 19 or 20.

The Pacific Beach has a unique feature, unmatched by any hotel in Hawaii: a three-story, 280,000-gallon indoor oceanarium with more than 70 different species, ranging from the 2-inch cleaner wrasse to the 4-foot Hawaiian stingray. Some 52-feet long and 32-feet wide, this oversized aquarium is the focal point of the hotel, and can be seen from the lobby and several restaurants. Check it out even if you don't stay here. The fish are fed six times a day.

The hotel consists of two towers: the Beach Tower, built in 1969, and the Oceanarium Tower, built in 1979. The front desk to this complex is located off the entrance on Liliuokalani Street, right by the giant oceanarium. Every room has a lanai, full bathroom with tub and shower, refrigerator, and coffeemaker. Nonsmoking rooms are available. You can get a room with a city, mountain, or ocean view. The oceanview rooms increase in price with each ascending floor. The deluxe oceanview rooms begin on the 10th floor (worth the extra money for the panoramic views).

Dining/Diversions: The hotel has three restaurants and lounges: the Oceanarium Restaurant for casual, family dining; Neptune, for continental fare; and Shogun, a Japanese steak and seafood restaurant with sushi bar.

Amenities: Room service (7 to 10am and 11am to 10pm), professionally designed tennis courts, swimming pool, 24-hour health club, whirlpool spa, and 17 shops.

MODERATE

Aston at the Waikiki Banyan. 201 Ohua Ave. (on mountain side, at Kuhio Ave.), Honolulu, HI 96815. ☎ **800/922-7866** or 808/922-0555. Fax 808/922-8785. www.aston-hotels.com. 307 units. A/C TV TEL. $145–$205 double. Extra person $18. Seniors 50 and older get 25% off and 7th night free, depending on availability; ask about Island Hopper rates that give you 25% off if you stay at Aston properties for 7 or more consecutive nights. AE, CB, DC, DISC, JCB, MC, V. Parking $5. TheBUS: 19 or 20.

This property combines the homey comforts of a condo apartment with the amenities of a hotel: daily maid service, bell service, front desk, coin-op laundry, a sundry store, and much more, including an enormous sixth-floor recreation deck complete with pool, tennis court, sauna, barbecue areas, snack bar, and a children's play area—a great boon for families. Your entry to this two-tower, 38-story complex is through the open-air lobby with impressive lacquer artwork, hand-carved and hand-painted in Hong Kong. The units have full kitchens (refrigerator, oven, microwave, rice cooker, toaster, coffeemaker, and utensils), a comfortably furnished living room (with sofabed), and a separate bedroom with two double beds or a king. The bedroom is separated from the living room by sliding doors, which can be opened to make one big unit. The one we stayed in had an old-fashioned air conditioner in the wall, but it did the job, and we could control the temperature. The apartments open out to a fairly good-size lanai with chairs and a small table; there's a partial ocean view (buildings obstruct it).

✪ **New Otani Kaimana Beach Hotel.** 2863 Kalakaua Ave. (ocean side of the street just Diamond Head of the Waikiki Aquarium, across from Kapiolani Park), Honolulu, HI 96815. ☎ **800/35-OTANI** or 808/923-1555. Fax 808/922-9404. www.kaimana.com. 124 units. A/C MINIBAR TV TEL. $115–$272 double; $180–$632 suite. Extra person $15. AE, CB, DC, DISC, JCB, MC, V. Valet parking $8. TheBUS: 19 or 20.

This is one of Waikiki's best-kept secrets: a boutique hotel right on a lovely stretch of beach, at the foot of Diamond Head. Kapiolani Park is right across the street. Robert Louis Stevenson's description of the beach fronting the hotel, Sans Souci, holds true today: "If anyone desires lovely scenery, pure air, clear sea water, good food, and heavenly sunsets, I recommend him cordially to the Sans Souci."

The hotel has two buildings: On the Waikiki side, the rooms open to an atrium courtyard, and on the Diamond Head side, they feature kitchenettes. The Waikiki-side rooms are tiny, but tastefully decorated in pale pastels, and they open out to large lanais with ocean and park views. Since the hotel overlooks Kapiolani Park, guests have easy access to outdoor activities; kayaking and snorkeling are available at the beach. The hotel also arranges for visitors to climb to the top of Diamond Head. The airy lobby opens onto the alfresco Hau Tree Lanai restaurant, a delightful beachfront restaurant that's one of the most romantic spots in Hawaii, set under the same banyan tree that sheltered Robert Louis Stevenson a century ago (see chapter 6, "Dining"). The beachfront ✪ **Sunset Lanai Lounge** is great for cocktails.

This is a nice hotel, but I had a couple of complaints when I stayed here: The air conditioner was positioned right over the bed, so you had either frigid air blowing on you all night or nothing, and the check-out staff at the front desk was not only slow but extremely unhelpful—and we've received a few letters from our readers with the very same complaints.

✪ **Outrigger Prince Kuhio.** 2500 Kuhio Ave. (on the Diamond Head, mauka side of Kuhio at Liliuokalani Ave.), Honolulu, HI 96815. ☎ **800/OUTRIGGER** or 808/922-0811. Fax 800/ 622-4852. www.outrigger.com. 625 units. A/C MINIBAR TV TEL. $150–$285 double; $195– $215 Voyager Club; $400–$700 Voyager Club suite. Extra person $25. Children under 18 free in parents' room with existing bedding. Seniors 50 and older get 20% off and members of AARP get 25% off. Free rent-a-car when booking at rack rates. Maximum of 4 persons per room. AE, CB, DC, DISC, JCB, MC, V. Parking $8. TheBUS: 19 or 20.

The Prince Kuhio is one of the best hotels in the Outrigger chain. Completely renovated in 1997, the 37-story Prince Kuhio is in the center of the Waikiki shopping scene, and only a few blocks from Waikiki Beach and the Honolulu Zoo. The regular guest rooms come with a king or two double beds, refrigerators, black-out drapes, coffeemaker, and lanais. The rooms on the Voyagers Club floors (the top four floors) have views to die for, and guests have use of a private lounge that serves continental breakfast and complimentary pupus in the evening. Voyagers Club guests also have complimentary privileges at the Outrigger Beach Club & Fitness Center. Eight floors in the complex are designated as nonsmoking, and 24 rooms are available for the disabled. Guests with children may or may not be happy to learn that all rooms come equipped with Nintendo.

Queen Kapiolani Hotel. 150 Kapahulu Ave. (at Lemon Rd., across from Kapiolani Park), Honolulu, HI 96815. ☎ **800/367-5004** or 808/922-1941. Fax 808/922-2694 or 800/ 477-2329. www.castle-group.com. 315 units. A/C TV TEL. $107–$165 double; $157–$180 studio with kitchenette; $250–$402 one-bedroom suite with kitchenette (sleeps up to 4). Extra person $17. AE, CB, DC, DISC, JCB, MC, V. Parking $7. TheBUS: 19 or 20.

Named for Queen Kapiolani (1834–99), the wife of Hawaii's last king, David Kalakaua (1836–91), this hotel hearkens back to the days of the Hawaiian monarchy. The 10-foot chandeliers in the main dining room and a full-size portrait of the queen in the lobby reflect some of the 19th-century flavor of the hotel. The plush decor, however, doesn't extend up to the budget rooms, which are quite small. You'll have a view of the shoreline through louvered windows, and each room has a small refrigerator and coffeemaker. The location is great: just across the street from Kapiolani Park (which was donated by King Kalakaua and named for his beloved wife), a half block to the beach, and within walking distance of the Honolulu Zoo, the aquarium, and the action of Waikiki. A large swimming pool and sundeck are on the third floor.

Waikiki Resort Hotel. 2460 Koa Ave. (at Liliuokalani Ave.), Honolulu, HI 96815. ☎ **800/ 367-5116** or 808/922-4911. Fax 808/922-9468. www.superpages.gte.net. 296 units. A/C TV TEL. $105–$145 double; $145–$155 double with kitchenette; $315–$470 penthouse suite. Extra person $15; children under 17 stay free using existing bedding. Excellent package deals, including room-and-breakfast buffet for $115–$125 and room/car package for $115–$125; room/car/breakfast packages are $125–$135. AE, DISC, JCB, MC, V. Parking $5. TheBUS: 19 or 20.

On a quiet street 1 block from the beach stands this 19-story hotel, offering quality rooms at budget prices. Owned by Korean Airlines, the recently renovated hotel has a huge marble lobby dominated by a stained-glass mural of the ocean. The rooms are decorated with tropical textiles and come with refrigerators, lanais, safes, and either two double beds or a king. The higher the floor, the better the view—and of course, the higher the price. If you're on a budget, consider getting a room with a kitchenette, which will save you money on food; these are also the corner units, which have great views. There are two on-site restaurants, including the Camellia Restaurant, one of Waikiki's few Korean restaurants. There are also two lounges: one at poolside, and one featuring dancing nightly. Other amenities include a freshwater pool, sundry and gift shops, an activities desk, laundry, and free transportation to the airport upon departure. Front-desk personnel are fluent in English, Korean, and Japanese.

INEXPENSIVE

✪ **Diamond Head Bed & Breakfast.** Noela Dr. (at Paki Ave., off Diamond Head Rd.), Honolulu. Reservations c/o Hawaii's Best Bed & Breakfasts, P.O. Box 563, Kamuela, HI 96743. ☎ **800/262-9912** or 808/885-4550. Fax 808/885-0559. www.bestbnb.com. 2 units. TV TEL. $100 double (includes large breakfast). Extra person $25. 2-night minimum. DISC. Free parking. TheBUS: 2.

Hostess Joanne and her long-time family housekeeper Sumiko offer a quiet, relaxing place to stay on the far side of Kapiolani Park, away from the hustle and bustle of Waikiki. Staying here is like going back to a Hawaii of 50 years ago, when *kamaaina* (native-born) families built huge houses with airy rooms, which opened outward, via sliding wooden screen doors, to big lanais and tropical gardens. The house is filled with family heirlooms and Joanne's artwork. One room features the beyond king-size koa-wood bed that once belonged to Princess Ruth, a member of the royal family. Other conveniences in the large room include a refrigerator and a bathroom big enough to dance in, complete with an old-fashioned tub; off the bedroom is a large lanai facing the greenery of Diamond Head. The other room in the house has two double koa beds, a lanai overlooking Waikiki through sweet-smelling plumeria trees, refrigerator, and another large bathroom. Sumiko, who speaks fluent Japanese, whips up a hearty breakfast, which may include fish if they're biting.

2 Honolulu Beyond Waikiki

ALA MOANA
MODERATE

Ala Moana Hotel. 410 Atkinson Dr. (at Kona St., next to Ala Moana Center), Honolulu, HI 96814. ☎ **800/367-6025** or 808/955-4811. Fax 808/944-6839. www.alamoanahotel.com. 1,169 units. A/C TV TEL. $125–$225 double; from $250 suite. Extra person $20; children under 18 stay free. AE, CB, DC, DISC, JCB, MC, V. Valet parking $12; self-parking $8. TheBUS: 19 or 20.

This hotel is big—1,169 rooms on 36 floors make it feel like a metropolis. Its proximity to Waikiki, the downtown financial and business district, the new convention center, and Hawaii's largest mall, Ala Moana Shopping Center, makes it a popular spot for out-of-state visitors and locals alike. Lots of Asian tourists choose the Ala Moana Hotel, probably because the management does an excellent job of making sure foreign guests feel welcome by providing a bilingual staff and translators. Shoppers, mostly from neighboring islands, also make up a good percentage of the guests (especially in December). The rooms vary in size according to price: The cheaper rooms are on the smaller side, but all come with two double beds, refrigerator, safe, phones with voicemail, and computer jacks. As a full-service hotel, the Ala Moana offers everything:

concierge, room service, valet, laundry, valet parking, a sundeck and pool, game room, and more. With four restaurants, a nightclub, and a Polynesian revue on-site, some guests rarely venture off-property.

INEXPENSIVE

Pagoda Hotel. 1525 Rycroft St. (between Keeaumoku and Kaheka sts.), Honolulu, HI 96814. ☎ **800/367-6060** or 808/923-4511. Fax 808/922-8061. www.pagodahotel.com. 361 units. A/C TV TEL. $90–$100 double; $115 one-bedroom double (sleeps up to 4); $145 one-bedroom deluxe double (sleeps up to 6); $145 two-bedroom double (sleeps up to 5). Extra person $25. Free breakfast packages available and excellent car/room packages. AE, DC, DISC, MC, V. Parking $3. TheBUS: 5 or 6.

This is where local residents from neighboring islands stay when they come to Honolulu. Close to shopping and downtown, the Pagoda has been serving Hawaii's island community for decades. All rooms have a full bathroom and refrigerator; the studios and one and two bedrooms also have kitchenettes. The property features two swimming pools, shops, self-service or valet laundry, and three different restaurants. There's easy access to Waikiki via TheBUS—the nearest stop is just a half-block away. Ask about the car packages: For the price of most rooms, you can get a free rental.

DOWNTOWN
EXPENSIVE

✪ **Aston at Executive Centre Hotel.** 1088 Bishop St. (at S. Hotel St.), Honolulu, HI 96813. ☎ **800/92-ASTON** or 808/539-3000. Fax 808/922-8785. www.aston-hotels.com. 114 all-suite units. A/C TV TEL. $170–$195 suite; $220–$245 executive suite. Rates include local calls and newspaper. Extra person $18; children under 17 stay free. AE, CB, DC, DISC, JCB, MC, V. Parking $10. TheBUS: 1, 2, 3, 9, 12.

Located in the heart of downtown, this is the perfect hotel for the business traveler. Not only is it close to Honolulu's business and financial centers, but the staff goes out of its way to make sure every need is met; there's even a staffed 24-hour business center.

The rooms occupy the top 10 floors of a 40-story, glass-walled tower; each room boasts unobstructed views of the city, the mountains, or Honolulu Harbor. Each is large enough to qualify as a mini-suite, with three phones (with private voicemail), safe, whirlpool bath, hair dryer, iron and ironing board, and coffeemaker. The executive suites feature full kitchens, washer/dryer, and VCR. All guests awaken to find the local newspaper outside their door. Free local phone calls make this hotel a huge plus for the business traveler.

Dining/Diversions: The New Eagle Café, on the lobby level, offers breakfast, lunch, and dinner.

Amenities: Concierge, coin-op laundry, same-day laundry and dry cleaning. The Business Services Center provides a full range of office and secretarial services: personal and laptop computers with a variety of word processing programs, printers, copy machines, typewriters, and more. There are also a 20-meter outdoor pool and Jacuzzi with sundeck, 24-hour fitness center with free weights, aerobic equipment, men's and women's saunas, as well as small to medium rooms for business meetings and gatherings, and two corporate-style boardrooms.

NEAR HONOLULU INTERNATIONAL AIRPORT

If you have a long layover between flights, or if your flight gets delayed, consider the services of the **Airport Mini-Hotel** (☎ **808/836-3044;** fax 808/834-8986). It's the perfect answer to a traveler's dilemma: The clean, comfortable single rooms come with nothing more than a bed, a nightstand, and a private shower. Bring your ear plugs, though; it tends to be noisy, even at night. They provide a wake-up call if you need it,

Bed-and-Breakfast Reservation Agencies

For a more intimate experience, try staying in a bed-and-breakfast. Accommodations on Oahu calling themselves "bed-and-breakfast" vary from a room in a house (sometimes with a shared bathroom) to a vacation rental in a private cottage. Breakfast can be anything from coffee, pastries, and fruit to a home-cooked gourmet meal with just-caught fresh fish.

If you don't want to go through the hassle of calling around and trying to match your dream accommodation to what is available, use a bed-and-breakfast booking agency. We recommend the following:

Bed & Breakfast Hawaii, P.O. Box 449, Kapaa, HI 96746 (☎ **800/ 733-1632** or 808/822-7771; fax 808/822-2723; e-mail www.bandb-hawaii. com), offers a range of different accommodations (from vacation homes to bed-and-breakfast units), starting at $65 a night on Oahu.

✪ **Hawaii's Best Bed & Breakfast,** P.O. Box 563, Kamuela, HI 96743 (☎ **800/ 262-9912** or 808/885-4550; fax 808/885-0559; www.bestbnb.com), is operated by Barbara Campbell, who did the marketing for the luxury Kona Village Resort for decades. It chooses only the crème de la crème of bed-and-breakfasts across the state. Rates on Oahu begin at $85 a night.

and there's always coffee brewing to get you going. If you have something that needs refrigeration (medication or flowers to bring home), the management is happy to help out. Rates are $33 for 8 hours ($5.50 for each additional hour); you can rent showers only for $8.25. There are only 17 rooms, so book in advance. The hotel does not provide transportation to the terminal, but it's just a short walk away.

MODERATE

Honolulu Airport Hotel. 3401 N. Nimitz Hwy. (Rodgers St.), Honolulu, HI 96819. ☎ **800/ 800-3477** or 808/833-0661. Fax 808/833-1738. www.honoluluairporthotel.com. 308 units. A/C TV TEL. $112–$122 double. Extra person $20. AE, DISC, MC, V. Free parking. Free shuttle to and from the airport. TheBUS: 19 or 20.

Just minutes from the airport via a free shuttle, this convenient airport hotel is actually the best of the lot, but it's still not a luxury resort, just a place to stay overnight. Two four-story buildings wrap around an outdoor swimming pool and garden; there are also a restaurant and lounge with entertainment on-site. There are noise problems here, though; the walls seem thin. If you don't have a lot of luggage, ask for a room well away from the elevator (late at night, lively guests tend to get louder). Non-smoking and wheelchair-accessible rooms are available.

INEXPENSIVE

Best Western—The Plaza Hotel. 3253 N. Nimitz Hwy. (at Paiea St.), Honolulu, HI 96819. ☎ **800/800-4683** or 808/836-3636. Fax 808/834-7406. www.bestwestern.com. 274 units. A/C TV TEL. $97–$108 double. Extra person $20. AE, DC, DISC, JCB, MC, V. Free parking. Free shuttle van to and from airport. TheBUS: 19 or 20.

If you've got a flight that arrives late or leaves early, this is a good place to spend the night. The rooms are fairly standard, with refrigerator and, if requested, a microwave. Other conveniences include room service, a pool for a quick dip, coin-operated laundry for that last-minute wash, a restaurant, and free shuttle service to the airport (less than 5 minutes away).

Pacific Marina Inn. 2628 Waiwai Loop (at Lagoon Dr.), Honolulu, HI 96819. ☎ **800/ 367-5004** or 808/836-1131. Fax 808/833-0851 or 800/477-2329. www.castle-group.com. 119 units. A/C TV TEL. $88 double; $104 suite for 2; $104 quad for 4. Extra person $17. AE, CB, DC, DISC, MC, V. Free parking. Free shuttle to and from airport. TheBUS: 19 or 20.

In dire need of renovations, this inexpensive hotel is okay in a pinch, but you wouldn't want to spend more than a night here. The main attraction is convenience—just minutes to the airport via a free shuttle. The Pacific Marina is a clean, affordable hotel featuring tiny, basic rooms with showers. Don't look for a lot of amenities; just soap and a shower cap are all you will find in the bathroom. Noise and people arriving and departing in the middle of the night are part of the "charm" of this transient facility, so bring ear plugs. Facilities include swimming pool, sun deck, two restaurants, and karaoke fun in the evening. Keehi Lagoon Park, with free tennis courts and picnic areas, is next door.

MANOA
MODERATE

Manoa Valley Inn. 2001 Vancouver Dr. (at University Ave.), Honolulu, HI 96822. ☎ **800/ 535-0085** or 808/947-6019. Fax 808/946-6168 or 800/633-5085. marc@marcresorts.com. 8 units (3 with shared bathroom; 5 with private bathroom). TV TEL. $99–$120 double with shared bathroom; $140–$190 double with private bathroom (shower only). Rates include continental breakfast and evening wine service. AE, DC, JCB, MC, V. Free parking. TheBUS: 4 or 6.

It's completely off the tourist trail and far from the beach, but that doesn't stop travelers from heading to this historic 1915 Carpenter Gothic home on a quiet residential street near the University of Hawaii. Saved from demolition by Rick Ralston (the Red Adair of historic renovation in Hawaii) in 1978, this eight-room Manoa landmark— it's on the National Register of Historic Places—offers a glimpse into the lifestyles of the rich and famous in early Honolulu.

Those who prefer to avoid resorts find the eclectically furnished inn refreshing. Each room has its own unique decor, and has been named for a prominent figure in Hawaii's history. The John Guild suite, for instance, has a turn-of-the-century parlor with antiques and old-fashioned rose wallpaper; the adjoining bedroom has a king-size koa bed, and the bathroom features an old-style tub as well as a separate modern shower. The three top-floor rooms share a full bathroom, and the others have private bathrooms. Some of the rooms have safes.

A genteel ambience pervades here. Guests regularly gather in the parlor to listen to the Victrola or play the nickelodeon. There's also an antique billiards table, a piano in the living room, and croquet set up in the backyard. As the sun sets, complimentary wine and cheese are served on the quiet veranda. The innkeepers ask that children staying here be at least 14 years old.

TO THE EAST: KAHALA
VERY EXPENSIVE

✪ **Kahala Mandarin Oriental Hawaii.** 5000 Kahala Ave. (at Kealaolu Ave.), Honolulu, HI 96816. ☎ **800/367-2525** or 808/739-8888. Fax 808/739-8800. www.mohnl.com. 402 units. A/C TV TEL. $295–$650 double; from $590 suite. Extra person $80; children 17 and under stay free. AE, CB, DC, DISC, JCB, MC, V. Parking $12.

Since 1964, when Conrad Hilton first opened it as a place to relax far from the crowds of Waikiki, the Kahala has always been rated one of Hawaii's premiere hotels; a venerable who's who of celebrities have stayed here, including every president since Richard Nixon. Now owned by the Mandarin Oriental chain, renowned for its excellent service, and with $75 million in renovations (completed in March 1996), this grande dame of hotels has reached a new level. It retains the traditional feeling of an earlier time in Hawaii—which defined the Kahala for a generation—accenting it with exotic Asian touches; the result is a resort hotel for the 21st century, but with the grace and elegance of a softer, gentler time. The location offers a similarly wonderful compromise: Situated in one of Oahu's most prestigious residential areas, the Kahala offers the peace and serenity of a neighbor-island vacation, with the conveniences of Waikiki just a 10-minute drive away.

All the guest rooms have been totally remodeled with 19th-century mahogany reproductions, teak parquet floors with hand-loomed Tibetan rugs, overstuffed chairs, canopy beds covered with soft throw pillows, and artwork by local artists adorning the grass-cloth-covered walls. Views from the floor-to-ceiling sliding glass doors are of the ocean, Diamond Head, and Koko Head. Some of the more modern conveniences in the rooms include two-line phones, computer and fax connections, 27-inch TV, and Super Nintendo. The large bathrooms include vintage fixtures, a freestanding glass shower, a large soaking tub, "his" and "hers" dressing areas, plush bathrobes and slippers, a hair dryer, and an illuminated makeup mirror.

Dining/Diversions: At Hoku's, the main dining room, every table has an ocean view and features Pacific and European cuisine (see chapter 6, "Dining"). Plumeria Beach Cafe serves both creative and traditional cuisine in a casual, open-air setting; its specialty is Sunday brunch. There's also a poolside snack bar, an oceanfront bar, and a lobby lounge with nightly entertainment.

Amenities: The lush, tropical grounds include an 800-foot crescent-shaped beach, a swimming pool, and a 26,000-square-foot lagoon, home to two bottle-nosed dolphins, sea turtles, and tropical fish. There's also 24-hour room service, valet and self-parking, nightly turndown, in-room safe, fax and modem connections, baby-sitting, concierge, foreign exchange facilities, Hawaiian cultural program, massage, multilingual personnel, business center, shops, banquet and meeting rooms, and shuttle service to Waikiki and major shopping centers. Free scuba lessons in pool; daily dolphin-education talks by a trainer from Sea Life Park; fitness center with steam rooms, dry sauna, Jacuzzis, weight room, Stairmasters, treadmills; Kahala Keiki Club for kids.

HAWAII KAI
INEXPENSIVE

J&B's Haven. Kahena St. (at Ainapo St., off Hawaii Kai Dr.), Hawaii Kai. Reservations: P. O. Box 25907, Honolulu, HI 96825. ☎ **808/396-9462.** www.hits.net/~babe. 2 units. TV TEL. $65–$75 double. Rates include continental breakfast. Extra person $10. 2-night minimum. No credit cards. Free parking. TheBUS: 1.

Englishwomen Joan and Barbara Webb have had a successful bed-and-breakfast on Oahu since 1982. Both Joan, who moved to Hawaii in 1981, and her daughter Barbara, who has been living here since 1970, are very knowledgeable about Oahu's attractions and enjoy meeting new people and introducing them to the Hawaii they love. They recently moved to this beautiful house in Hawaii Kai, just 15 minutes east of Waikiki (on the other side of Diamond Head) and close to Hanauma Bay, Sandy Beach, and Sea Life Park, as well as within easy reach of three shopping centers with excellent restaurants. There are two rooms in the house: the large master bedroom, with private bathroom, king bed, mini-refrigerator, and microwave, and a smaller room with a small refrigerator. *Note:* This is a smoke-free house for non-smokers only.

PEARL CITY
INEXPENSIVE

✪ **Rainbow Inn.** 98–1049 Mahola Pl. (off Kaonohi St., 2 miles from Kamehameha Hwy.), Pearl Ridge, Aiea, HI 96701. ☎ and fax **808/488-7525.** E-mail: gsmith3777@aol.com. 1 unit. A/C TV TEL. $65 double. Rates include refrigerator stocked with breakfast items. Extra person $10. 3-night minimum. No credit cards. Free parking. TheBUS: 20, 50, 51, or 52.

This private tropical garden studio, downstairs from the home of retired military officer Gene Smith and his wife Betty, has panoramic views of Pearl Harbor, the entire south coast of Oahu, and the Waianae and Koolau mountains. A large deck and full-size pool is just outside the apartment's door; inside, the apartment features a double bed, washer/dryer, and kitchen. The Smiths are happy to lend their guests beach and picnic equipment—ice chest, beach mats and chairs, even wine glasses. Located close to Pearl Ridge Shopping Center, Rainbow Inn is freeway-close to all of Oahu's attractions, yet far enough away to give you lots of peace and quiet. This is one of Oahu's best bed-and-breakfast deals. Reserve early—bargains like this book up fast.

3 The Windward Coast

KAILUA

Pat O'Malley of **Pat's Kailua Beach Properties,** 204 S. Kalaheo Ave., Kailua, HI 96734 (☎ **808/261-1653** or 808/262-4128; fax 808/261-0893; www.10kvacation-rentals.com/pats), books a wide range of houses and cottages on or near Kailua Beach, from a million-dollar beachfront estate to studio cottages on or close to the water. Rates start at $70 a day for a studio cottage near the beach and go up to $425 per day for a multimillion dollar home right on the beach with room to sleep up to eight. All units are fully furnished, with everything from cooking and dining utensils, to telephone and TV, even washers and dryers.

MODERATE

✪ **Ingrid's.** Pauku St. (across from Enchanted Lakes School), Kailua. c/o Hawaii's Best Bed & Breakfasts, P.O. Box 563, Kamuela, HI 96743. ☎ **800/262-9912** or 808/885-4550. Fax 808/885-0559. www.bestbnb.com. 1 apt. TV TEL. $125 double. Rate includes continental breakfast. Extra person $15. 2-night minimum. DISC. Free parking. TheBUS: 56 or 57.

Ingrid has impeccable taste. Upstairs, past the Japanese garden and through a private entrance, is the cute one-bedroom apartment that she keeps immaculate. Decorated in Japanese modern style, this place is straight out of a magazine: The pristine white walls and cabinets are accented with such dramatic touches as black tile on the counter top, black-and-white shoji doors, and a black Oriental screen behind a king bed dressed in white quilts and red, red throw pillows. The tiled bathroom is done in complementary gray and has a luxurious soaking tub. The kitchenette includes a dishwasher, refrigerator, microwave, and coffeemaker. A huge tiled deck extends out from the apartment, and a small alcove is off the bedroom for a third person. Fresh flowers are everywhere.

The place is gorgeous, but the best part is Ingrid (who isn't Swedish, but Portuguese). A former advertising sales manager for a local TV station, Ingrid is one of the friendliest and most helpful people you'll meet in Hawaii. People return year after year because of her welcoming warmth.

INEXPENSIVE

✪ **Lanikai Bed & Breakfast.** 1277 Mokulua Dr. (between Onekea and A'ala drs., Lanikai), Kailua, HI 96734. ☎ **800/258-7895** or 808/261-1059. Fax 808/262-2181. www.lanikaibb.com.

2 units. TV TEL. $80 studio double; $90 apt. Rates include breakfast items in units. Extra person $10–$20. 3-night minimum. MC, V. Free parking. TheBUS: 56 or 57 with 70 shuttle to Lanikai.

This old-time bed-and-breakfast, a *kamaaina* (native-born) home that reflects the Hawaii of yesteryear, is now into its second generation. For years, Mahina and Homer Maxey ran this large, comfortable island-style residence. Today their son Rick and his wife, Nini, are the hosts. The recently renovated 1,000-square-foot upstairs apartment is decorated in the style of an old Hawaii bungalow. With a king bed in the bedroom, separate den, large living/dining room, and big bathroom, it easily accommodates four. It has all the modern conveniences—including a kitchenette—and oversized windows let you enjoy wonderful views. Or you can follow the ginger- and ti-lined path to a 540-square-foot honeymooner's delight, with a queen bed and sitting area and a new kitchen. The units are stocked with breakfast fixings (muffins, juice, fruit, coffee, tea) and all the beach equipment you'll need (towels, mats, chairs, coolers, water jugs). Access to picture-perfect Lanikai Beach is across the street, bus routes are close by, and a 2.5-mile biking/walking loop is just outside.

Schrader's Windward Marine Resort. 47–039 Lihikai Dr. (off Kamehameha Hwy.), Kaneohe, HI 96744. ☎ **800/735-5711** or 808/239-5711. Fax 808/239-6658. 19 units. A/C TV TEL. $50–$149 one-bedroom double; $110–$150 two-bedroom double; $160–$210 three-bedroom. Rates include continental breakfast. Extra person $7.50. 2-night minimum. AE, DC, DISC, JCB, MC, V. Free parking. TheBUS: 55, 56 or 57.

This older cottage-style motel is nestled in a tranquil, tropical setting on Kaneohe Bay, only a 30-minute drive from Waikiki. Despite the name, the ambience here is more motel then resort, but Schrader's offers a good alternative for families. Many of the guests are military families visiting nearby Kaneohe Marine Corps base. Cottages have kitchenettes with refrigerator and microwave. Prices are based on the views; depending on how much you're willing to pay, you can look out over Kahuluu fish pond, the Koolau Mountains, or Kaneohe Bay. Lots of watersports are available at additional cost. *Tip:* When booking, ask for a unit with a lanai; that way, you'll end up with at least a partial view of the bay.

4 The North Shore

Team Real Estate, 66–134 Kamehameha Hwy., Suite 1, Haleiwa, HI 96712 (☎ **800/982-8602** or 808/637-3507; fax 808/637-8881; www.teamrealestate.com), manages vacation rentals on the North Shore. The units range from affordable cottages to oceanfront homes. The rates start at $85 per night and go up to $275 per night. A minimum stay of 1 week is required for some properties, but shorter stays are available.

EXPENSIVE

✪ **Hilton Turtle Bay Resort.** P.O. Box 187, (Kuilima Dr., off Kamehameha Hwy. [Hwy. 83]), Kahuku, HI 96731. ☎ **800/HILTONS** or 808/293-8811. Fax 808/293-9147. www.hilton. com. 485 units. A/C TV TEL. $165–$265 double; $285–$600 cabana; from $400 suite. Extra person $30; children stay free. AE, CB, DC, DISC, ER, JCB, MC, V. Valet parking $9; self-parking $5. TheBUS: 52 or 55.

An hour's drive from Waikiki and eons away from that tourist mecca is this luxurious oceanfront resort in a country setting. Sitting on 808 acres, this is a resort loaded with activities: 27 holes of golf, 10 tennis courts, and 5 miles of shoreline with secluded white-sand coves. The resort was built on Kalaeokaunu Point ("point of the altar"), where ancient Hawaiians built a small altar to the fish gods. Its remains are now at the Bishop Museum, but it is easy to see why the Hawaiians considered this holy ground.

Next to the point is Kuilima Cove, one of the safest swimming beaches on the North Shore, thanks to the large reef offshore.

The feeling of old Hawaii is carried through to the guest rooms, which are done in Polynesian decor and have a private lanai, all the amenities, and a great ocean view.

Dining/Diversions: The Palm Terrace is known for fabulous buffets. Sunday champagne brunch at the Sea Tide Room is a favorite. The Cove, which features continental and local cuisine, is best known for its excellent wine list. There's live entertainment nightly at the Bay View Lounge, and the Hang Ten Lounge is the place for poolside or sunset cocktails.

Amenities: Room service, concierge, many shops (including a branch of Liberty House), daily craft demonstrations, a children's program, sightseeing programs, and guided nature and Hawaiian reef walks. Oceanview championship 27-hole golf course, 10 Plexipave-court tennis complex, horseback riding, fitness center, idyllic beach, two pools, snorkeling, scuba diving, and windsurfing.

MODERATE

Ke Iki Hale. 59–579 Ke Iki Rd. (off Kamehameha Hwy.), Haleiwa, HI 96712. ☎ **800/ 377-4030** or 808/638-8229. 11 units, 5 one-bedroom, 3 two-bedrooms. $138–$165 one-bedroom double; $185 two-bedroom double. Extra person $15. 2-night minimum. MC, V. Free parking. TheBUS: 52.

This collection of rustic one- and two-bedroom duplex cottages has a divine location, snuggled on 1½ acres with its own 200-foot stretch of beach between two legendary surf spots—Waimea Bay and Banzai Pipeline. The winter waves at both of these spots are rough stuff; we regular folks can swim only in the flat summer seas. But there's a large lava reef nearby with tide pools to explore, and on the other side, Shark's Cove, a relatively protected snorkeling area.

The North Shore doesn't have many accommodations; Ke Iki Hale is a good choice for those who enjoy the beach. It's not for everyone, though. Kitchens, barbecues, hammocks, and laundry facilities provide some of the comforts of home. The furnishings are modest, but clean, homey, and comfortable. The one-bedrooms have two single beds in the living room, two beds in the separate bedroom, and a full kitchen. Nearby are tennis courts and a jogging path. The downside is that the units are subject to constant salt spray, which adds to their evident deterioration. None have TV or phones (there's a pay phone in the parking lot). *Tip:* Don't stay in one of the noisy streetside units; instead, spring for one closer to the water.

INEXPENSIVE

✪ **Santa's By The Sea.** Ke Waena Rd. (off Kamehameha Hwy.), Haleiwa. c/o Hawaii's Best Bed & Breakfasts, P.O. Box 563, Kamuela, HI 96743. ☎ **808/885-4550** or 800/262-9912. Fax 808/885-0559. www.bestbnb.com. 1 unit with shower only. TV TEL. $110 double. Rate includes breakfast items in refrigerator. Extra person $5. 2-night minimum. Free parking. TheBUS: 52.

This certainly must be where Santa Claus comes to vacation, and for good reason: St. Nick knows a bargain when he sees it. The location, price, and style make this place a must-stay if you plan to see the North Shore. It's one of the few North Shore B&Bs right on the beach—and not just any beach, but the famous Banzai Pipeline. You can go from your bed to the sand in less than 30 seconds to watch the sun rise over the Pacific.

Hosts Gary and Cyndie renovated this vacation hideaway into an impeccable one-bedroom unit with finely crafted woodwork, bay windows, and a collection of unique Santa figurines and one-of-a-kind Christmas items that Cyndie has assembled over the years; it may sound schlocky, but somehow it gives the apartment a country charm.

Honeymooners, take note: There's lots of privacy here. The unit has its own entrance; a living room with VCR and stereo; a full kitchen with everything a cook needs; and an adjacent dining room. Fruit, cereals, bread, coffee, tea, and juice are provided on the first morning to get you started.

Santa's also features a covered gazebo for non–sun worshipers, a moss-rock outside shower (with hot water), and a tranquil setting that would cost you four times as much if this were a hotel rather than a private B&B. The only sound you'll hear is the waves gently lapping on the beach in summer or thundering onto the shore in winter.

5 Leeward Oahu: The Waianae Coast

☺ **Ihilani Resort & Spa.** At Ko Olina Resort, 92–1001 Olani St., Kapolei, HI 96707. ☎ **800/ 626-4446** or 808/679-0079. Fax 808/679-0080. www.ihilani.com. 423 units. A/C TV TEL. $285–$575 double; from $800 suite. Extra person $35. Children under 18 stay free using existing bedding. AE, CB, DC, JCB, MC, V. Free parking. No bus service. Take H-1 west toward Pearl City/Ewa Beach; stay on H-1 until it becomes Hwy. 93 (Farrington Hwy.); look for the exit sign for Ihilani Resort; exit road is Alinui Dr., which goes into the Ko Olina Resort; turn right on Olani Pl.

In December 1993, some 17 miles and 25 minutes west of Honolulu Airport—and worlds away from the tourist scene of Waikiki—the first hotel in the 640-acre Ko Olina Resort community opened to much speculation. It's so far from Waikiki and Honolulu, critics charged, who would want go all the way out there? Lots of people, it turns out. The Ihilani has been well booked ever since. Located in the quiet of Oahu's West (leeward) Coast, Ihilani ("heavenly splendor") is nestled between the Pacific Ocean and the first of four manmade beach lagoons. Featuring a luxury spa and fitness center, plus tennis and golf at Ko Olina, it's a haven of relaxation and well-being.

Rising some 15 stories along the virgin coastline, it's hard to get a bad room here— some 85% of guest rooms enjoy lagoon or ocean views. The luxuriously appointed rooms are larger than most (680 square feet) and come with huge lanais outfitted with comfortable, cushioned teak furniture (chaise longue, chairs, and table). The rooms feature a state-of-the-art comfort control–system panel (to operate the ceiling fans, air-conditioning, lights, and so on) built into the three phones, CD player, minibar, and in-room safe. Luxurious marble bathrooms have deep-soaking tubs, separate glass-enclosed showers, hair dryers, yukata robes, and many more amenities.

Dining/Diversions: Extraordinary cuisine, using the freshest local ingredients is found in all three Ihilani restaurants. The jewel is Azul, an intimate terrace overlooking the ocean serving Mediterranean-inspired cuisine. There's open-air dining on light, tropical fare at an informal poolside restaurant, and a low-fat, low-calorie menu is served at the Spa Cafe. Island artists provide entertainment and music to dance by in the resort's two lounges.

Amenities: Concierge, 24-hour room service, daily newspaper, business services, transportation to Waikiki and Ala Moana Shopping Center. Keiki Beachcomber Club is a year-round program for toddlers to teens, housed in its own ground-floor facility, with a wide variety of outdoor adventures and indoor learning activities, including a Computer Learning Center, a 125-gallon fish tank, an evening lounge for teen-themed parties, and more. Championship 18-hole Ko Olina Golf Course, designed by Ted Robinson and recognized as one of Hawaii's premier courses; a tennis club with pro shop; shopping arcade; 3-mile coastal fitness trail; two pools; and a stretch of four white-sand beaches.

The world-class Ihilani Spa offers just about everything to enhance your health, fitness, and well-being, including thalassic treatments, Swiss showers, Grand Jets, Vichy showers, and Roman pools. Shiatsu, Swedish, and Hawaiian Lomi Lomi massages and herbal bodywraps are offered. Complete fitness and relaxation programs can be custom-designed. For us, the spa alone is reason enough to come here.

6 Oahu's Campgrounds & Wilderness Cabins

Camping is a year-round experience on Oahu, thanks to the balmy weather. There is, however, a wet (winter) and dry (summer) season. You should be prepared for rain year-round. You also need to be ready for insects (have a good repellent for mosquitoes), water purification (boiling, filtration, or iodine crystals), and sun protection (sunscreen, a hat, and a long-sleeve shirt).

If you don't plan to bring your own camping equipment, you can rent or buy equipment at **The Bike Shop,** at 1149 S. King St. (oceanside between Piikoi and Pensacola streets; ☎ **808/595-0588**).

Oahu is the only Hawaiian island with a public transportation system that serves the entire island (see "Getting Around" in chapter 4, "Getting to Know Oahu," for details). However, one problem with getting to a camping site on TheBUS is that carry-ons must fit under your seat or on your lap. Metal-frame packs are not permitted on TheBUS. Drivers do use discretion, but be forewarned.

The best places to camp on Oahu are listed below. You can find them on the map titled "Beaches & Outdoor Activities on Oahu" in chapter 7, "Fun in the Surf & Sun."

HONOLULU
SAND ISLAND STATE RECREATION AREA

Believe it or not, there is a campground in Honolulu. It's located just south of Honolulu Harbor at a waterfront park. Don't be put off by the heavy industrial area you have to drive through to reach this 102-acre park with grassy lawns, ironwood trees, and sandy beaches. Campers have great views of the entire Honolulu coastline all the way to Waikiki, better than some of the guests in the $400-a-night hotel rooms in Waikiki. In addition to the scenery, the most popular activity here is shoreline fishing, especially along the west shore of Sand Island. Swimming is an option, but watch out for the rocks along the shoreline bottom; the water quality is occasionally questionable, too.

The park is also an excellent location from which to enjoy the attractions in Honolulu; it's just 15 minutes from Waikiki or Pearl Harbor.

Only tent camping is allowed in this park. There are picnic tables (some under small covered shelters), rest rooms with cold showers only, and potable water. You'll need a permit; applications are accepted no earlier than 30 days in advance. Write to the **Department of Land and Natural Resources,** State Parks Division, P.O. Box 621, Honolulu, HI 96809 (☎ **808/587-0300;** www.hawaii.gov). Permits are limited to a 5-day stay in every 30-day period. Camping is allowed only on Friday, Saturday, and Sunday nights. The gates close at 6:45pm in the fall and winter (from the weekend after Labor Day until March 31) and 7:45pm in the spring and summer (April 1 to Friday after Labor Day). The gates do not open until 7am the next morning; cars cannot enter or leave during that period. TheBUS 19 stops at Nimitz Highway and Puuhale Road, just over a mile walk to the park entrance.

To get here from the Honolulu International Airport, take Nimitz Highway toward Honolulu and Waikiki. Turn right at the Sand Island Access Road (Hwy. 64) and follow it to the end of the road and the park entrance.

CENTRAL OAHU
KEAIWA HEIAU STATE RECREATION AREA

At the southern end of central Oahu, above Halawa Heights, this 385-acre wooded park offers a cool mountain retreat with hiking trails and picnic facilities. This area, in the foothills of the Koolaus, is filled with eucalyptus, ironwood, and Norfolk pines. The remains of the *heiau ho'ola* (temple of treating the sick) are on the grounds, and specimens of Hawaiian medicinal plants are on display. An excellent 5-mile hiking trail, the Aiea loop, offers magnificent views of Pearl Harbor and the mountains. There's tent camping only; campers have the choice of flat, open grassy areas or slightly sloping areas with shade trees. Facilities include picnic tables, rest rooms with cold showers, outdoor grills, a dishwashing area, a covered pavilion, drinking water, and a public phone. Supplies are available in Aiea, 2 miles away.

You'll need a permit; applications are accepted no earlier than 30 days in advance. Write to the **Department of Land and Natural Resources** (see "Sand Island State Recreation Area," above for address and telephone number). Permits are limited to a 5-day stay in every 30-day period. Camping is permitted Friday through Tuesday nights; no camping on Wednesday and Thursday nights. The gates close at 6:45pm in the fall and winter (from the weekend after Labor Day until March 31) and 7:45pm in the spring and summer (April 1 to Friday after Labor Day). The gates do not open until 7am the next morning; cars cannot enter or leave during that period.

To get here from Waikiki, take the H-1 Freeway to Highway 78 and exit at Aiea (Exit 13A). Follow Moanalua Road to Aiea Heights Drive and turn right; the park entrance is at the end of the road. There is no bus service to this area.

WINDWARD
HOOMALUHIA BOTANICAL GARDENS

This relatively unknown windward-side camping area, outside Kaneohe, is a find. *Hoomaluhia* means "peace and tranquility," an apt description for this 400-acre botanical garden. In this lush garden setting with rare plants and craggy cliffs in the background, it's hard to believe you're just a half-hour from downtown Honolulu. The gardens are laid out in areas devoted to the plants specific to tropical America, native Hawaii, Polynesia, India–Sri Lanka, and Africa. A 32-acre lake sits in the middle of the scenic park (no swimming or boating is allowed, though), and there are numerous hiking trails. The Visitors Center can suggest a host of activities, ranging from guided walks to demonstrations of ancient Hawaiian plant use. The facilities for this tent-camp area include rest rooms, cold showers, dishwashing stations, picnic tables, grills, and water. A public phone is available at the Visitors Center, and shopping and gas are available in Kaneohe, 1 mile away.

Permits are free, but stays are limited to Friday, Saturday, and Sunday nights only. For information, contact **Hoomaluhia Botanical Gardens,** 45–680 Luluku Rd. (at Kamehameha Highway), Kaneohe, HI 96744 (☎ **808/233-7323**). The gate is locked at 4pm; it is open again from 5:30 to 6:30pm, and then closed for the night after that. The gates open again at 9am. TheBUS no. 55 (Circle Island) stops 4 miles from the park entrance. To get here from Waikiki, take H-1 to the Pali Highway (Hi. 61) and turn left on Kamehameha Hwy. (Hi. 83); at the fourth light, turn left on Luluku Road.

KUALOA REGIONAL PARK

Located on a peninsula on Kaneohe Bay, this park has a spectacular setting. The gold-sand beach is excellent for snorkeling, and fishing can be rewarding (see "Beaches," in chapter 7, for details). There are two campgrounds: Campground A—in a wooded area with a sandy beach and palm, ironwood, kamani, and monkeypod trees—is mainly used for groups, but has a few sites for families, except during the summer (June through August), when the Department of Parks and Recreation conducts a children's camping program here. Campground B is on the main beach; it has fewer shade trees, but a great view of Mokolii Island. Facilities at both sites include rest rooms, showers, picnic tables, drinking fountains, and a public phone. Campground A also has sinks for dishwashing, a volleyball court, and a kitchen building. Gas and groceries are available in Kaaawa, 2½ miles away. The gate hours are 7am to 8pm; if you're not back to the park by 8pm, you're locked out for the night.

Permits are free, but limited to 5 days (no camping on Wednesday and Thursday). Contact the **Honolulu Department of Parks and Recreation,** 650 S. King St., Honolulu, HI 96713 (☎ 808/523-4525; www.co.honolulu.hi.us), for information and permits. Permits are not issued until 2 weeks before your camping dates. Kualoa Regional Park is in the 49–600 area of Kamehameha Highway, across from Mokolii Island. To get here, take the Likelike Highway (Hi. 63); after the Wilson Tunnel, get in the right lane and turn off on Kahakili Highway (Hi. 83). Or you can take TheBUS 55.

KAHANA BAY BEACH PARK

Under Tahiti-like cliffs, with a beautiful, gold-sand crescent beach framed by pine-needle casuarina trees, Kahana Bay Beach Park is a place of serene beauty. You can swim, bodysurf, fish, hike, and picnic, or just sit and listen to the trade winds whistle through the beach pines.

Tent and vehicle camping only are allowed at this oceanside oasis. Facilities include rest rooms, picnic tables, drinking water, public phones, and a boat-launching ramp. Do note that the rest rooms are at the north end of the beach, far away from the camping area, and there are no showers. There's no fee for camping, but you must get a permit, which is also free; the limit is 5 nights. Camping is allowed Friday through Tuesday nights; no camping on Wednesday and Thursday nights. You can get a permit at the **Department of Land and Natural Resources,** State Parks Division, P.O. Box 621, Honolulu, HI 96809 (☎ **808/587-0300;** www.hawaii.gov).

Kahana Bay Beach Park is in the 52–222 block of Kamehameha Highway (Hi. 83) in Kahana. To get here from Waikiki, take the H-1 west to the Likelike Highway (Hi. 63). Continue north on the Likelike, through the Wilson Tunnel, turning left on Hi. 83; Kahana Bay is 13 miles down the road on the right. You can also get there via TheBUS 55.

WAIMANALO BAY STATE RECREATION AREA

Just outside the town of Waimanalo is one of the most beautiful beachfront camping grounds on Oahu: Steep verdant cliffs in the background, a view of Rabbit Island off shore, and miles of white-sand beach complete the picture of Waimanalo Bay State Recreation Area. This campground is close to Sea Life Park and relatively close to Hanauma Bay, Makapuu, and Sandy Beach.

Ocean activities abound: great swimming offshore, good surfing for beginners, and plentiful fishing grounds. There is tent camping only at the 12 sites, which ensures plenty of privacy. The campsites (in numbered slots) are all in the open grassy lawn between the ironwood trees and the shoreline. Each campsite has its own picnic table, barbecue grill, and garbage can. Other facilities in the area include a central rest room with showers, water fountains, and a dishwashing sink. A public telephone is located by the caretaker's house.

Permits are free, but limited to 5 days (no camping on Wednesday and Thursday). Contact the **Honolulu Department of Parks and Recreation,** 650 S. King St., Honolulu, HI 96713 (☎ **808/523-4525;** www.co.honolulu.hi.us), for information and permits. Permits are not issued until 2 weeks before your camping dates.

TheBUS 57 stops on Kalanianaole Highway (Highway 72), about a mile walking distance to the park entrance. To get here from Honolulu, take the H-1 Freeway east until it ends. Continue on Highway 72 into Waimanalo. Turn right on Whiteman Road and then right again on Walker Road, which leads to the park entrance.

THE NORTH SHORE
MALAEKAHANA BAY STATE RECREATION AREA

This beautiful beach camping site has a mile-long gold-sand beach (see "Beaches," in chapter 7, for details). There are two areas for tent camping. Facilities include picnic tables, rest rooms, showers, sinks, drinking water, and a phone. Permits are free, but limited to 5 nights, and can be obtained at any state parks office, including the **Department of Land and Natural Resources,** State Parks Division, P.O. Box 621, Honolulu, HI 96809 (☎ **808/587-0300;** www.hawaii.gov). Camping is allowed Friday through Tuesday nights; no camping on Wednesday and Thursday nights. For your safety, the park gate is closed between 6:45pm and 7am; vehicles cannot enter or exit during those hours. Groceries and gas are available in Laie and Kahuku, less than a mile away.

The recreation area is located on Kamehameha Hwy. (Hi. 83) between Laie and Kahuku. To get there, take the H-2 Freeway to Hi. 99 to Hi. 83 (both roads are called Kamehameha Hwy.); continue on Hi. 83 just past Kahuku. Or take TheBUS 55.

CAMP MOKULEIA

A quiet, isolated beach on Oahu's North Shore, 4 miles from Kaena Point, is the centerpiece of this 9-acre campground. Camping is available on the beach or in a grassy, wooded area. Activities include swimming, surfing, shore fishing, and beachcombing.

Facilities include tent camping, cabins, and lodge accommodations. The tent-camping site has portable chemical toilets, a water spigot, and outdoor showers; there are no picnic tables or barbecue grills, so come prepared. The cabins have bunk beds and can sleep up to 14 people in the small cabins and 22 in the large cabins. The lodge facilities include rooms with and without a private bathroom. The cabins are $125 per night for the 14-bed cabin and $160 per night for the 18-bed cabin. The rooms at the lodge are $45 to $50 for a shared bathroom and $55 to $60 for a private bathroom. Many groups use the camp, but it's still a very peaceful place. The tent area is separated from the buildings—but you can use all the facilities if you opt for it—and there's a real sense of privacy. Tent camping is $5 per person, per night (children 5 and under stay free). Reservations for permits are needed; contact **Camp Mokuleia,** 68–729 Farrington Hwy., Waialua, HI 96791 (☎ **808/637-6241;** fax 808/637-5505).

Camp Mokuleia is located on Farrington Highway, west of Haleiwa. To get here from Waikiki, take the H-1 to the H-2 exit; stay on H-2 until the end. Where the road forks, bear left to Waialua on Hi. 803, which turns into Hi. 930, to Kaena Point. Look for the green fence on the right, where a small sign at the driveway reads CAMP MOKULEIA, EPISCOPAL CHURCH OF HAWAII.

Dining

6

by Jocelyn Fujii

Honolulu, the Rodney Dangerfield of the Hawaiian Islands, has many underrated and underappreciated features. One of them is the Koolau Mountains. The other is its plethora of restaurants in all categories, from plate lunch to Provençal. Even with the state's sluggish economy, you can hardly get a table at Alan Wong's Restaurant, Chef Mavro Restaurant, or Jimbo's, the noodle house the chefs go to when they leave their own busy kitchens. Even for a late bloomer like Honolulu, dining out is a top priority—not only for pleasure, but also because Hawaii has one of the highest percentages of working mothers in the nation.

More than ever, chefs once trained and celebrated in Hawaii's top resorts are moving into their own spheres beyond hotel properties and walk-in traffic, creating their own destinations and loyal clienteles who are willing to venture to unexpected neighborhoods and urban niches. Newest among them is Chef Mavro Restaurant in McCully, where celebrated chef George Mavrothalassitis, formerly of Halekulani's La Mer and the Four Seasons Wailea's Seasons, has opened his own temple of fine dining a few blocks from where Alan Wong put out his shingle a few years ago. And Wong, owner/chef of what is arguably Honolulu's most popular restaurant, has broken new ground again, this time with the announcement that he will take over Liberty House's restaurants in Ala Moana: a Hawaii Regional Cuisine eatery (with wood-burning oven and kitchen) to replace the Garden Court on the third floor, a gourmet marketplace on the fourth floor, and a coffee bar on the second floor. Philippe Padovani, formerly of Halekulani, Ritz-Carlton Mauna Lani (now Orchid at Mauna Lani), and Manele Bay Hotel, has also returned to Honolulu with his Padovani's Bistro and Wine Bar in the Alana Hotel. Chefs such as Mavrothalassitis, Wong, Padovani, Jean-Marie Josselin, Sam Choy, and Roy Yamaguchi are worth renting a car to find, but so are Oahu's many great plate-lunch palaces for casual dining on the run. See "A Table of Hawaii" in the Appendix for more information on the culinary scene in Hawaii.

The recommendations below will lead you to the few noteworthy hotel dining rooms, neighborhood hangouts worth seeking out, ethnic winners, and isolated marvels in all corners of the island.

CHAIN RESTAURANTS L&L **Drive-Inn** (corporate ☎ **808/521-3044**) is plate-lunch heaven, with 38 locations in Hawaii (32 on Oahu alone). You know L&L is great by the long lines of policemen and students. **Zippy's Restaurants**—at last count 21 of them on Oahu (corporate ☎ **808/973-0880**)—is the dine-and-dash maestro with a surprisingly good selection of fresh seafood to complement its saimin, chili, and American and local fare. It's hard to spend more than $7 for the French and Vietnamese specials at the **Ba-le Sandwich Shops:** *pho* (the noodle soup that's a national ritual in Vietnam), croissants as good as the espresso, and wonderful taro/tapioca desserts that have won an islandwide following. Branches include Ala Moana Center (☎ **808/944-4752**); 333 Ward Ave. (☎ **808/591-0935**); Kahala Mall, 4211 Waialae Ave. (☎ **808/735-6889**); Manoa Marketplace, 2855 E. Manoa Rd. (☎ **808/988-1407**); and Chinatown at 150 N. King St. (☎ **808/521-3973**). *Tip:* The Manoa Marketplace branch now serves a terrific selection of Thai dishes in an enlarged dining area, making it as much a restaurant as a place for take-out food.

Like the spaceship *Enterprise* in a cloud of java, **Starbucks Coffee** has descended in a big way, with locations in Waikiki (corner of Lewers and Kalakaua), Ward Village (across from Ward Centre), Kahala Mall, Manoa (across from Manoa Marketplace), downtown (1000 Bishop St.), Pearlridge Shopping Center, and other locations. The high-profile **Boston's North End Pizza Bakery** chain has an enthusiastic following among pizza lovers, and not just because it boasts "Hawaii's largest slice." Boston's reasonable prices and hefty sizes (19 in. and 3 lb.!) add extra value, and fans swear by the sauces and toppings. Voted Hawaii's best pizza in the *Honolulu Weekly*'s annual "Best of Honolulu" awards for 1998, Boston's can be found in Kaimuki, Kailua, Kaneohe, Wahiawa, Kapolei, Pearlridge, and Salt Lake, with plans for Mililani and Hawaii Kai (corporate ☎ **808/263-2253**). In Waikiki, the local **Hard Rock Cafe** is at 1837 Kapiolani Blvd. (☎ **808/955-7383**), and **Planet Hollywood Honolulu** is nearby at 2155 Kalakaua Ave. (☎ **808/924-7877**). At the Ala Moana end of Waikiki, **Red Lobster** (☎ **808/955-5656**) is crustacean central, a bustling family-style seafood haven at 1765 Ala Moana Blvd., in the same building as the new **Outback Steakhouse** (☎ **808/951-6274**), a Roy Yamaguchi/Ed Wary/Shep Gordon partnership that serves textbook-perfect steaks and is always full. On downtown's Restaurant Row, beef eaters can also chow down at **Ruth's Chris Steak House,** 500 Ala Moana Blvd. (☎ **808/599-3860**). In Kahala Mall, you can taste the medley of toppings offered by the local branch of **California Pizza Kitchen,** 4211 Waialae Ave. (☎ **808/737-9446**).

Otherwise, the streets of Waikiki are lined with famous fast-food joints, from Denny's to McDonald's, from Burger King to Jack in the Box. Oahu also has most of the familiar sit-down chain restaurants and pubs.

FOOD COURTS   Several shopping centers have food courts where you can grab a quick, cheap meal on the run. The largest is the newly renovated Makai Court in **Ala Moana Shopping Center,** at Ala Moana Blvd. and Atkinson Dr. (☎ **808/946-2811**). There are nearly two dozen different types of eateries in this busy, noisy complex on the ground floor of the rambling mall, including the new **Panini Grill Too, Orleans Express,** and old-timer **Thirst Aid Station.** Our favorites: **Tsuruya Noodles** (the Tenzaru is excellent), **Sbarro's pizza,** and **Yummy Korean BBQ.** Korean, Italian, Thai, Chinese, and other ethnic foods, as well as health foods, are also available. Open Monday to Saturday from 9:30am to 9pm, Sunday from 10am to 5pm.

1 Waikiki

VERY EXPENSIVE

✪ **La Mer.** In the Halekulani, 2199 Kalia Rd. ☎ **808/923-2311.** Reservations recommended. Jackets required for men. Main courses $36–$45; prix-fixe $85, $105. AE, CB, DC, JCB, MC, V. Daily 6–10pm. NEOCLASSIC FRENCH.

Expectations run high at La Mer, the only AAA Five-Diamond restaurant in the state—and they should. Honolulu's most sumptuous and expensive dining takes place

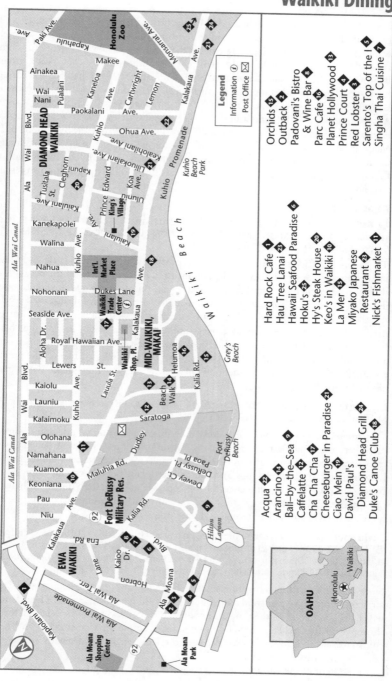

in the hushed elegance of this second-floor, open-sided oceanside room with views of Diamond Head and the sunset beyond palm fronds. Classical French influences meld seamlessly with the fresh island ingredients that La Mer has always celebrated. Some samplings from the rarefied world of Michelin-award–winning chef Yves Garnier: Beluga caviar ($105), sautéed foie gras ($34), bouillabaisse ($40), hamachi (yellowtail tuna) médaillons with Maui pistachio nuts ($42), filet of kumu (goatfish) in rosemary salt crust ($43), breast of Barbary duck with lavender honey ($38), whole roasted Atlantic monkfish ($36), and a host of other wonders in the à la carte and prix-fixe menus of the evening. Also notable are the wine list, desserts (try the Symphony of La Mer and lilikoi souffle), and service, which is formal without being stiff. Although Garnier brings his own signature to this dining room, it is clearly not an easy task to fill the shoes of former chef George Mavrothalassitis, who has opened his own restaurant not far away.

EXPENSIVE

✪ **Bali By the Sea.** In Hilton Hawaiian Village, 2005 Kalia Rd. ☎ **808/941-2254.** Reservations recommended. Main courses $22.50–$31.25. AE, CB, DC, DISC, JCB, MC, V. Mon–Sat 6–9pm. CONTINENTAL/PACIFIC RIM.

This is one of Waikiki's most memorable oceanfront dining rooms—pale and full of light, with a white grand piano at the entrance and sweeping views of the ocean. It's a shame it's no longer open for breakfast and lunch. But dinner is a winner, with offerings that merge island cooking styles and ingredients with chef Jean-Luc Voegele's Alsatian roots: herb-infused rack of lamb encrusted with macadamia nuts, escargots in phyllo, and fresh seafood in sauces hinting of plum wine, kaffir lime, black bean–ginger, and lemongrass. Poached opakapaka, roast duck with green peppercorns, and linguine and lobster are among the items on the sophisticated menu. The presentation and execution—not to mention the eye-popping setting—make Bali a good choice for foodies of all stripes.

Caffelatte. 339 Saratoga Rd. ☎ **808/924-1414.** Reservations recommended. Prix-fixe $35. MC, V. Wed–Mon 6:30–10pm. NORTHERN ITALIAN.

Owner-chef Laura Proserpio makes everything from scratch and to order; you wouldn't catch her near a microwave oven. As a result, you won't find a better bruschetta, pasta carbonara, marinara, or risotto in Honolulu. Thanks to her generations-old recipes and long hours of simmering soups and sauces, the menu is built on uncompromising basics. The prix-fixe–only dinner consists of appetizer or salad, soup (usually fish, lentil, or vegetable, and reliably wonderful), and the entree, which could be a porcini risotto, homemade ravioli, or any of several veal selections.

David Paul's Diamond Head Grill. At the Colony Surf Hotel, 2885 Kalakaua Ave., 2nd floor. ☎ **808/922-3734.** Reservations recommended. Main courses $14–$19 at lunch; $26–$30 at dinner. AE, DC, DISC, JCB, MC, V. Mon–Fri 11:30am–2:30pm; daily 5:30–10pm; Tues–Sat light menu 10–11:30pm; entertainment 8:30pm–midnight. NEW AMERICAN.

Sleek and chic, with a serpentine martini bar and baby grand piano, David Paul's attracts not only lovers of good food, but the after-dinner crowd as well. The offerings, which are good much of the time (but not all), include David Paul's specialties: tequila shrimp with firecracker rice, Maui onion-crusted seared ahi, kalua duck, and Kona coffee–roasted rack of lamb. (We also love the Kula corn chowder with Yukon gold potatoes and the triple-berry pie.)

To the right of the entrance, a glass-enclosed private dining room holds a table for seven or more for the chef's arranged-in-advance degustation dinners of five or nine courses. At center front is the main dining room, with large windows looking out over Kapiolani Park and the flanks of Diamond Head.

Hau Tree Lanai. In New Otani Kaimana Beach Hotel, 2863 Kalakaua Ave. ☎ **808/ 921-7066.** Reservations recommended. Main courses $19–$32.50. AE, CB, DC, DISC, JCB, MC, V. Mon–Sat 7–11am, 11:30am–2pm, and 5:30–9pm; Sun 7–11:30am, noon–2pm, and 5:30–9pm; late lunch in the open-air bar, daily 2–4pm. PACIFIC RIM.

Its outdoor setting and earnest, although not extraordinary, menu have made the Hau Tree a popular informal dining spot. The centerpiece of this terrace on the sand is an ancient hau tree that provides shade and charm for diners, most of whom are busy observing the diverse parade of beachgoing bodies at Sans Souci Beach. Breakfast here is a must: salmon Florentine, served on spinach and a fresh-baked scone; poi pancakes and Belgian waffles; eggs Benedict; and the Hawaiian platter of miniature poi pancakes, eggs, and a medley of island sausages. Lunchtime attractions include house-cured Atlantic salmon and an assortment of burgers, sandwiches, salads, and fresh-fish and pasta specialties. At dinner, choices include entrees of fresh moonfish, red snapper, opakapaka, ahi, and meats (ginger-steamed chicken breast, sesame-crusted hoisin rack of lamb).

Hy's Steak House. 2440 Kuhio Ave. ☎ **808/922-5555.** Reservations recommended. No beachwear. Main courses $17.95–$49.95. AE, CB, DC, DISC, MC, V. Sun–Thurs 6–10pm; Fri–Sat 6–11pm. AMERICAN.

Call it old-fashioned or call it a survivor, but there's no denying that Hy's has demonstrated admirable staying power in a cult of the low fat. This dark and clubby steak house still scores high among carnivores and even offers a grilled vegetable platter for carniphobes, a relief for the arteries among the Chateaubriand, beef Wellington, shrimp scampi, and other fruits de mer and terre. "The Only" is its classic best, a New York strip steak kiawe-grilled and served with a mysterious signature sauce. Garlic lovers swear by the Garlic Steak, a richly endowed rib eye with sliced mushrooms, herbs, and garlic aplenty. For an appetizer, you can order Thai-style scallops, buttery escargots, or wonderful salads: an excellent Caesar, warm spinach, and seafood-and-avocado. Hy's is a great choice for steak and seafood lovers; in its inimitable way, without giving an inch to faddism, it manages to please nearly everyone.

Miyako Japanese Restaurant. In New Otani Kaimana Beach Hotel, 2863 Kalakaua Ave. ☎ **808/923-4739.** Reservations recommended. Main courses $30–$40. AE, CB, DC, DISC, JCB, MC, V. Daily 6–9:30pm. JAPANESE.

Ikebana arrangements accent the dining room, and servers in gorgeous kimonos bustle to bring you brisk, courteous service. The food presentation is flawless: lacquer trays, precious sake cups, and esthetically arranged morsels reminiscent of imperial dining in Kyoto. Offerings include make-your-own hand-sushi rolls (*temaki*) from a tray of vegetables, mountain yam, crab, king clam, sashimi, nori, and salmon roe; prearranged kaiseki dinners; and several combinations of tempura, sashimi, shrimp, fresh lobster, soup, and pickled vegetables. This is a pretty room on the second floor of the hotel, with the Waikiki skyline glittering in the distance.

Nick's Fishmarket. In Waikiki Gateway Hotel, 2070 Kalakaua Ave. ☎ **808/955-6333.** Reservations recommended. Main courses $17.95 to market price; complete dinners $27.95– $55.95. AE, CB, DC, DISC, JCB, MC, V. Sun–Thurs 5:30–10pm, cafe menu 5:30pm–midnight; Fri–Sat 5:30–11pm, cafe menu 5:30pm–midnight. SEAFOOD.

With its extensive menu and lobster specialties, Nick's will always be the restaurant for seafood lovers with upscale tastes. A perennial award-winner, Nick's has a Kalakaua Room with windows for Waikiki people-watching and a menu that remains one of Honolulu's finest examples of Neptunian muscle. Appetizers range from Beluga caviar to escargot, ahi tartare and salmon carpaccio, and blackened sashimi. Whether Alaskan king crab or roast chicken, filet mignon or rack of lamb, or one of the impressive lobster combinations, the entrees are familiar but appealing. Fresh fish, Nick's trade-mark, comes grilled, seared, and sautéed, in preparations ranging from green pepper-corn to Oriental ginger. A keiki menu appeals to families, pasta and risotto to less-formal tastes, and the late-night entertainment with live music makes Nick's a magnet for the after-dinner crowd, too (see chapter 10, "Oahu After Dark").

✪ **Orchids.** In the Halekulani, 2199 Kalia Rd. ☎ **808/923-2311.** Reservations recom-mended. Dinner main courses $18.50–$35. AE, CB, DC, JCB, MC, V. Daily 7:30–11am, 11:30am–2pm, and 6–10pm; Sunday brunch 9:30am–2:30pm. INTERNATIONAL SEAFOOD.

The stunning oceanside ambience of this Honolulu landmark hasn't changed, but its menu has. (And the people-watching has never been better.) After several culinary incarnations, Orchids is now an international seafood house with a highly successful seafood bar. While viewing Diamond Head over crisp white linens or flickering can-dlelight, you can sample everything from gravlax to calamari, opakapaka Provençal to Oriental-style steamed onaga, shrimp spring rolls to sashimi and poke. At lunch, the crab cakes, calamari Caesar salad, and seafood curry are winners, but leave room for the lemon curd dessert. Dinner winners: fresh oysters on *ogo* (seaweed) topped with caviar; soft-shelled crab with tobiko remoulade; flawless opakapaka on a bed of wasabi mashed potatoes. Orchids' famous Kula tomato salad, rack of lamb, filet mignon, paella, and steak-and-seafood combinations ensure that no one is left out. Nightly live music, usually light jazz, is a new feature from 8:30 to 10:15pm, when the musicians move to the adjacent Lewers Lounge for after-dinner entertainment.

✪ **Padovani's Bistro & Wine Bar.** In the Doubletree Alana Waikiki Hotel, 1956 Ala Moana Blvd. ☎ **808/946-3456.** Reservations recommended. Main courses $20–$39; prix-fixe $48, $75. AE, DC, JCB, MC, V. FRENCH/MEDITERRANEAN.

Formerly of Halekulani's La Mer, the Ritz-Carlton Mauna Lani, and the Manele Bay Hotel, Philippe Padovani has opened a swanky room in Waikiki—his own, at last. A bamboo floor (à la Hoku's in the Kahala Mandarin), Frette linens, custom-made 1930s-style lamps, lavish upholstery, Riedel stemware, Bernardaud china, Christofle flatware, and a 16-bottle Cruvinet (which keeps wines fresh for by-the-glass orders) are among the impressive features of this Waikiki newcomer, open since December 1998. The à la carte, prix-fixe, and vegetarian menus are pure Padovani: *ogo* (seaweed) bread, fresh artichoke hearts with tabouleh salad, poached moi with fiddlehead ferns and aïoli sauce, sautéed tiger shrimp with mushroom-herb polenta, and a host of fresh seafood, meats, and vegetables in spirited preparations. Padovani's way with fennel (as in the peppercorn-crusted tenderloin), chervil, and other herbs is masterful, and his fresh-clam chowder with ogo is the best we've ever had. (Lunchtime entrees cost the same as at dinner, which makes for an expensive lunch!)

At press time, the Wine Bar upstairs from the restaurant (crafted by partner J. P. Damon, an oenophile of considerable means) was scheduled for imminent opening with its 50 wines by the glass, extensive and rare after-dinner liqueurs, and Old World cart service. The bistro's dress code (collared shirts, no shorts or jeans, covered shoes) and understated, clubby atmosphere suggest an effort to clone the exclusive Pacific Club, bastion of Hawaii's old money—an ambitious undertaking given the restau-rant's location and low ceilings. Padovani's brother, Pierre, is an incomparable pastry chef, and wife, Pierrette, has a warm touch as maitre d'.

Prince Court. In Hawaii Prince Hotel Waikiki, 100 Holomoana St. ☎ **808/944-4494.** Reser-vations recommended. Main courses $18–28; prix-fixe $58, $60. AE, DC, JCB, MC, V. Daily 6–10:30am and 6–9:30pm; Mon–Fri 11:30am–2pm; Sat–Sun brunch 11:15am–1pm. HAWAII REGIONAL.

Executive chef Gary Strehl's departure for the mainland leaves the future of Prince Court up in the air. We have always enjoyed this restaurant and hope that Strehl's successor will maintain the same high quality that has kept Prince Court on the culinary map. The gorgeous harbor view is a plus any time of the day or night, but particularly at sunset or on Friday nights when fireworks light up the skies from Waikiki shores. On Monday through Wednesday, diners can sample the shellfish appetizer bar with a demi entree from the varied à la carte menu, featuring fresh island seafood, Hawaii regional specialties (melt-in-your-mouth ahi carpaccio, whole island moi in ginger-sesame-soy), and excellent grilled and roasted meats, such as fork-tender New York steak. The "marina buffet" on Friday and Saturday evenings ($36), seafood buffet brunch on Saturday and Sunday ($24.50), and daily highlights (such as the shrimp-scallop-Kona lobster with wild rice and saffron sauce) keep diners coming to this pleasant harborfront room.

Sarento's Top of the I. In Ilikai Hotel Nikko Waikiki, 1777 Ala Moana Blvd. ☎ **808/ 949-3811.** Reservations recommended. Main courses $16–$34.95. AE, DC, DISC, JCB, MC, V. Sun–Thurs 5:30–9:45pm, bar until 11pm; Fri–Sat 5:30–10:30pm, bar until 11:30pm. ITALIAN.

The ride up the glass elevator is an event in itself, but Sarento's is not all show. A sister restaurant to Nicholas Nickolas and Nick's Fishmarket, Sarento's is fancier than a trattoria, with brisk professional service and good food to match the ambience. Diners rave about the romantic view of the city, the stellar Caesar salad, the opakapaka al forno, and the seafood fra diavolo—spicy and delectable. From pasta (veal and spinach ravioli, capellini pomodoro, penne with fresh basil, eggplant, sausage, and tomatoes) to pizza (grilled chicken, prosciutto and mushroom, crabmeat, and sausage with artichokes) to veal (scaloppine, saltimbocca, veal chop), Sarento's covers most of the bases and covers them well. On the lighter side, the smoked salmon Italiano and black and blue ahi are pleasers.

MODERATE

Acqua. In Hawaiian Regent Hotel, 2552 Kalakaua Ave. ☎ **808/924-0123.** Reservations recommended. Main courses $11.95–$24.95; specials can cost more. Sunset special, a 3-course dinner from 5:30–6:30pm nightly, $24.95. AE, DC, DISC, JCB, MC, V. Sun–Thurs 5:30–9pm; Fri–Sat 5:30–10pm; bistro menu in lounge 5:30pm–closing. MEDITERRANEAN/PACIFIC.

Acqua's cross-cultural touches and innovative menu make it a worthy and enjoyable stop—a good way to ward off tastebud atrophy with the latest in culinary seductions. We like the chef's way with taro (as in clam, taro, and corn chowder, and garlic taro mashed potatoes), Hawaiian hearts of palm, guava barbecue sauce, and local traditions, such as steamed seafood *lau-lau* (fish, lobster, prawns, scallops, crab, taro, and spinach). Winners include the guava baby-back ribs and king crab and the Acqua Pacific Sampler, a platter of guava prawns, duck spring roll, and eggplant-mozzarella cake—grand enough for four. The dining around the open kitchen is casual, and the late-night live entertainment on Thursday, Friday, and Saturday has featured some prominent names in island music.

Arancino. 255 Beach Walk. ☎ **808/923-5557.** Reservations strongly recommended; required for parties of 6 or more. Main courses $6.50–$14.50. AE, CB, DC, JCB, MC, V. Daily 11:30am–2:30pm and 5–10pm. ITALIAN.

When jaded Honolulu residents venture into Waikiki for dinner, it had better be good. And for the price, Arancino is worth the hunt. Here's what you'll find: a cheerful cafe of Monet-yellow walls and tile floors, respectable pastas, fabulous red-pepper salsa and rock-salt focaccia, we-try-harder service, and reasonable prices. The risotto changes daily and the pizza, when it's gorgonzola-asparagus, is memorable. If lobster linguine is on the menu, don't miss it. Arancino is frequently filled, with a line outside—a testament to the success of its intimate, convivial atmosphere of fairy lights on potted trees and its good food at affordable prices.

Ciao Mein. In Hyatt Regency Waikiki, 2424 Kalakaua Ave. ☎ **808/923-2426.** Reservations recommended. Main courses $14–$35; prix-fixe $26–$36. AE, CB, DC, DISC, JCB, MC, V. Daily 6–10pm. ITALIAN/CHINESE.

The cross-cultural connection seemed gimmicky at first, but Ciao Mein has pulled it off in a large, pleasing dining room with efficient service, surprisingly good Chinese food (especially for a hotel restaurant), and award-winning menu items that make this a haven for noodle lovers. If you're feeling extravagant, the honey-walnut shrimp, with snap peas and honey-glazed walnuts, is worth every penny of its $21.50 price. The crisp fried noodles with chicken and lobster make up a dish hailed by fans, and few Honolulu festival-goers will forget the spicy wok-fried Szechwan eggplant ($6.75) that won accolades and helped put Ciao Mein on Honolulu's culinary map. Sweet tooths, take note: The celebrated tiramisu lives up to its reputation.

✪ **Duke's Canoe Club.** In Outrigger Waikiki Hotel, 2335 Kalakaua Ave. ☎ **808/922-2268.** Reservations suggested for dinner. Main courses $9.95–$19.95; breakfast buffet $9.95. AE, DC, MC, V. Daily 7am–1am. STEAK/SEAFOOD.

This is what dining in Waikiki should be. Named after fabled surfer Duke Kahanamoku, this casual, upbeat oceanfront hot spot buzzes with diners and Hawaiian music lovers throughout the day, some of them wandering in from the beach, where they overheard slack-key guitar riffs that were too good to resist. Open-air dining provides a front-row view of the sunset. Duke's specializes in affordable fresh seafood (fresh catch for $16.95) in an oceanfront setting with good music—who could ask for more? The dinner fare is steak and seafood, with high marks for the prime rib, macadamia-crab wontons, and several preparations of the daily catch. Open for breakfast, lunch, and dinner, Duke's is also loved for its barefoot bar with topnotch island entertainment and its kamaaina, island-style ambience: Koa-lined walls, lauhala ceilings, and Hawaiian memorabilia accent the interior. The Concerts on the Beach series (Friday to Sunday 4 to 6pm) features top-notch island entertainers, and there is live entertainment daily in the dining room.

✪ **Hawaii Seafood Paradise.** 1830 Ala Moana Blvd. ☎ **808/946-4514.** Reservations recommended. Main courses $7–$32. AE, DC, JCB, MC, V. Daily 6:30am–3am. CHINESE/SEAFOOD.

You can dine as simply or as lavishly as you choose in this quirky, unpretentious restaurant that serves nine kinds of roast duck (I'd stake my life on the Peking duck); peerless shrimp-fried rice; many selections of chicken, noodles, and seafood; sizzling platters; an impressive selection of abalone and clam dishes; and "hot pot" casseroles with everything from lamb to lobster and fish. Top quality in the more than 200 Cantonese and Szechwan selections makes this a mecca for Chinese-food aficionados, including those speaking their native dialects—a sure sign of good Chinese food. A few of the best items on the menu are written in Chinese with no English translation, so don't be afraid to ask questions. There are Thai selections as well, among them the delectable, spicy Tom Yum soup with whole prawns, a hint of coconut, and lemongrass—rich but irresistible and one of the great finds on the Chinese-language menu.

Keo's in Waikiki. 2028 Kuhio Ave. ☎ **808/951-9355.** Reservations recommended. Main courses $8.95–$12.95; fixed-price dinners for 2–10 people, $23.95 per person. AE, DC, DISC, JCB, MC, V. Sun–Thurs 5–10:30pm; Fri–Sat 5–11pm. THAI.

Keo Sananikone's move to Waikiki caused an immediate elevation in the esthetic and gustatory level of Waikiki. With the oceans of fresh flowers that mark his restaurants, his freshly spiced and spirited dishes, and his familiar menu of Thai specialties, Keo's has arrived in Waikiki with a splashy tropical ambience. Sate shrimp, evil jungle prince (shrimp, chicken, or vegetables in a basil-coconut-chile sauce), Thai garlic shrimp with mushrooms, basil-infused eggplant with garlic, pad Thai noodles, and the ever-delectable panang curries are among the abiding delights. Most of the fresh flowers, herbs, fruits, vegetables, and spices are grown on his North Shore farm.

☻ Parc Cafe. In the Waikiki Parc Hotel, 2233 Helumoa Rd. ☎ **808/921-7272.** Reservations recommended. Buffets $12.50–$25.50. AE, DC, MC, V. Mon–Sat 6:30–10am and 11:30am–2pm; Sun 6:30–9:30am and 11am–2pm (brunch); daily 5:30–9:30pm. BUFFETS/BRUNCH.

The Halekulani's sister hotel has made a name for itself as Honolulu's top spot for buffets, with food and prices so good it has won over even the most dedicated buffet bashers. Regulars flock to the dining room for the Wednesday and Friday Hawaiian buffet, the finest such spread around: lau-lau, lomi salmon, kalua pig, steamed fresh catch, mashed Molokai potatoes, Kauai taro au gratin, and dozens of salads. Chafing dishes notwithstanding, this is gourmet fare using fine, fresh ingredients. A carving station serves up rotisserie duck and prime rib. The seafood soup is reliably wonderful, and the squid luau, with coconut milk, taro tops, and a brilliant smattering of tomatoes, is arguably the best in Hawaii. Otherwise, there are breakfast and luncheon buffets (the latter featuring salads, sandwiches, pasta, and rotisserie chicken). The prime rib and seafood dinner buffets are also a roaring success: sashimi, poke, and oysters on the half shell; a wok station and fresh catch; a carving station for prime rib and rotisserie chicken; the cafe's famous salads, from Oriental chicken to duck and charbroiled eggplant; and many other selections, including smashing desserts.

☻ Singha Thai Cuisine. 1910 Ala Moana Blvd. (at the Ala Moana end of Waikiki). ☎ **808/941-2898.** Reservations recommended. Main courses $11–$27. AE, CB, DC, DISC, JCB, MC, V. Daily 4–11pm. THAI.

The Royal Thai dancers arch their graceful, boneless fingers nightly in classical Thai dance on the small center stage, but you may be too busy tucking into your Thai chili, fresh fish, or blackened ahi summer rolls to notice. Indeed, the flavors and sights are rich here; imaginative combination dinners and the use of local organic ingredients are among the special touches of this Thai-Hawaiian fusion restaurant. Complete dinners for two to five cover many tastes and are an ideal way for the uninitiated to sample this cuisine, as well as the elements of Hawaii regional cuisine that have had considerable influence on the chef. Some highlights of the diverse menu are local fresh catch with Thai chili and light black-bean sauce; red, green, yellow, and vegetarian curries; ginseng chicken soup; and many seafood dishes. Such extensive use of fresh fish (mahi-mahi, ono, ahi, opakapaka, onaga, and uku) in traditional Thai preparations is unusual for a Thai restaurant. The entertainment and indoor-outdoor dining add to this first-class dining experience.

INEXPENSIVE

Cha Cha Cha. 342 Seaside Ave. ☎ **808/923-7797.** Complete dinners $7–$11. MC, V. Daily 11:30am–2am. MEXICAN/CARIBBEAN.

With its heroic margaritas and cheap happy-hour beer, pupus, and all-around lovable menu, we should all cha-cha-cha to this Waikiki treasure. There's nothing wimpy about the flavors here; the chiles and zesty Caribbean spices make Cha Cha Cha more than plain ol' Mex, adding zing to the Jamaican jerk chicken, blackened swordfish, and the spicy beef, pork, and vegetable dishes. Tacos, tamales (steamed in banana leaves and served with Jamaican red beans, rice, and sour cream), quesadillas, wraps and "unwraps" (served in crisp red tortilla shells on a bed of warm black beans) are the general categories, but don't miss the specials. Blackened fish and fresh veggies in a spinach tortilla, curried fresh grilled vegetables, blackened fish tacos, and homemade desserts (including a creamy toasted-coconut custard you won't want to miss) make this one of Waikiki's enduring delights. Located across from two of Waikiki's three movie theaters, it's perfect for a quick before- or after-dinner meal.

Cheeseburger in Paradise. 2500 Kalakaua Ave. ☎ **808/923-3731.** Reservations accepted for large parties. Main courses $6.50–$10.95. AE, MC, DISC, V, JCB. Daily 8am–11pm; cocktails until midnight. AMERICAN.

Maui's Front Street Cheeseburger was such a hit that they've brought their burger bonanza to Waikiki. Cheeseburgers (about ⅓ pound!) are the bestseller, made of certified Angus beef with a choice of mushrooms, chili, bacon, and grilled pineapple to build your own high-rise. For the more cautious, Chinese chicken salad is a big seller, too. There's live music nightly at 6:30pm, ranging from solo guitarist to acoustic quartets. The owners hope to turn this into a rock-'n-roll mecca like their Maui counterpart, so keep your ears to the ground.

2 Honolulu Beyond Waikiki

ALA MOANA & KAKAAKO
EXPENSIVE

✪ **A Pacific Cafe Oahu.** At Ward Centre, 1200 Ala Moana Blvd. ☎ **808/593-0035.** Reservations recommended. Lunch $8–$14; 3-course lunch special $12.95; dinner main courses $16.50–$26.75; prix-fixe $34.50. AE, DC, DISC, MC, V. Mon–Thurs 11:30am–2pm and 5:30–9pm; Fri 11:30am–2pm and 5:30–10pm; Sat 5:30–10pm; Sun 5:30–9pm. HAWAII REGIONAL.

Chef-owner Jean-Marie Josselin is known for his excellent appetizers (firecracker salmon rolls, tiger-eye ahi sushi tempura) and his seasoned hand with island produce and seafood. Great for lunch or dinner, this Ward Centre staple keeps a creative edge with its signature sesame- and garlic-crisped mahi-mahi, Josselin's staple statewide; seared sea scallops with white truffle mashed potatoes; seared ahi salad; and firecracker salmon roll with house kim chee and sweet-sour sauce. A triathlete, Josselin keeps health-conscious and vegetarian items on the menu as well as excellent pizzas from a wood-burning oven and extensive Pacific Rim specialties that change daily. Last time we looked, Pacific Café was celebrating a Tongan vanilla bean festival and serving kalua pork potstickers, grilled beef tenderloin with feta-herb crust, Pacific salmon with griddled rice cakes and miso ginger vinaigrette, and organic Kealakekua lamb with kabocha pumpkin ravioli.

✪ **Mariposa.** In the Ala Moana Center, 1450 Ala Moana Blvd. ☎ **808/951-3420.** Reservations recommended. Main courses $8–$26. AE, MC, V. Daily 11am–3pm; dessert menu 3–5pm; Mon–Thurs 5–10pm; Fri–Sat 5–11pm; Sun 5–9pm. PACIFIC RIM/SOUTHWESTERN.

Once you get past the gourmet food department of the new Neiman Marcus, you will be in Mariposa, the hottest new lunch spot in town. High ceilings for indoor diners and tables on the deck with views of Ala Moana Park and its art deco bridges (with the ocean beyond) add up to a pleasing ambience, with or without the shopping. Instead of Neiman Marcus attitude, you'll find cordial service, nearly four-dozen reasonably priced wines by the glass, and a menu of Pacific and American (called "heritage cuisine") specialties that include everything from smoked pork ribs with mashed potatoes to ahi carpaccio and seared salmon salad. Chef Doug Lum's mashed potatoes are legendary, and the Hamakua Myer lemon tart is a force of nature. Mariposa's beef tenderloin and scallop linguine (with a clever undertone of wasabi) are each a tour de force, but the lunchtime favorite is invariably the starter of chicken broth. Like the towering, eggy "popover" with poha-berry butter, it's too good to be true.

Nicholas Nickolas. In Ala Moana Hotel, 410 Atkinson Dr. ☎ **808/955-4466.** Reservations recommended. Collared shirt, slacks, and shoes required for men. Main courses $19–$42. AE, CB, DC, DISC, JCB, MC, V. Daily 5:30–11:30pm; live music Sun–Thurs until 2am, Fri–Sat until 3am. AMERICAN/CONTINENTAL/SEAFOOD.

Take the express elevator to the 36th floor, where the circular dining room reveals the city in its mountain-to-sea splendor. The menu is spare and to the point, strong on appetizers and seafood: crab cakes (a bestseller), the signature Cajun-seared ahi, clams casino, and ahi spring rolls in exotic sauces. Beluga caviar is for the luxury-minded, sashimi for everyone else. Blackened onaga has always been a house specialty, seared in Cajun spices and baked. The herb-infused mahi-mahi is another Nicholas Nickolas notable, and for the undecided, the seafood mixed grill or surf-and-turf à la Nick. Meat lovers are not neglected: Rack of lamb, New York steak, and veal, pork, and chicken round out the menu. You'll dine at tables along the edge of the dining room or at cozy booths along the interior, and when dinner's over, the dancing begins.

☺ Sushi Sasabune. 1419 S. King St. ☎ **808/947-3800.** Reservations recommended. Sushi $3.90–$7. DC, JCB, MC, V. Mon–Fri 12–2pm and 5:30–10pm; Sat 5:30–10pm. SUSHI.

The new lunch specials are divine: four choices, ranging from three sushi rolls (crab, salmon belly, and tuna) for $7.50 to the sushi combo (seven pieces and one roll) for $12.50. The $10.50 chirashi special is brilliant, a perfect ensemble of warm rice topped with nori and several kinds of fresh fish and teriyaki octopus, daintily presented in a rectangular "box" as though you were in Japan. Besides being exquisitely fresh and delectable, the specials come with seaweed salad, miso soup, and azuki bean ice cream. You can always choose to dine at the sushi bar, where Seinfeld's "soup Nazi" has found his match in the Sasabune way, otherwise known as "trust-me" sushi: Obey the chef, eat what's served, and God help you if you drop a grain of rice or dip in wasabi without permission. When you make a reservation at this small, informal sushi bar, you will be told that there is no California roll, avocado, or anything not authentically Japanese. If you want to order from a menu, sit at a table; if you're brave enough to sit at the sushi bar, you get what the chef serves, which is freshly shipped in that day. Whether it's salmon from Nova Scotia, sea urchin from Japan, halibut from Boston, Louisiana blue crab, or farmed oyster from Washington, chef Seiji Kumagawa's sushi comes with a strict protocol: Dip only with permission, and then with some restraint. From the first bite of bluefin tuna in ponzu to the final morsel of eel cooked in egg, this is an extraordinary experience for sushi aficionados, a journey into new tastes, textures, and sensations, expensive (at dinner) but well worth it. A master stroke: warm rice, which sets off the coldness of the fish and lends a titillating new dimension to sushi.

MODERATE

☺ Akasaka. 1646B Kona St. ☎ **808/942-4466.** Reservations recommended. Main courses $10–$19. AE, DC, DISC, MC, V. Mon–Sat 11am–2:30pm and 5pm–2am. JAPANESE.

Cozy, busy, casual, and occasionally smoky, with a tiny tatami room for small groups, Akasaka wins high marks for sushi, sizzling tofu and scallops, miso-clam soup, and the overall quality and integrity of its Japanese cuisine. The zesty, spicy tuna hand-roll (*temaki*) is excellent, and many claim the California roll, scallop roll with flying-fish

Honolulu Area Dining

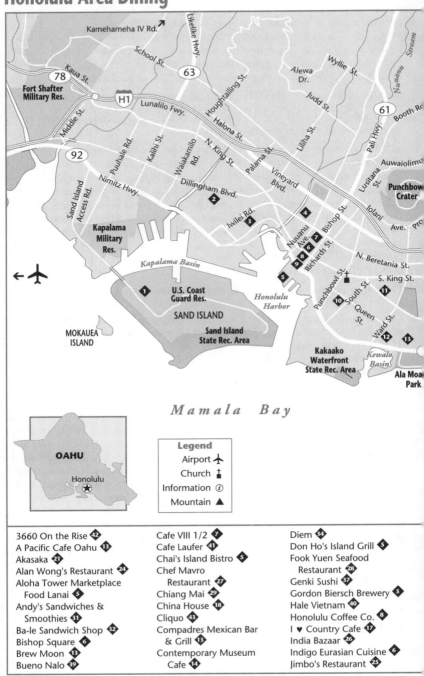

Legend
Airport ✈
Church ⭧
Information ⓘ
Mountain ▲

3660 On the Rise ㊷
A Pacific Cafe Oahu ⑬
Akasaka ㉑
Alan Wong's Restaurant ㉔
Aloha Tower Marketplace
  Food Lanai ⑤
Andy's Sandwiches &
  Smoothies ㉛
Ba-le Sandwich Shop ㉜
Bishop Square ⑥
Brew Moon ⑬
Bueno Nalo ㊴

Cafe VIII 1/2 ⑦
Cafe Laufer ㊶
Chai's Island Bistro ⑤
Chef Mavro
  Restaurant ㉗
Chiang Mai ㉙
China House ⑱
Cliquo ㊸
Compadres Mexican Bar
  & Grill ⑬
Contemporary Museum
  Cafe ⑭

Diem ㉞
Don Ho's Island Grill ⑤
Fook Yuen Seafood
  Restaurant ㉘
Genki Sushi ㊲
Gordon Biersch Brewery ⑤
Hale Vietnam ㊵
Honolulu Coffee Co. ⑧
I ♥ Country Cafe ⑰
India Bazaar ㉖
Indigo Eurasian Cuisine ⑥
Jimbo's Restaurant ㉕

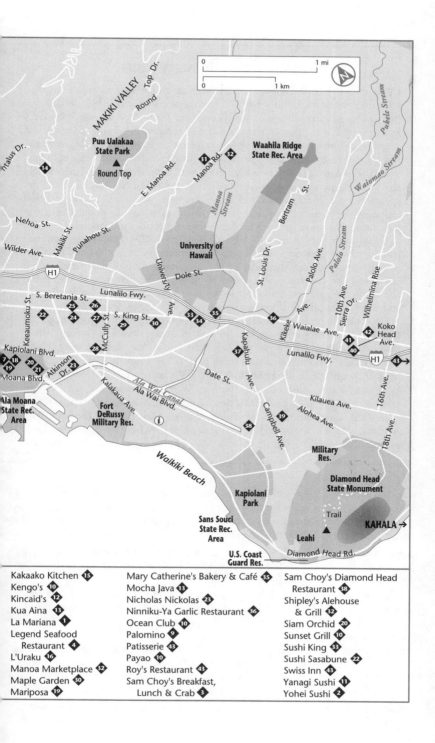

Kakaako Kitchen **15**	Mary Catherine's Bakery & Café **45**
Kengo's **10**	Mocha Java **13**
Kincaid's **12**	Nicholas Nickolas **23**
Kua Aina **13**	Ninniku-Ya Garlic Restaurant **36**
La Mariana **1**	Ocean Club **10**
Legend Seafood	Palomino **9**
Restaurant **4**	Patisserie **43**
L'Uraku **16**	Payao **10**
Manoa Marketplace **32**	Roy's Restaurant **43**
Maple Garden **30**	Sam Choy's Breakfast,
Mariposa **19**	Lunch & Crab **3**

Sam Choy's Diamond Head
Restaurant **38**
Shipley's Alehouse
& Grill **32**
Siam Orchid **20**
Sunset Grill **10**
Sushi King **33**
Sushi Sasabune **22**
Swiss Inn **43**
Yanagi Sushi **11**
Yohei Sushi **2**

Family-Friendly Restaurants

Honolulu is constantly battling its image as an expensive destination. It's true that accommodations on Oahu are pricey, but the abundance of ethnic restaurants (born of burgeoning new ethnic populations) and the high percentage of working mothers in Hawaii paint an entirely different scenario for dining. Even with a sluggish economy, residents eat out—because they're busy, because they want to, and because many popular ethnic traditions aren't so easy to duplicate at home. What makes a good family restaurant in Hawaii? More than the presence of high chairs, we think it's friendliness, affordability, and menu choices that take into consideration the tastes and preferences of more than one generation. Not including the usual fast-food burger joints that are prosaically popular with the kids, here are some suggestions for family-friendly eateries in Honolulu.

Genki Sushi (900 Kapahulu Ave.; ☎ 808/735-8889) is part entertainment, part assertiveness training, and part culinary pleasure. Kids love to lunge for their favorites among the freshly made, individually wrapped sushis that parade by on conveyor belts, and the slower ones who miss out the first time around get a chance on the next revolution. Sit with your family around the curvy counters and empty your plates without emptying your pocketbook. (See p. 129.)

Our observation is that Blockbuster Video outlets are often adjacent to places that kids and teenagers love. And because this may mean less cooking, these places are popular among parents, too. Adjacent to Ala Moana Center, Honolulu's busiest Blockbuster is smack dab next to **I ♥ Country Cafe** (451 Piikoi St., Ala Moana Plaza; ☎ 808/596-8108). I ♥ Country Cafe offers everything from meat loaf to shoyu chicken, burgers, vegetarian dishes, and stir-frys, for takeout or dining in—and there's a new branch in Kahala Mall. (See p. 118.)

In Ward Warehouse, the classic pre-teen pleaser is **Old Spaghetti Factory** (1050 Ala Moana Blvd.; ☎ 808/591-2513), where kids have been sucking in spaghetti and meatballs for years. Ornate Italianate decor, beveled glass everywhere, and an

roe, and hamachi are also at the top of the list. During soft-shell crab season, lovers of these spiny delicacies can order them in sushi—a novel, tasty treat. Fresh ingredients at the sushi bar make this a good bet for top-notch Japanese fare, and lunch and dinner specials can help ease the bite of the bill.

Brew Moon. In Ward Centre, 1200 Ala Moana Blvd. ☎ **808/593-0088.** Reservations recommended. Main courses $8–$27.50. AE, DC, MC, V. Mon–Sat 11am–2pm and 4–10pm; Sun 9am–2pm and 4–10pm. PACIFIC RIM/AMERICAN.

Award-winning beers and an eclectic menu of sandwiches, pizza, seafood, and ethnic specialties (jambalaya, Moroccan-spiced chicken, tofu-veggie stir fry) make up this strange industrial-tropical architectural phenomenon in the Ward Centre. Prepare yourself for more hype than culinary excellence, and you won't be disappointed. Food isn't the strong suit here (especially the pastas), but it's still amazingly popular. Diners can sit indoors or on the terrace to sample the wide-ranging menu. After dark, the bar area is a singles mecca. Highlights: pizza and the single-malt scotches. The Sunday Jazz Brunch, featuring live entertainment, is held weekly from 10am to 1pm.

China House. 1349 Kapiolani Blvd. ☎ **808/949-6622.** Reservations recommended for large parties. Main courses $8.95–$28. AE, MC, V. Mon–Fri 10am–10pm; Sat–Sun 9am–10pm. CHINESE.

affordable menu of "Dino meals" (for ages 6 and younger, served on a dinosaur plate) and "Junior meals" (for 6- to 12-year-olds), plus pasta, salads, and sandwiches for the post-dino set, have kept this spot on the family circuit.

Downtown, the faithful still gather at **Kengo's** (Restaurant Row, 500 Ala Moana Blvd.; ☎ **808/533-0039**), buffet central with kids' rates and tastes for all generations—and many ethnic traditions and tastes. (See p. 122.)

At the gateway to Waikiki, **Hawaii Seafood Paradise** (1830 Ala Moana Blvd.; ☎ **808/946-4514**) is open late (until 3am) but is popular with the pre-curfew set, too. Families love to sit at the circular tables and order the works from a menu of more than 200 items—enough to please several dynasties and more than a few generations. Excellent fried rice, noodle dishes, sizzling platters, soups, lemon chicken, several selections of duck, and many other delicacies are among Paradise's offerings. (See p. 110.)

On the outskirts of Honolulu, **Swiss Inn** (5730 Kalanianaole Hwy., Niu Valley Shopping Center; ☎ **808/377-5447**) is another family favorite—not just for its children's-portion spaghetti for $4, but also because it serves European-style frankfurters, with Swiss potato salad or French fries, for $5.75. Parents and children can feel much more elegant dining here than at a sandwich shop, and they don't have to dress up. Martin and Jeanie Wyss have always welcomed families with a combination of good value, pleasing service, and good food, including a cheese fondue for those too young to consider cholesterol. (See p. 131.)

Finally, we come to **Zippy's,** the mecca of chili and saimin. There are nearly two dozen of them on Oahu alone (call ☎ **808/955-6622** for the one nearest you). All locations feature cheap, tasty chili, burgers, sandwiches, salads, and all-day American fare that is popular among parents and kids. Tasty vegetarian chili and meatless, smoky Boca Burgers are among the healthy choices for vegetarians.

Cavernous and noisy and synonymous with dim sum, China House is a beehive of activity: servers pushing carts with bamboo steamers and trays of exotic delicacies, the clatter of plastic chopsticks, brusque service, and much craning of necks and raising of voices to hear above the din. But this is one of Honolulu's major purveyors of the dainty Chinese delectables, with dozens of choices and some surprises: mochi-rice chicken pouch, spinach-and-scallop dim sum, pan-fried turnip cake, and fresh scallop roll, as well as the more commonly known varieties. Future plans call for a luncheon buffet.

Compadres Mexican Bar & Grill. At Ward Centre, 1200 Ala Moana Blvd. ☎ **808/591-8307.** Reservations recommended. Main courses $8–$13. DC, JCB, MC, V. Mon–Thurs 11am–11pm; Fri–Sat 11am–midnight; Sun 11am–10pm; bar daily 11am–2am, business pending. MEXICAN.

There should be a national holiday around the Compadres margarita—it is memorable, served in a festive atmosphere with one wall of glass windows looking out toward Ala Moana Park. Tequila festivals, Cinco de Mayo, fund-raisers, live entertainment on Fridays, and every excuse for a party make this place an all-around good deal. Huevos rancheros are a must any time of the day, but there are many other choices, including eight different types of enchiladas; steak, chicken, and fish combination plates; fajitas; carnitas; and notable nachos. For the reckless: the back-bar margarita, made with Gold tequila, Grand Marnier, fresh lime, sweet-and-sour, and orange juice.

Kincaid's Fish, Chop and Steakhouse. In Ward Warehouse, 1050 Ala Moana Blvd. ☎ **808/591-2005.** Reservations recommended. Lunch $8.95–$15.95; dinner main courses $14.50–$45.95. AE, DC, JCB, MC, V. Daily 11am–10pm (later for pupus); lounge Sun–Thurs 11am–midnight, Fri–Sat 11am–1:30am; sunset menu 5–6pm daily. SEAFOOD/STEAKS.

Kincaid's is always winning surveys for one thing or another—best place for a business lunch, best seafood restaurant—because it pleases wide-ranging tastes and pocketbooks. Brisk service, a pleasing harbor view, and an extensive seafood menu keep the large dining room full. Among the highlights: great fresh-fish sandwiches, seafood chowders and French onion soups, kiawe-grilled and herb-buttered salmon, fresh mahi-mahi with key-lime butter, seafood sampler, and oven-roasted garlic prawns. Steaks are big here too, and so is the mushroom garden burger—but we also love the romaine-and-blue-cheese salad and the devil-may-care Dungeness crab and artichoke sandwich—open-faced, rich, and fabulous. You might want to save room for the signature dessert, the original burnt creme—custardy and high in calories, with a glazed sugar topping. Kincaid's is also a popular happy-hour rendezvous, with inexpensive beer and appetizers. On Friday and Saturday from 9:30pm, live local entertainment draws crowds.

✪ **L'Uraku.** 1341 Kapiolani Blvd. ☎ **808/955-0552.** Reservations recommended. Lunch main courses $8.95–$12.50; dinner main courses $15–$28; prix-fixe $32. Daily 11am–2:30pm; 5:30–10:30pm. EURO-JAPANESE.

L'Uraku's pleasant, light-filled dining room and expanded fusion menu make it a great spot for lunch—not overly fussy, casual enough, but with the right touch of elegance for dining in style without breaking the bank. Chef Hiroshi Fukui, born in Japan and raised in Hawaii, was trained in the formal Japanese culinary tradition called *kaiseki*, and he uses this training to great advantage with fresh island ingredients and European cooking styles. Although dishes such as wild mushroom pasta, seafood udon, grilled salmon, and seared sea scallops with local greens go for under $10 at lunch, the $15 "Weekender lunch" cannot be beat. Crab cake, green salad, an entree (choice of shrimp katsu, almond-crusted fresh snapper, steak pilaf, pescatore, garlic steak (for $1.50 more), and misoyaki butterfish (for $3 more) are offered in this multi-course meal, plus dessert and iced tea. The dinner menu inches upward, with novelties such as arare- (mochi-cracker) crusted opakapaka; steamed whole moi ($23.50); crunchy corn flake shrimp (a $6.50 appetizer); spiced duck breast with Maui onion ($22); open-faced chicken ravioli ($17.50); and a vegetarian's dream of portabello mushrooms, tomato, and eggplant served on green tea noodles, all for $16.75.

INEXPENSIVE

I ♥ **Country Cafe.** In Ala Moana Plaza, 451 Piikoi St. ☎ **808/596-8108.** (Also in Kahala Mall, ☎ 808/735-6965.) Main courses $5–$9.50. AE, DISC, MC, V. Mon–Thurs 10am–9pm; Fri–Sat 10am–9:30pm; Sun 10am–9pm. INTERNATIONAL.

Give yourself time to peruse the lengthy list of specials posted on the menu board, as well as the prodigious printed menu. Stand in line at the counter, place your order and pay, and find a Formica-topped table, or wait about 10 minutes for your takeout order to appear in a Styrofoam plate heaped with salad and other accompaniments. This is a beehive with a mind-boggling selection that includes garlic mahi-mahi, Cajun meatloaf, Thai curries, stir-fry galore, shoyu chicken, two-dozen plate-lunch selections, kalua pork cabbage, and a long list of other choices spanning many cultures and tastes.